FROM JAILER TO JAILED

*My Journey from
Correction and Police Commissioner
to Inmate #84888-054*

Bernard B. Kerik

Threshold Editions

NewYork London Toronto Sydney New Delhi

Threshold Editions
A Division of Simon & Schuster, Inc.
1230 Avenue of the Americas
New York, NY 10020

First Threshold Editions hardcover edition March 2015

THRESHOLD EDITIONS and colophon are trademarks of Simon & Schuster, Inc.

For information about special discounts for bulk purchases, please contact Simon & Schuster Special Sales at 1-866-506-1949 or business@simonandschuster.com.

The Simon & Schuster Speakers Bureau can bring authors to your live event. For more information or to book an event, contact the Simon & Schuster Speakers Bureau at 1-866-248-3049 or visit our website at www.simonspeakers.com.

Interior design by Robert E. Ettlin

Manufactured in the United States of America

1 3 5 7 9 10 8 6 4 2

ISBN 978-1-4767-8370-3
ISBN 978-1-4767-8372-7 (ebook)

For Besim Aydin, whose life was cut short long
before his time; my wife, Hala, for being the mother
that every child wihes they had; and for Angelina,
who keeps me young and thinking.

CONTENTS

CONTENTS

PART III: Reform

Introduction

My name is Bernard B. Kerik.

I was the fortieth commissioner of the New York City Police Department and was nominated by President George W. Bush for the cabinet position of secretary of the U.S. Department of Homeland Security.

Now I am former federal prison inmate #84888-054.

I served my time. I'm back with my family. I still have good friends and supporters. I'm speaking out for criminal justice reform, writing this book. But part of me still feels lost. I'm not sure I'll ever feel whole again. The system beats you down in a way that remains, in a way you can't fully grasp and don't realize even when you're a part of it.

For more than thirty years, I served in various law enforcement positions. I was once a correction officer in a New Jersey county jail, later a beat cop in Times Square. In the late 1990s I ran the New York City Department of Correction—a jail system that includes Rikers Island, a massive penal colony with a history of mismanagement and violence. Then I ran the New York City Police Department at fifty-five thousand strong. These are two of the largest law enforcement institutions in the country.

In the line of duty I've rescued people from burning buildings,

been stabbed, been shot at. I saved my wounded partner in a gun battle. I've survived a bomb plot in Iraq, been the target of death threats, seized tons of cocaine and millions of dollars from the Cali cartel. I've brought cop killers, drug lords, and terrorists to justice.

I believed in public order. I believed in the public good. I felt pride standing against the dangerous, the lawless. But then I was convicted of violating the public's trust: tax fraud, false statements, lying to the White House. I was sentenced to four years in federal prison.

I am accountable and responsible for how my life has turned out thus far—the good, the bad, the rage, the heartache, the bitterness, the luck. I'm far from an angel. My mistakes and scandals are many, as the press has widely publicized. But far greater is my professional service and love for this country.

Even after having served my time and paid a high price for my errors, as an ex-convict in many ways I remain disgraced. I've lost some of my basic civil and constitutional rights—the right to vote, hold public office, or obtain a law license. I cannot work in law enforcement for a government agency ever again. In many states, I can never work for the government or obtain a barber's license or become a physical therapist. I've joined the growing demographic of Americans tagged for life as ex-convicts.

With this new book I aim to fill in the public and historical record, to tell my side of my story, taking readers on the tumultuous ride of the action-packed last thirteen years of my life, the paradox of a jailer being jailed, a prison builder becoming a prison reformer.

This is not just about me. It's about all the men and women on both sides whom I've met and worked with during my career. It's

about how shortsighted, inefficient, and cruel our criminal justice system is, how badly in need of reform. I didn't see the system this way when I was a warden, a cop, a commissioner. I could have. I should have. But you really can't, not fully, not unless you experience having your freedom taken from you, what it's like to live on the other side of the bars.

They say that a conservative is a liberal who's been mugged, and a liberal is a conservative who's been indicted. So change is possible, and both sides agree: It's time for positive and substantial reform. This is my goal.

PART I

The Other Side of the Bars

1

Despair

The screams were bloodcurdling.

"Por favor! Saqueme de aqui! Saqueme de aqui!"

Please get me out of here!

The young Hispanic prisoner's desperation echoed through the ninth floor of the Special Housing Unit, the SHU, of the Metropolitan Correctional Center in lower Manhattan. I listened from my solitary confinement cell just a few locked doors down the corridor from him. By that point, autumn of 2012, I had served more than two years of my four-year federal sentence for tax fraud and making false statements on a White House vetting application. I was serving my time at the federal prison in Cumberland, Maryland, and had just been transferred back to New York City, to the MCC, to serve as a witness in the perjury trial of Frank DiTommaso, who had gotten caught up in the legal troubles that had led me to prison.

The young Hispanic inmate must have been lying on the floor of his cell as he yelled, kicking the base of the solid steel door, each blow sounding like a thundering explosion.

Other prisoners began screaming and beating on their doors, too, yelling for the correction officers to do something for this desperate young man.

I lay on my bed shivering, listening to this kid scream bloody murder. His cries echoed the strains I felt inside, the desperation, the despair, even the fear of madness.

I looked around my own trap. My box, hole, or cage, as most of the prisoners called them. A twelve-by-eight-foot solid steel box, with a bed, a stainless-steel sink and toilet, and a small metal writing table and stool. On the door there was a four-by-twenty-four-inch window that gave me a limited view of the corridor, and a tiny barred window in the back that allowed me a small glimpse of the free world outside that wretched place.

I could see the steps of the U.S. Federal Courthouse, and a sign that read PEARL STREET.

The MCC was the U.S. Justice Department's New York City detention center. For the most part it held pretrial inmates for federal court in the Southern District of New York. On one side of the building was New York City Police Headquarters, where my commissioner's office had been. On the other side of the building was the Manhattan House of Detention, once named in my honor for my achievements in the New York City Correction Department. Not even when it had my name did I really think about what it would be like to pass days and months and years in those boxes, to be on the other side of the treatment, to have your freedom and contact with the world taken in such a stark and complete way.

I was slipping into despair. In my head I kept going over and over the series of events that had put me there, that had led to my conviction. What could I have done differently? Why did they need to bury me? Why am I in solitary with murderers and terrorists?

———

Among an inmate population of about eight hundred, fifty to sixty of my fellow MCC inmates were considered some of the most wanted and dangerous men in the world.

To the right of my cell was an Afghan by the name of Khan. Across from me was Wasami, a Somali. Both being held on terrorism charges. There was "G," a thirty-four-year-old Puerto Rican from the Bronx, and a short black man in his mid-thirties from Tennessee—both charged with multiple murders. To the left and at the end of our small wing that held eight prisoners was an NYPD officer named Gilberto Valle, who'd been charged with conspiring to cook and eat his girlfriend. The press had dubbed him the "Cannibal Cop." He was scared to death. I could see it in his face and hear it in his voice. When his toilet wouldn't stop flushing, he panicked and screamed for help. The facility's medical and psychological staff were constantly at his cell door, trying to calm him down. One day when the correction officers were busy, he got locked in the shower for about twenty minutes and was screaming and crying out for help.

Most of our cells were the same: corroded with massive amounts of rust at the seams where the metal walls met the concrete floors and ceilings, from prior inhabitants flooding the cells to get the attention of the staff.

You could see and feel the history of each cell: the burn marks where prior inmates had started fires, the personal notes written on the walls that documented the feelings of hopelessness and despair:

"Live with the pain."

"Be strong for those who are weak."

"Have faith—God loves you."

It was an eerie feeling reading these messages from men who

were probably spending the rest of their lives in a cell like this. I couldn't tell if it was the strain of isolation or the frigid cold that was making me shiver uncontrollably. Just two days before, Hurricane Sandy had torn through the Northeast. Now the MCC had no heat or hot water and was running on minimal generator power. My toes and nose were numb. The four blankets were no match for the frigid cold magnified by the solid steel cell.

The on-duty correction officers wore coats, scarves, and watch caps, many working double shifts for coworkers who couldn't make it in due to the storm. From my window, I saw a pitch-black city; the only lights were those of the passing cars trying to maneuver through a blacked-out lower Manhattan. Staring into that darkness I found myself deeper in paranoia and anxiety, even hallucinating, talking to myself at times. I entertained myself by playing with three or four mice that would come into my cell nightly to capture the bran flakes I'd dropped during breakfast.

These were the lowest moments of my life. Hopelessness and failure covered me. I was nothing. I was worthless. The mind-altering nature of prison, of the deprivation of freedom—intensified by solitary confinement—makes you say and do and think things that you would never otherwise say or do or think. I confess that I was pretty close to the edge then, in those darkest moments in the darkness of lower Manhattan. My battleground. I remember thinking, How could I do this, end this senseless emptiness and suffering? But how could I do it quickly enough so that the COs wouldn't rush in and save me before it was over?

2

═══

Cumberland

I've been called arrogant, obnoxious, and defiant by my critics. But I'm also fair, generous, and sentimental, particularly when it comes to matters of the heart, my family, my wife and children, and my country. My love for my family and especially my children, Joe, Celine, Angelina, and Lisa, is so profound that at times it's difficult for me to understand. Having lived through what I have, I don't fear too much. But the thought of my family in pain is so heartbreaking to me that it defies description.

I'm often pained by the thought that I inspired my son, Joe, to follow in my footsteps, into a job that could ultimately cause his death. On the day he took his oath with the Newark Police Department, I held the Bible and beamed with pride. Yet at the same time, as his father, I was overcome with a fear that only a cop would know, of the dangers of the job. I pray every day for his safe return from duty.

I hope that I'm long gone before they are. I would gladly give my life for theirs to allow them to live in peace. This is the strongest emotion in my body. It's immeasurable.

───

• • •

In the spring of 2010, as the day of my self-surrender to federal prison in Cumberland, Maryland, approached, I had Celine and Angelina watch *Rocky Balboa*, the sixth and last movie in Sylvester Stallone's series. Both girls had autographed pictures of Stallone. On Celine's he'd written, "The only man tougher than Rambo is your dad. Love, Sly." I wanted the girls to see the scene in the movie where Rocky talks to his son about life and how difficult it is—to let them know that our family had to stand strong in the face of what was about to happen, their dad going away for several years to serve a prison sentence. They didn't know what I had been convicted of. At seven and ten years old, all they knew was that "Daddy didn't pay taxes for Mari," their nanny. They had no idea what that meant.

The next morning as I was kissing them good-bye, I said, "Don't forget, the next time Daddy comes home I'm here to stay. And what did you learn last night?"

"Life is not all sunshine and rainbows," they said in unison. It broke my heart.

• • •

On May 17, 2010, I arrived at the Federal Correctional Institution in Cumberland, Maryland. It's located in sweeping farmland in the western part of the state, a six-hour drive from New York City. I drove down with Hala, Albert and Caroline Manzo, Simon Cohen, and Nathan Berman, four of my closest friends. Jon Cumbo, a retired NYPD detective; John Picciano, known as Pitch, my corrections and police chief of staff; my brother, Don; Jimmy Grillo, one of my standout captains at Rikers; and Athan Tsimpedes, an attorney, met us in Cumberland for support.

———

Cumberland has two facilities: a minimum-security camp, where I was going, and down the hill a medium-security prison. The camp could almost pass for an elementary school—maybe the very first part of the generally immature, even childish atmosphere: salmon-colored stone blocks under teal roofs. The other inmates and I had complete freedom to come and go from our cubicles, the various buildings. There were no locks on any of the doors. It made the captivity all the stranger. Any inmate really could, if he wanted to, just walk out.

At the reception center Don gave the correction officer, or CO, five hundred dollars to put into my account. I was processed and then driven up to the minimum-security camp in a small white truck by Jason Courtney, my prison counselor, or supervising CO, for the dormitory I'd been assigned. He was about forty years old and had a Clark Kent look—dark hair, blue eyes, glasses. He was in the standard dark blue pants and light blue shirt of the COs. His walkie-talkie crackled with static and snatches of reports from around the prison. Courtney would become my link to the staff at Cumberland, one of the closest connections I made during my sentence.

"Was it all political?" he asked, turning his head to glance at me as he drove. He was matter-of-fact. I didn't know what to say. I'd just met him and hadn't expected the question. Later, I learned that Courtney and other Bureau of Prisons (BOP) staff at the camp had already researched my case and knew many of the details. My confirmation hearing, the vetting, my unclaimed nanny, the renovations to my Bronx apartment by an allegedly mob-connected company, the tax charges.

Inside I was still reeling from what I was now facing. The sign over the door of the Message Center read FEDERAL PRISON CAMP.

———

Courtney walked alongside me as we got out of the truck and entered the small building. He showed me around and walked me out into a courtyard that looked very much like a college campus, with a bunch of prisoners in green maintenance uniforms and black boots just milling around.

As we passed by the laundry, cafeteria, and library on our walk to my new home for the next three years, a middle-aged white inmate passed Courtney and said something under his breath to him. I didn't hear what he said, but I could tell Courtney caught it immediately. That inmate kept walking, but Courtney turned back to me as though we were in midconversation. Just then a tall, thin, young black inmate passed us. As he did Courtney pointed to a building on our left and told me to go inside and wait for him there. As I obeyed, I turned to see Courtney take off at a clip after the black inmate, who was now entering the building on our right. Then it dawned on me that the white inmate must have tipped off Courtney that the other guy had some contraband on him. Cigarettes, probably.

As this was going down and in the immediate days to come, I was gradually realizing that regardless of the term *prison camp*, where minimum-security prisoners are held by the U.S. Federal Bureau of Prisons, much of the population here seemed not very different from the inmates that I once held on Rikers Island. Most of the inmates on Rikers were pretrial; at Camp Cumberland, they were already convicted but either had shorter sentences and lower classifications or were at the end of longer sentences, and so were housed in our minimum-security camp. Many of them were or will become career criminals and they'll return to prison. Maybe not Cumberland, but there's a strong chance they'll be back. Many

won't have much choice, because the collateral cost of their convictions will prevent them from ever successfully re-entering society—from being given a fair chance to do so. With no other path available, they'll be forced to return to crime.

After Courtney snatched up and handcuffed the inmate he was tailing, he came back to where I stood waiting at G Building, Wing 1. He took me inside what resembled military quarters and showed me the bunk bed I was assigned in a four-man concrete cubicle split into two sides.

Courtney had assigned me to the cubicle of Anthony Dorsey, Sr., a heavyset sixty-one-year-old black man from Baltimore. Shortly after we introduced ourselves, he asked me, "Was nine-eleven a conspiracy?" I laughed and thought to myself, "Everything's a conspiracy, man." But Dorsey seemed well-read and well-spoken. Some didn't like him because he was a bit of a know-it-all, liked to talk against the government a lot. But that kind of stuff doesn't bother me unless it's being hammered into my face. No, Dorsey was mostly just a nice old man, and he and I got along fine for the next six months, when he was moved to another wing in the building.

Like me, Dorsey was in for tax evasion. "Nowhere in our constitution does it say anything about paying taxes," he argued, cleaning his trumpet.

"But the bottom line is you gotta pay taxes," I told him. "If you don't, you come here." Ironic, coming from a guy serving time for tax fraud. But I believe it. I believe in paying taxes. And I did pay my taxes, but over the years I also missed things and my accountants made mistakes. If I could do it over I wouldn't have hired a nanny, first of all, but if I did hire a nanny, I'd pay taxes on her. I

would be much more careful. But I also felt that I was prosecuted criminally for what are essentially civil violations. I was willing to and agreed to pay back taxes I was determined to owe, and the penalties assessed. Unlike Dorsey and a lot of the other inmates, I didn't hate the government. My tax issues weren't part of any struggle against the United States.

. . .

Dorsey loved to play chess. He kept himself occupied with that, that and his trumpet, which he spent many hours playing in a small music room on the other side of the compound.

After Dorsey, one of the first characters I met in our building was Gary Antonino, an Italian from Pittsburgh. A stocky fifty-five-year-old with gray hair, he came right up and punched me lightly in the shoulder. "Hey, Bernie Kerik, right? I'm Gary Antonino. We've been waiting for you."

I liked his style. He'd been a senior vice president for MetLife and was sharp. Gary and I hit it off and talked often. He'd gotten eighty-seven months for a bank fraud charge. He'd never had so much as a parking ticket before. The government said he owed $2 million in restitution, then they gave him more than seven years in prison, during which time he couldn't do anything to pay that back—just be here in this empty institution, I kept thinking, for eighty-seven fucking months.

There were hardened criminals and thugs in Cumberland. But I was quickly seeing too many guys who just seemed ridiculously misplaced.

Like Bob Lumpkin, a fifty-five-year-old commercial fisherman from Maryland, doing fourteen months for violating the Lacey Act. The Lacey Act became law in 1900. In lay terms, it means

Bob caught more fish than he was allowed to, or they were bigger than legally permitted, or he crossed state lines in the commission of his criminal fishing.

He reminded me of a combination of Gomer Pyle and Red Skelton, with thinning red hair, powder blue eyes, and a blotchy red complexion, obviously from the sun and sea air over the past forty years. In an aw-shucks southern drawl, he said, "I caught my first fish with my granddaddy at seven years old and I was hooked. I've never been in trouble my entire life and look where I am today." Father of two, married for more than thirty years, Bob sat in front of the dormitory television with tears in his eyes as he watched the BP oil disaster in the Gulf Coast unfold on the morning news. The oil that was killing the wildlife was killing Bob Lumpkin as well. "Now something isn't right," I thought. "This guy is in here, and BP has destroyed one-fifth of our country's coastline."

Or Terence McLaughlin, who'd been a banker for close to twenty-five years and had no criminal history. He was convicted of manufacturing and selling cigarettes and failing to pay taxes, sentenced to a year and a day.

Prison is supposed to make you stop and think, but I tried not to think about my case or the past. It haunts you, though, creeping in every day. I lay on my bed, staring at the white walls, at nothing, poring over my case, trying to understand better just what I had done, what had happened. And the other guys asked me questions, like Courtney did at the start, bringing it all back. "Hey, Bernie, I saw this on TV . . ." or "I read that you . . ." Stuff about 9/11, New York, Iraq, my prosecution. Nearly every inmate had at least an inkling of who I was. Many of them knew about my police and corrections past, too. But it felt safe in Cumberland, for the most part. Sure, if another inmate had wanted to try to

make some kind of name for himself by attacking me, he might have had a chance to try. But overall the guys in Cumberland were on their better behavior, close enough to going home, not wanting to get transferred down the hill to Cumberland's rougher medium-security facility (whose more infamous inmates include Jeffrey MacDonald, the former army doctor who was convicted of butchering his pregnant wife and two daughters; the subject of the acclaimed books *Fatal Vision*, by Joe McGinniss, and *The Journalist and the Murderer*, by Janet Malcolm).

To be honest, Cumberland wasn't such a shock. From the moment the grim process of the criminal investigation starts, it depletes you, diminishes your work ability, your social capacity, your social acceptance, so that by the time you get to prison you're already demoralized. I felt beaten down before I got there, beaten down by the state and federal investigations, the public shame. I'd risen high and fallen far.

. . .

Six, six-thirty, I'm up. Dorsey, too. Older people tend to get up early. For me it's energy, restlessness, everything I've got to do. The cubicle is just the bunk bed and the desk. All made of something like formica. The air is stale and timeless. I clean the cube, straighten up, make my bed tight. I'm a military policeman again, walking the perimeter in South Korea. I'm back at Fort Bragg. I'm doing all I can not to go fucking crazy.

I make myself coffee, dried instant espresso. I eat in the cube instead of the mess hall. I usually did.

Every prison mess hall, including in a minimum-security camp, is a part of the system that helps institutionalize the inmates, where much of the food is outdated and wouldn't be eaten on the out-

side. You eat off a plastic tray, with plastic forks and spoons. Guys stuff their pockets with plastic baggies full of vegetables, bread, and meat to take back to their dormitories. It's part of turning you into an animal—the stale food, the stagnant environment, guys acting like kids as they go from table to table, joking around, talking a lot of nonsense.

I hated the mess hall and went as little as possible.

After breakfast, I go on the computer in the email room in our wing, check my messages, my vital link to the outside world. At five cents a minute, a lot of guys couldn't afford it. After emailing I head to the gym.

Back to our building at 10:30 a.m. for recall and a head count. Soon, lunch. I eat in my cubicle again, chicken or tuna from commissary.

Nothingness and monotony. I'm seeing the massive waste. I'm noticing it very early and that's not a good sign. Rikers was full of jails, not prisons. In the NYC correction system, we had jails and detention centers. We didn't hold long-term inmates. I'm embarrassed to learn this way that we are, by the powers of the federal government, basically just wasting away time and days, years and lives and billions of dollars.

There is a mandatory count at 4:00 p.m., dinner at 5:00, and then recall again at 8:30 p.m. Night. Another day. Friends and family members would drop items, packages, cigarettes, and food on the road that borders the prison. Guys would run down to the road to pick stuff up and come back. When they got caught, they were transferred to other facilities. I watched this action sometimes from the outside track, walking laps, little pieces of glass in the dirt. Cumberland was formerly the site of a glass factory.

———

. . .

Thank God for books. It was in books that I could get lost and escape the daily mental grind. I read a lot at night in my bunk, more than I'd read in my entire life. I told a friend of mine the titles I was interested in and he'd send them to me: *The Last Lion*, a trilogy on Winston Churchill; *The Last Lecture*, by Randy Pausch; *Night*, by Elie Wiesel; George W. Bush's *Decision Points*; Barack Obama's *Dreams From My Father*. I loved Alexandre Dumas's classic *The Count of Monte Cristo*. What I found so interesting was that although it was written hundreds of years ago, in a different country, the themes of injustice and revenge were the same, easily recognizable.

I read a number of excellent criminal justice books, which had a special impact, including those written by my friend Andrew Napolitano. The Heritage Foundation's *One Nation Under Arrest* shines a spotlight on overcriminalization. The book's subtitle spells it out: *How Crazy Laws, Rogue Prosecutors, and Activist Judges Threaten Your Liberty*. Michelle Alexander's *The New Jim Crow* convincingly makes its point. Then again, I had the evidence all around me—the destruction of the black community in particular by an unjust and prejudiced legal system. Another book that took me to some difficult places was *The Autobiography of an Execution*, by David Dow, a law professor and litigation director of the Texas Defender Service.

One of my favorite books that I read in prison was actually a set of three, written by the brilliant historian Edmund Morris, dealing with U.S. politics, New York City, the NYPD dating back to the 1800s, and one of the best-remembered U.S. presidents, Theodore Roosevelt. Roosevelt is a hero to many, but to me and the thirty-nine New York City police commissioners who held that office before me, the connection is just a little more personal knowing that Roosevelt once carried a shield or badge like the one

I did, and because for a time I occupied his desk in the commissioner's office at police headquarters in Manhattan.

Most guys in our wing, on the first floor, read at night. The other three wings were a lot louder, with the lights on until four in the morning—guys running around, playing cards and chess, music on. Some called those other wings upstairs the "jungle habitat" because they were so raucous at night. We were more civilized—but still animals. Yes, even in a supposedly cushy federal prison camp you still feel that, in ways large and small.

During my first few weeks I met Cumberland's other prime candidate for most infamous inmate.

The first thing I noticed was the black yarmulke on the man walking ahead of me in prison greens. He wore a coat that was about four sizes too big. His pants were about three inches too long and dragged on the ground as he shuffled along. Someone yelled, "Hey, Jack!" and the man stopped to speak to a few prisoners milling about. As I got closer they all stopped talking and turned their attention to me, the new guy in the camp.

Seeing him up close, I immediately recognized the man wearing the yarmulke. Jack Abramoff, the notorious D.C. lobbyist once dubbed "The Man Who Bought Washington." He was heavier than I imagined. Although we had never met before, there were no introductions necessary, thanks to the abundant press on the two of us, independently, over the years. "You okay?" he asked me as we shook hands. He excused us from the few inmates around us and motioned me to follow him into a small office in the prison chapel. It was a plain square room with cabinets filled with props for the various religions practiced.

"I can't believe they put you in here," Abramoff said.

Then his serious tone disappeared and he made light of our

new surroundings, our outfits, the thugs walking past the open door of the office we sat in. He was charming and hysterically funny, but with all his humor and charm he still couldn't hide his hatred for many of the inmates and the camp itself.

"They're animals," he said. "They should blow this entire place up." I'd once read that Abramoff was a racist, but that's not what I got from that first conversation or the many that followed before they let him go. He was an equal-opportunity hater. He was a stone patriot and didn't like liberals or thugs, didn't matter if they were black, white, or Hispanic. If you fell into one of those two categories (and neither is necessarily easy to define), he didn't like you. He spoke his mind, like it or not, and I noticed quickly that the other prisoners respected him and kept their distance, even the bullies.

"They're afraid of me because I speak to the staff," Abramoff told me with a devious smile. "And I will if they act like idiots." He would mock their ghetto slang and go into a thirty-minute tirade about America today and our educational system and its failures. "Here's the future of our country," he said mockingly as a young Arab kid walked into the chapel looking for some juice. We laughed, even the Arab kid. Later I learned that this kid was the camp's supplier of cell phones, tobacco, and other contraband.

Although I had read a lot about Jack and his case over the years, my own experience with the press left me unsure of what to believe. But in Gary S. Chafetz's fascinating book *The Perfect Villain*, I learned that Jack played the same game as thirty-five thousand other registered lobbyists. He did what they were doing and continue to do today, but he was made a target. It's hard to feel that any justice was done when prosecution seems so selective.

I got to sit with Jack frequently during the three weeks before his release. I found him to be forthright, patriotic, and profoundly religious. In my view, whatever mistakes he'd made, he'd paid for them by serving his years in prison.

Before he left Cumberland, Abramoff met with the chaplain—a young guy who was not an inmate—and convinced him to let me replace Abramoff as the clerk in the chapel. The chapel clerk's primary job was to maintain the religious props and prevent inmates from hiding contraband in there. Both the chaplain and Courtney confirmed that I had the job. It would be perfect—a small office where I could work, read, and focus on the future. I might even have access to a typewriter.

The following Monday my hopes were dashed. Courtney called me into his office. "Listen, I know we talked about you being the clerk in the chapel, but it's not happening. You've been assigned to kitchen duty, either washing dishes or mopping floors." I asked him what happened, why the sudden switch. Courtney just hunched his shoulders as if to say *shit happens*. I learned later that it was on orders from the unit manager, a woman who oversaw the camp.

I couldn't help but wonder what was behind this. When I got back to the wing, I told some of the other guys about it. "They did the same thing to Jack when he first got here," they told me, talking about Abramoff. Right there it felt like the prison was going too far to simply degrade and demean me, by giving me the shittiest job they could. To show me who was boss. Of course I understood that feeling very well. I felt it many times when I struggled and fought with inmates in the Passaic County Jail. *Show 'em who's boss.* Iron fist. I felt it and thought it when I inspected Rikers. *Show 'em who's boss.* But I knew I couldn't act on that impulse. I knew—and

this was a huge part of my success in running the NYC jail system—that if you demean and try to disrespect inmates, regardless of what they've done and how you feel about them morally, you will get the same thing back. Not as a cop, or as a correction officer, or as warden, or as commissioner did I go out of my way to degrade and demean lawbreakers or inmates, because I wanted to be good at those jobs, and that meant avoiding trouble, not creating it, and staying smart, understanding how respect is exchanged.

Apparently, when the unit manager found out about my chapel assignment, she basically said, "He ain't getting that job." I think she took it as a badge of honor, that she could make me mop floors for the next six months.

I told Jack about it. "They do it because they can," he said.

Just some extra punishment. The kind that some of the staff, like the bad apples back in the halls of Rikers, liked to dole out. All the little degradations that go into creating life for the inmate after the sea change of losing your freedom, having it taken. Prison doesn't need to be like this, I found myself thinking in ways I never had before. You have already been punished tremendously, mentally and physically, with the loss of your freedom. But some correctional staff believe it's their job to break you more once you're there, to degrade, demean, and demoralize you further. Unfortunately, they're too stupid to realize, as is anyone who agrees with such treatment of lawbreakers and convicts, that this behavior in fact hurts the prison facility, the families involved, and most of all society when the inmate is released. More than 90 percent of America's prisoners will return to society.

This insidious attitude was reflected in something as simple as the way one of the case managers for the camp walked around

The inmates had their sense of being in there. They may hate your guts, but if you don't disrespect them, and you give them what they're supposed to get, the arrangement can work. You won't have problems. If you disrespect them, it'll get dangerous.

One reason some of the Cumberland staff, too many of them, from both my inmate and warden perspectives, could be disrespectful or neglectful was that they could transfer us, or just threaten to transfer us, down the hill to the medium-security facility. No inmate in the camp wanted that to happen.

Courtney, our Clark Kent counselor, was different. He was firm but fair. That really is the best way to sum up and praise Courtney. We had a secretary in our building named Tammy Miller. She was another member of the staff who was cordial and fair, as were Anthony (Tony) Welsh and William Pugh. They were among the staff members whom an inmate could speak to and be treated with decency. They didn't look at you or treat you as morally inferior. They wouldn't say or do anything to rub your face in your punishment, which was being exacted every moment you were there and not free.

· · ·

Gary Antonino, the former MetLife executive, and I would walk into Courtney's plain office in our building and sit with him. On the floor next to his file cabinets would always be bags of stuff he'd confiscated on his passes through the dorm: cigarettes, sneakers, unauthorized clothes. Always a bag of shit on his desk or the floor. That was his job. Those were the rules. Courtney didn't enforce them condescendingly. He didn't talk down to you. He'd been

with an aura of disdain for every one of us. I couldn't figure out which she hated more, us or her job. She seemed to go out of her way to demean us. As case manager she was supposed to help us with our programming, help prepare us for getting out of the system (who doesn't want this?), coordinate with halfway houses. But she would resist giving any of that assistance. It was painfully clear that hers was not the right personality for the job. You didn't need to have run a prison to see that.

This woman would literally look down or away when I passed her and said hello politely. Like I wasn't even there. She did it to all of us.

This might sound trivial to you, but hold on. These are the things that can make or break an institution—the staff, how they interact with the inmates. All the little things. Rikers had shown me that. You can't disrespect people and think they are going to respond nicely or do what you want.

When this case manager disciplined people for having contraband, she took their good time, the days off their sentence that they'd earned from programs and other allegedly rehabilitative activities. The CO can take your phone time, your commissary, but no, she liked to take away your good time, the most precious thing of all.

Actually, that kind of sticking it to the inmates wouldn't work in a high- or medium-security prison. People like that wouldn't stay on the job, because you can't disrespect inmates like that. They will wait and they will come after you.

This is why I always told my staff at Rikers, "Do not disrespect the inmates. You might disrespect them, antagonize them, and you go home, but the next poor CO walks through the door, and he gets knifed."

a state correction officer in West Virginia, I think it was. He and I talked shop—criminal justice, prison management, crime. I would complain about the federal system to him all the time. He didn't respond; he'd just look at me with his intense blue eyes and nod. He also never disagreed with me. Anybody with exposure to the federal system, who is honest, would have to agree. There aren't enough programs. It is a colossal waste of time and life. I didn't understand this when I was warden or commissioner, I'm embarrassed to say. I didn't see it, not with this focus, with these words and this perspective. Being an inmate showed me this. Prison was the finishing touch in my education on these matters. Cumberland was teaching me a bad lesson very quickly, in mind-numbing days.

But I still had hope that first year, before my appeal. I still thought that somewhere down the line I was going to get some reduction on my four-year sentence. I was going to be able to get back to my family sooner. The nothingness could last only so long.

. . .

I'm standing in a cluster of inmates in the hallway entrance as a CO stands in front of us handing out mail. My nerves are jumping. The CO hands me a card from Celine. On the front of the card is one word: POSITIVE.

Dear Dad,

You will never know how much I love you. Please stay strong. I know you are a strong guy but everybody has feelings.

What I would like to say is keep a positive attitude and I will always be there for you.

———

*Family, friends, fans, and I all love you. I was looking for the
right card and I found it.*
POSITIVE

Love,
Celine

I finish reading the card. I'm breathless, like I've gotten the wind
knocked out of me. I turn my head from the other men and quickly
walk away, hiding the tears streaming down my face.

3

Eyes Open

Have you ever wondered what your world would be like without you in it?

Think about all the things that happen in your daily life and what it would be like if you weren't around to deal with them. Could your spouse and children do without you? What would it be like for you to have a bird's-eye view of this world, your world, with you missing? What would you see if you died with your eyes open?

Before my imprisonment, I never considered this. At Passaic County, as a CO, I'd come and go. Inspections at Rikers, walking through, coming out, not staying behind, not locked behind the doors I walked past, whose keys I turned. I know these places, what a cell block feels like. I've looked in at and spoken to the men and women behind those doors and barred windows. But even doing all of that doesn't mean you then know what it's like to be an inmate.

"This is like dying with your eyes open." When my fellow in-

mate Eric Ring uttered these words to me one day in Cumberland, I felt like someone had frozen me on the spot. He was right. That was how it felt, like a kind of waking death.

He and I were in Cumberland's cavernous gym. I was doing pull-ups on a bar while he sat on a Ping-Pong table next to me, waiting for his turn. His muscular tattoo-covered arms shone in the July heat. I'd seen Eric but had never spoken to him before that day. He was just another of the roughly three hundred minimum-security inmates in the camp, and he didn't appear to be someone I would want to hang out with. He was shaved bald, was covered from his neck down with tattoos, and walked with a slow prison swagger that gave you the impression he came from the wrong side of the tracks. But that preconception disappeared as soon as he spoke.

"I worked two jobs, supported my wife and two kids," he told me. He said he owned his own house. He'd been arrested for a first-time low-level drug offense by state authorities in Maryland—possession of nine grams of cocaine, if I remember correctly. Just before he was supposed to show up in court, where his attorney said that he'd probably get probation and a possible fine, his attorney informed him that his case had been turned over to the federal government for prosecution. Threatened with a lengthy prison term, Eric wound up accepting a plea deal for thirty-six months. As it would turn out, that punishment was only the beginning of his troubles.

"So I lost both my jobs," he said, wiping the sweat off his face. "Then my wife became ill. She can't work."

He applied for a compassionate furlough from Cumberland to accompany his wife to the hospital, and requested additional halfway house time, which would get him back to his family sooner.

Both requests were denied, and he received a note from the warden telling him to avail himself of Cumberland's psychological services, or the chaplain's, neither of which could do anything to assist his family.

As Eric sat there explaining all this to me, in what was our first real conversation, I couldn't help feeling horrible for this man, his wife, and their children. I told him as much. As someone who had put plenty of people in prison for drugs, I had mixed feelings about his situation. I believe he should have been held accountable for his actions, but it was nine grams of cocaine—roughly the weight of seven or eight sugar packs in a coffee shop—and it was his first offense. There was no violence involved in his crime. He was working two jobs and had a home and a family to take care of. In light of all this, I thought his thirty six month sentence was excessive. Given his wife's condition, and the fact that they had no one else to take care of their kids, why couldn't Eric have been given home detention, been allowed to work and take care of his family? He had already been punished by his conviction, along with the resulting collateral economic costs.

Where I might have arrested a guy like Eric before, in my other life, now I was his fellow convict. It was as if I was seeing the whole judicial process all the way through. Here was the result of the punishment. Those men I had arrested and put into the system, this was what it did to them. Those inmates I had watched and counted and managed for years, this was what was happening to them. Here was the other side.

Every day I watched Eric walk in circles around the gym, do pull-ups and push-ups, unable to do anything to help his family or benefit society. Nothing.

Dying with your eyes open.

I understood exactly what Eric meant.

I usually called home from Cumberland daily to speak to Hala and the girls. When I called one evening in the summer of 2011, Hala told me that my brother-in-law Besim Aydin was going into the hospital to have a cyst removed from his spine. I figured I'd call him to say hi.

Besim was married to Hala's oldest sister, Maysoun, and was one of the nicest people I'd ever met. He couldn't say a negative word about anyone, and his entire life was dedicated to his wife, his eighteen-year-old son, and his triplet boys, who were thirteen at the time.

Besim was matter-of-fact but cheerful on the phone as he explained to me the routine procedure he was going to have. He was more concerned about me than himself, and we agreed that the following weekend after the surgery he and his family would come down to Cumberland to see me.

He went into surgery on a Thursday morning, and when I called Hala that night, she told me Besim was doing fine. I spoke to her again that weekend, and Besim was recovering nicely.

Then on Monday afternoon I called her just to say hi, and she answered sobbing uncontrollably into the phone. I could hear women in the background crying loudly. "He's in a coma!" Hala blurted out before I had a chance to ask her anything. "His heart stopped. He wasn't breathing, and now he's in a coma."

I was floored. I tried to console her, but she cut me off and said she had to get off the phone. I started calling back every few hours to see what was going on; each time the news was grim. I felt horrible. I couldn't be there for Hala and my daughters, who were terrified, but worse, I couldn't be there for Besim's wife and

four sons. This went on for eleven days. I felt absolutely helpless, a sickening powerlessness.

When I called home early on the morning of the twelfth day, it only got worse: Hala told me that Besim had died in the early morning hours. Hala now had to take care of her grieving sister, her sons, and our daughters as well.

When I asked my case manager to be considered for a furlough to attend the funeral, my request was denied. When I asked for additional phone minutes, over the three hundred minutes we were allowed each month, so that I could spend more time on the phone with Hala and the girls, that request, too, was denied.

No matter what you have been incarcerated for, or how long your sentence, the one thing that is certain is that you will immediately be cut off from the outside world, including from those you love and anyone or anything that depended on you. No matter what problem or emergency might arise, no matter how devastating a circumstance might be for your family and children, the only thing you can do from prison is watch their suffering from afar and pray for them to get through it on their own.

This is a terrible collateral punishment that wounds not only the lawbreaker and inmate but also the innocent, and in turn society as a whole. The federal prison system encourages inmates to spend as much time as possible with their families, and then turns around and does many things to prevent them from doing that. Take phone calls: You can buy up to three hundred minutes of phone time per month. But think about it, if you have a family of four, for example, and they're older children, and you have ten minutes total a day, that's about three minutes a day with each person. Plus, you pay twenty-three cents per minute. From my house now in New Jersey, I can call China for five cents.

———

People have said to me, "But you were a guy who put people away. You were part of that system that took people away from their families."

I have no problem looking back over my career and recalling that I put people in prison, some for a long time. In my mind this was justified. They were bad people who did bad things. They were guys who killed people, guys who were selling tons of cocaine. They were a threat to society, a threat to innocent people, so I don't feel regrets there. But that doesn't mean that those individuals can't be treated with more thought and attention in prison; it doesn't mean that they can't be treated as more than animals, given ways to grow and improve.

In the aftermath of Besim's death, I hoped and prayed that if anything else bad was going to happen, it would at least wait until I was home so that I could be there to help.

A few months later, I realized my prayers would not be answered. In Cumberland's computer room, where inmates have access to the BOP Internet service, I opened an email from my son, Joe.

"Call me ASAP," it read. When he answered the phone, I knew it was bad. I could hear the heaviness in his voice.

"Have you heard? Mike Morgan is dead," he told me. I was floored. Couldn't get my head around it. Michael Morgan was a thirty-two-year-old detective in the Newark Police Department, one of Joe's colleagues and closest friends. He had just been shot and killed during an armed robbery.

I had helped bury and eulogize the twenty-three cops who worked for me and died on 9/11. In the aftermath of those attacks I attended hundreds of funerals, memorials, and wakes. Over my thirty-year career as a law enforcement officer I've attended doz-

ens of funerals for cops, correction officers, and firefighters killed in the line of duty around our country. But when my son needed me most for his own loss, I couldn't be there for him. It felt wrong and I felt terrible. I did everything I could to console Joe, and to help him understand that at times like that it was up to him and his colleagues to take care of the family of the cop who was killed. I did the best I could from where I was. I had my voice still. I could be there disembodied over the phone, but I felt powerless to help. I had died with my eyes open.

I lay on my bunk in our cube, thinking about Eric, Besim, and Mike Morgan, staring wide-eyed at the ceiling.

4

Time Stands Still

I often stayed up until midnight or 1:00 a.m. reading and writing in my bunk. Like a lot of guys, I slept with earplugs in, just trying to shut it all out. I walked or ran most days around the grass and gravel track outside, summer and winter. Five times around was a mile. David Johnson, a fifty-two-year-old engineer who worked for the U.S. Department of Defense for more than thirty years, would walk around that track for an hour or two a night, and four or five hours on weekends. He'd invested in a computer kiosk company that asked him to speak with potential investors over the phone. The business became the target of a federal investigation and David got forty-two months in prison for failing to inform the people he spoke with that he was being paid to talk to them. Outside on the track he was a man possessed. I watched him in disbelief at times. He could've walked to fucking China and back in the thirty months he was at Cumberland.

About a year and a half into my sentence I met a new inmate, Joe Burchfield from Rhode Island. Joe and I used to walk the

track together. A former city councilman, he'd been arrested and charged with bribery. Out of all the men I met at Cumberland, he turned out to be one of the best.

Joe was sentenced to five years, which struck me as another example of overpunishment. Yes, he broke the law, made a mistake, did something stupid, but he showed himself to be a compassionate and decent man: helping others when they arrived in the camp; looking out for the men in his cube; teaching parenting and AA classes. In meting out punishment, our prosecutors, judges, and courts should take an honest and complete look at the defendant. To my mind, Burchfield didn't need to be imprisoned for five years to be taught the error of his ways. He learned parts of his lesson the day he was arrested, then facing public humiliation, then surrendering to federal prison to be strip-searched and put into prison living conditions. And still after that, five more years in the nothingness.

Later, Joe stopped walking and switched to a cross-fitness regimen with some other inmates, doing high-intensity powerlifting, gymnastics, and calisthenics. Because the exercise equipment was so limited, Joe and the guys had to do a lot of improvising.

I stuck with my calisthenics and push-ups, doing between four hundred and a thousand every few days. By the end I'd lost about eighty pounds. Joe lost sixty, and of the three hundred guys in Cumberland, he might have been in the best shape.

I'd shaved my mustache before reporting to prison, not because I was marking this dramatic change in my life, but simply because I messed it up while trimming it. I'd worn a mustache ever since I was fifteen, with the exception of a brief stint in the Cumberland County (irony not lost on me), North Carolina, sheriff's office, which didn't allow patrolmen to wear one.

I needed contact with Hala and my daughters. Initially, for about the first six months, they visited me once a month. Thereafter it was about once every two or three months. Time, distance, and money were the big factors.

Of course there was the excitement and anticipation of their visits, but those precious meetings were roller coasters of emotion.

We sat in the visiting room on plastic chairs. Quilts sewn by inmates at Cumberland hung from the walls. A little sign said:

STRESSED IS DESSERTS SPELLED BACKWARDS.

TAKE IT ONE BITE AT A TIME.

We ate snacks, frozen hamburgers and chips, from the vending machine—only I wasn't allowed to stand up. The rule is the inmate must remain seated. So if you want something to eat, your family, your visitor, has to get up and get it for you and heat it up in the microwave, adding to the general humiliation and strangeness. Mind you, this is in a minimum security camp. So even during your visit, what is supposed to be a positive, constructive time for you and your family, you're still under the thumb of the prison authorities. And not just you, but your family, too. Your wife and kids may have been wanded and patted down on their way in. Then there is their confusion—"Daddy, why can't you get up yourself? Why won't they let you stand?" They get an early, up-close view of institutionalization. It's a humiliation for you and them just being there.

Piper was a CO in the visiting area who was always courteous and professional. She did her job, but she didn't treat your family like inmates, with that kind of obvious distaste. There were other COs who did.

———

One of the most painful things to see at Cumberland was a family united for the first time in the visiting room. Mothers, fathers, wives, and children all coming in for their first visit with one of the men in the camp. I would often try to look the other way, just so I didn't have to see the tears, the children who would scream and cling to their fathers as they were about to leave. It was horrifying for the children. They would leave that room as if they were never going to see their fathers again. I knew those feelings throughout my life, with my mother, my oldest daughter, my little girls and wife, my son.

On their visits, Hala and I had conversations about personal issues that were a strain on the family: about my appeal, the kids, my release, our finances, not having any income. Some of these conversations were obviously upsetting, but you don't want to show the kids you're upset. Also, if the kids are acting out or behaving badly in some way, you don't want to correct them or say anything negative to upset them, because then they leave and you're left in that nothingness like a basket case with your conscience playing on you.

Hala and I tried everything in our power to keep Celine and Angelina stabilized without putting any added pressure on them. Thank goodness we were able to keep our house back in New Jersey throughout everything.

When they walk out of the building at the end of the visit and you go back to your cube, a complete depression comes down on you. You don't sleep that night. Your mind wanders in a thousand different directions. Hala herself would sometimes drive the girls down to see me. I'd be a mess worrying about them for the six hours the drive back home would take them.

But of course, the more support and care an inmate has out-

side, the easier it is to survive. I was lucky enough to have some very supportive friends who helped me and my family get through my sentence. A lot of guys don't have that. I know how blessed I've been.

. . .

I mopped floors, then went to work in the library.

A year and a half in, I moved into the cube next door, where lived a tiny sixty-six-year-old Puerto Rican from the Bronx whom I will call Rodrigo Gomez. He was quiet, clean, and courteous— a model prisoner. For the year and a half we were together Rodrigo only called me "Mr. Kerik." We talked a lot about his case, the cocaine conspiracy charge that was a prime example of a rigged plea. It had netted him ten years.

I tried to keep my head from spinning out of control.

I continued my almost daily conversations with Courtney in his office, with those bags of confiscated cigarettes and clothes on his floor, his calm demeanor and fairness, his understanding of the federal system's failings reminding me that all was not lost.

I noticed improprieties around the camp, especially involving one of the COs who worked in the camp's garage, where the BOP's vehicles were serviced. He was perhaps the most corrupt public officer I've ever seen in action. I understand there is a public perception that I am corrupt. Certainly my convictions feed that perception. But I will present the case later in this book, and you can make your own judgment about how corrupt I am.

This garage CO was one of those guards who would treat everyone like a piece of shit—barking orders, slamming doors, a scowl on his face. If you weren't a white country boy, he would treat you like garbage.

———

I stayed away from the garage, because I didn't want to be around this guy. I do believe that he would have stolen anything in the camp that wasn't nailed down. I once witnessed him load four brand-new tires from the garage into his truck. He'd also get the inmates who worked in the food warehouse to load up his own truck with taxpayer-funded food, twenty-pound turkeys, green beans. Who knows what he did with it.

One day at lunch in the mess hall, I watched this garage CO walk over to Rodrigo, my tiny sixty-six-year-old cube mate, who was on line and about to put some food on his tray. He stepped on Rodrigo's foot. "Are you wearing your steel-toed boots?" he asked Rodrigo. That was BOP policy.

"I only have these. I don't have steel-toed boots," Rodrigo told him, still holding his tray of food.

"You can't eat," he barked. "Get out of here. You can't eat unless you got steel-toes. Go!"

Rodrigo walked back to our dorm and found Courtney, told him what happened. Courtney marched right back to the mess with Rodrigo in tow, sat him down at a table near the door, walked right past the garage CO—who was glaring at both Courtney and Rodrigo—filled a tray with food, walked it back to where Rodrigo was sitting, put it in front of him, and then stood there while Rodrigo ate to make sure that the other CO couldn't fuck with him while he did.

I respected Courtney. You cannot get respect without giving it. This holds true even with convicts and wrongdoers. If the convicted are not treated fairly, and with a certain level of basic human respect, then our criminal justice system cannot truly be reformed. We as a society will not progress, and the United States will remain retrograde and unevolved in our practice of law, order, and justice. We are not who we say we are then.

———

. . .

My appeal in the *United States of America v. Bernard Kerik* was heard back in New York City in 2011, at the Daniel Patrick Moynihan Courthouse near City Hall, where I had once sat with the mayor and helped run this great city. I sat back in Cumberland and pored over my case, obsessing over every detail, every possible outcome.

It came to nothing. The judges sided with the prosecution, who said that the original judge, Stephen C. Robinson, had had the power and authority to sentence me to fifteen months above the negotiated plea agreement, just as he did.

After all your appeals are exhausted you come to the realization that you're staying there. One piece at a time your hope gets chipped away. You go into a different mode. A deeper depression sets in. This is something you can't get away from. No longer could I cling to those little hopes of getting out sooner rather than later. I'd be in Cumberland for the long haul.

My job in the camp's library was on the weekends, four hours on Saturday, four on Sunday. Eighteen cents an hour, the same as my kitchen pay. So in an hour I wouldn't earn enough for even a one-minute phone call, which cost twenty-three cents.

I was a clerk and sat at a desk and handed out forms. Thinking about it now brings back the sting of the humiliation and wasted time.

On Friday nights we would get crazy in the cubicle and make Mexican-style tortillas with mozzarella cheese, pepperoni, and to-mato sauce. Looking back, it was completely disgusting, but back then it was not so bad, something different from the monotony of our food and all our days.

———

5

Taming Rikers

How could I do my time in Cumberland without thinking back to when I ran New York City's Department of Correction in the 1990s? The parallels were obvious and dripping with irony—for me a cold irony. The jailer now jailed. The commissioner now an inmate.

But this gave me added insight. In Cumberland I thought often of Rikers Island, that sprawling penal colony, one of the largest in the world, in New York's East River, which still represents one of my greatest career achievements. I look back on that time with pride.

In 1994, just after I was appointed to the New York City DOC, I was told over and over by city officials, friends, and observers that I should never have taken the job. "Rikers is too big, too violent and out of control," they said. "It can never be fixed. Don't waste your time." The general sense was that the place was set to explode.

I recall the bridge out to the island, and how from the crest of

it you'd suddenly have a view of the enormous, forbidding sprawl ahead. I took my father to visit Rikers once, after I'd become first deputy commissioner in 1995, and as we crested that bridge, he looked out and said, "Where's the jail?" "Dad, that's the island," I told him. He was looking for one isolated building, when in fact Rikers is home to ten different jails, holding up to sixteen thousand inmates at any one time, a formidable city within the city. The entire New York City correction system consisted of sixteen jails, fifteen holding facilities, and four prison hospital wards. Roughly 133,000 inmates passed through the system each year, with a force of 13,000 correction officers running it. The responsibility was enormous.

I'd sometimes go out to Rikers at night, the darkness cut by the lights pointing out at the fences and the water. The only activity you'd see was the security on the outside. You knew what was inside, unseen within the walls: an enormous pent-up energy with deadly potential. Many of the pretrial inmates were there for acts of violence. Anything could happen at any moment. The island possessed a danger.

In the month in which I became first deputy, we had 130 stabbings and slashings in the system. This was average—several serious acts of violence a day. Six years later, during my final month before being appointed police commissioner and departing the DOC, there was only one such violent act. In those six years, New York City's jail system had gone from being one of the most violent, overcrowded, and mismanaged in the country to an international role model of efficiency, accountability, and safety. This success we achieved showed me that nothing is impossible. Change *is* possible.

In 1999 *City Journal* published a long article titled "Why the

Jails Didn't Explode," about Rikers Island and the way the Department of Correction under my leadership was able to tame that jungle. The *New York Times* ran the article "An Iron Hand at Rikers Drastically Reduces Violence." For the first time in decades, the largest and most violent jail system in America was under control.

I had the positive organizational experiences of having been in the U.S. military and the NYPD to inform my approach to the challenge of running Rikers. Morale, accountability, communication, and respect were the keys.

To address these critical issues—the high rate of violence that led, in turn, to high levels of employee overtime and absenteeism, low staff morale, and unsanitary conditions in the jails—in 1996 we implemented a new management concept that I had created: the Total Efficiency and Accountability Management System (TEAMS).

I had seen the results and efficiency of COMPSTAT in the NYPD. Created by the visionary Jack Maple and our current NYC police commissioner, Bill Bratton, in the mid-1990s, COMPSTAT used performance indicators (numbers and statistics gathered consistently and accurately) to achieve objectives and make the department more efficient.

With TEAMS—which would eventually be a finalist for Harvard's John F. Kennedy School of Government Innovations in American Government Award in 2000—the New York City Department of Correction under my command brought both order and high-quality services to the largest jail system in the country. Traditional thinking says that the only way to establish order is by cracking down on inmates, through extreme regimentation and taking away amenities and services. But we demonstrated that order and services were both obtainable, and that they in fact reinforce each other.

———

As "broken-window" policing and similar public-order philosophies had noted, the little details were crucial. We cleaned up Rikers and the other city jails, painting over the graffiti, much of it gang-related, putting in more lights and fans, constantly scrubbing the walls and floors until they were shipshape. I was notorious for my inspections, during which a burned-out lightbulb that hadn't been replaced would be a problem, because I'd make it one. I was a hard-ass, I was. I wanted things done right.

We washed and painted the DOC buses used to transport inmates. I introduced crisper uniforms, lending a paramilitary pride to the officers, who previously had often appeared slovenly, not much better dressed than the inmates. I was asking our agency to think of itself differently. New York City Correction, like many jail and prison systems elsewhere, was seen as the ugly stepchild of the overall justice system. It should not be treated as such; it should not be seen by the public that way either.

There was great resistance to change, as we still see. What got repeated all the time was "But we've always done it this way," and "That isn't the way we do it." When you hear that, you should be suspicious, whether you're running a pizza place or a prison. Those who didn't want to help effect the positive changes I was seeking, who didn't get with the new and necessary program, who didn't rise to meet their responsibilities, were demoted or fired. There was a lot of upheaval in the department, and I was not liked by everyone.

I demanded accountability, from both correction officers and inmates. With TEAMS, we identified and tracked hundreds of specific performance indicators (for example, the time it takes for an inmate to see a doctor; the number of slashings in a particular facility; rate of sick days and overtime), and then shared this timely

and accurate statistical information at monthly TEAMS meetings attended by department heads, all the different facility wardens, and the entire executive staff.

At the meetings, executive staff, using our statistical information, would question, discuss, praise, or reprimand managers based on the knowledge they displayed of their commands, their awareness of the issues, and the actions they'd taken since the last meeting. Uniformed and nonuniformed managers would conduct dialogues in a way that they'd never done before. Given that we collected our data and statistics daily, we could identify problems immediately and develop remedies for them on the spot. In this way, the department's decision-making process was streamlined and accelerated, because all agency decision-makers were there in the same room, on the same page. We all heard the same reports.

When my TEAMS meetings first began, senior uniformed staff felt threatened by the concept of accountability, by being held responsible for their command's performance. Managers were skeptical of the process, believing that it was only about one's ability to "know the numbers." The meetings were rough at times. At the very least, wardens had to know their inmate counts. They had to have answers to my questions. They couldn't continue to be managers in title only, who didn't involve themselves in the jails they were supposed to be responsible for.

The objective was not to embarrass people, or to measure their speaking skills. Instead, the meetings were about the substance of correction management: a forum to ensure efficiency and effectiveness in identifying, discussing, and solving problems.

For example, at one meeting we discussed the seizure of scalpels from inmates at Rikers. At the same meeting we identified where these weapons were coming from and devised on the spot

a plan of action and procedures to prevent this from occurring in the future—and with managers from all the jails there in the room, the problem was solved department-wide. It wasn't brain surgery.

If I learned that some inmate didn't get his food or medical attention on time on one occasion, that was one thing. But if it was a pattern over days or weeks, we would figure out why and who was at fault.

Once every two or three weeks, on Friday, my chief of staff, John Picciano, would pull the assignment rosters from the facilities, identify several COs working security posts that day, and then call the chief of department, the senior uniform manager in the agency, to pull those COs off their posts and send them to me. I'd wind up with twenty COs in my conference room. John would order pizzas and sodas. "Have something to eat. Relax. The commissioner wants to talk to you," he'd tell them. I'd come in, take out my commissioner's shield, and lay it on the desk. "Mayor Giuliani just gave you my job," I'd say. "If you were made commissioner, what would you do to make your job safer, easier?" Thirty percent of the answers would be off-the-wall, but a lot of those answers held great stuff. Those sessions empowered the COs, kept them thinking.

My management style was all about common sense: You treat staff the way you would want to be treated. You reward those who succeed, and you discipline those who don't. Our new approach gave officers and managers incentive. It empowered those who took on the challenge, who embraced their responsibility. I fed them these chances, and many of them ran with the ball and were duly rewarded and promoted.

Of course, stemming the tide of violence at Rikers was the most important task. If we could achieve that, we would improve

morale all around. To do this, we had to hold the inmates accountable. You can't put people in prison and then let them do crime inside. Aside from making these places dangerous hellholes for both staff and inmates, it sends the wrong message—that the authorities either are too weak to keep order and maintain the peace or just don't give a shit. People can't break the law in prison and think it's okay. It's not okay.

If you slash a guy in the face on the street, you're going to be charged with criminal possession of a weapon and with assault. Why is this tolerated in prison? It's simple logic, but before I became correction chief, inmates who committed violent acts usually faced no more punishment than the loss of certain privileges. You cannot allow lawlessness to prevail among those who have already broken the law. This mentality that this is just what happens in jail, that it's supposed to be a dangerous hellhole, is insidious and counterproductive.

Under my lead, we instituted a zero-tolerance, proarrest policy in the jails, sending a message to the inmate population that violent acts would likely result in criminal prosecution. We arrested violators and charged them and they went to court. Part of the resistance to doing this is financial. No one wants to spend money on these cases. What many fail to realize is that the money you spend now is a cost-saver later.

To deal with the rampant violence, I expanded our Emergency Services Unit, which now not only responded to emergencies, but also performed random searches, confiscating many weapons. I broadened the scope of the essential and highly effective Gang Intelligence Unit to include the identifying, tracking, gathering, and accessing of intelligence and information on gang members and their illegal activities throughout the jail system.

I also knew we had to equip our COs better, give them the tools to conduct their job more safely. I remember seeing photos of a riot at Rikers before I joined the DOC. In these photos the officers were holding brooms and garbage can lids as shields. I got them better equipment: pepper sprays and mace; soft tubes to cover the cuffed hands of violent inmates when they were being transported; 9mms instead of old revolvers; stun shields that briefly incapacitated violent or defiant inmates with a jolt of electricity; body orifice security scanning (BOSS) chairs that greatly reduced the need for cavity and strip searches.

Of course, we had to make sure that these new tools were not abused. We instituted strict protocols and trained officers to use them responsibly. Still, there was an outcry from the ACLU and other quarters about the use of the sprays and the stun shields, but these did not do any permanent damage to inmates, and their effects lasted only long enough for officers to gain control.

Also, I was well acquainted with the more brutal alternative: cracking the gate and going in to face an uncooperative, dangerous, and possibly armed inmate with your fists. As the commander of the Emergency Services Unit at Passaic County Jail in the early 1980s I was the go-to guy for cell extractions. If an inmate created problems, fought, lit someone on fire, refused to come out of his cell, I was the guy who had to go in and get him.

First I would talk to the inmate for a few minutes to try to get him to come out and behave peaceably. I didn't attack people for no reason, and if officers under my command at Rikers did, they would be held accountable and punished.

"You're coming out," I would tell the rebelling inmate. "There's no question about that. You can do it quietly and without a fight or I'm gonna come in there and get you." It didn't make a differ-

ence to me who the guy was or how big he was. Back then, cell extractions weren't as organized as they are today (and they still result in fatalities). There were times you'd have to go it alone, or with one other CO, go into the block, into the cell, no backup, no pads, no stun shield, no helmet. "Crack the gate," I'd say, and when it opened, it was on. It was between you and that guy, man-to-man, hand-to-hand combat.

I've had plenty of bruises, sprains, fortunately nothing too serious. I was a black belt in Japanese karate and in the Korean martial art of tae kwon do (I studied it in South Korea when I was stationed there as a military policeman in the U.S. Army) and had been a hand-to-hand combat instructor for Special Forces at the J.F.K. Unconventional Warfare Center. I knew plenty of COs who were injured much worse in these exchanges with inmates—which were demoralizing and dangerous for all involved.

At Rikers, before I improved the cell extraction procedure and brought in the new equipment, these exchanges often led to injuries, hospital stays, and overtime for other COs to cover for those injured, or frightened into taking frequent sick days, or detailed to watch injured inmates during extended hospital stays. I couldn't continue to let COs go into cells to subdue rebellious inmates. The stun shields and sprays actually made these unavoidable exchanges safer for both staff and inmates. They improved morale and discipline.

In an episode of *60 Minutes* on Rikers Island under my leadership, Mike Wallace raised the complaints about the use of the shields and sprays. I asked him if the concerned parties were also complaining that we weren't beating down inmates anymore, because in my opinion, that was far more inhumane.

A key to all this was treating the inmates with respect. This was

what I taught my officers: I didn't want them to physically or verbally abuse any inmate. I taught them to refer to inmates as "sir" or by their last name preceded by "mister." Much of the prison population is black and Hispanic. I grew up in the poor, mostly black neighborhood of Paterson, New Jersey, what most people would call the ghetto. I feel I understand these guys. I understand what they go through. I understand they're out there dealing drugs. Drugs is their profession. We're locking them up, but many of these individuals aren't violent criminals. I saw this as a street cop. These are mostly nonviolent guys who sell you a twenty-dollar bag of coke on the corner. They don't need to be treated like garbage or like animals, to be verbally and physically abused.

When we arrested guys for drugs and brought them into the precinct, I treated them like human beings. I made sure they got medical treatment if they needed it, made sure they had food, gave them cigarettes, coffee, even money out of my own pocket on a few occasions when they needed it.

The fact that they're suspects or prisoners doesn't mean you treat them like shit. This works only if your goal is to make monsters. Of course, some cops and correction officers do treat suspects and inmates like garbage, but it's wrong and they should be held accountable for such behavior, and some were on my watch. The argument is that prison is supposed to be rough; it's supposed to be hellish. This is what many law-and-order, tough-on-crime proponents say. But who really believes this? How can they? So you want prison to be tough? You want to break the wrongdoer, the inmate, mentally, and then you want to send him back into society? Only a moron would say that prison should be tough and nasty. Your objective is not to make prison rough. You've deprived the lawbreaker of his freedom already. This alone is more pro-

foundly affecting to the soul of a person than anyone who has not experienced it can ever fathom. Taking away someone's freedom is mind-altering.

Your objective should not be to treat these individuals like animals, but to prepare them for reintegration into society. Degrading and demoralizing lawbreakers—putting them in solitary without good reason; denying them contact with the outside world; making their living conditions miserable; giving them few if any productive outlets; punishing them with extra-long sentences—is not in the best interests of anyone involved, not even the misguided multitudes out there who still believe this is the proper course. People who believe that convicts need to be constantly degraded on top of having their freedom taken have got to wise up and think again. That ignorance is in many ways more dangerous than any thing else.

. . .

With TEAMS, under my leadership, the New York City Department of Correction achieved unprecedented results in all areas.

From the late 1980s through 1995, inmate slashings and stabbings ranged from 900 to 1,500 incidents each year. The entire year total for 2000, five years into our application of TEAMS, was less than the monthly average in 1995, while annual inmate admissions during those two years were essentially the same. The use of force by officers upon inmates declined markedly, from 453 incidents in 1995 to 125 in 2000. With this decline in violence came a rise in morale and a decline in sick time, leading to a reduction in overtime costs ($90 million in 1995 to $50 million in 2000). The number of beds dedicated to the department's substance abuse program increased. More inmates graduated from the residential

drug-treatment readiness programs. The time it took for an inmate to see a doctor was greatly reduced, part of a marked overall reduction in the number of inmate grievances filed.

TEAMS was adopted by the Inspector General's Office in the U.S. Department of Justice, the New Jersey State Department of Correction, and the Office of Pre-Trial Detention Services in Baltimore, Maryland, among other places. Its success is not based on conditions unique to the New York City jail system. All or parts of it can be replicated and retrofitted into any jail or prison system.

The overarching takeaway from my time at Rikers? *Nothing is impossible.*

If something's broken and needs to be fixed, and you have the right leadership and accountability in place, it can be done.

6

The Box and the Angel

On September 28, 2012, I was driven from Cumberland to the Metropolitan Correctional Center (MCC) in downtown Manhattan to serve as a state witness. At the beginning of all my legal problems, the Bronx district attorney targeted my brother's boss and my friend Frank DiTommaso. Now, six years later, the DA wanted me to testify in DiTommaso's trial.

Even though my classification was the lowest a federal prisoner could have, given my prior positions in law enforcement and high public profile, the Federal Bureau of Prisons mandated that I be designated a "Controlled Move" and "Three-Man Hold," meaning every time I left my cell to go to another part of the building, one lieutenant and two correction officers were required to escort me, during which time the entire facility had to come to a standstill, all eight hundred other prisoners on lockdown until I got to where I was going. The press played up the cop-in-prison-among-the-inmates story.

One inmate yelled to me through his cell door, "Hey, Commish, what the fuck are you doin' in here?"

I was doing my time, is what I was doing. Paying my debt. Locked in the box for twenty-four hours a day. We had showers on Monday, Wednesday, and Friday. One fifteen-minute phone call every thirty days, no access to the BOP's computer system, and an occasional offer of one hour of recreation, which was carried out in a fifteen-by-twenty-foot fenced steel cage. Every time I left my cell, my hands were cuffed behind my back, even going to the shower, which was a three-by-five-foot concrete and tile room, in which you were also locked. Breakfast was at 6:00 a.m., lunch at 11:00 a.m., and dinner at 4:30 p.m., all brought to your door and handed to you through a food slot.

For the most part, that was my main interaction with the staff, except when I was taken to the showers or had a visitor. Most prisoners in the SHU, or Special Housing Unit, were allowed visits, but when I arrived at MCC, I was informed by the captain that my visits, if I chose to have any, would have to be caged, to keep me away from other prisoners and their families. Initially, I didn't want Hala or my daughters to come to see me in a Hannibal Lecter–like scenario, but after no contact with the outside world for more than three weeks, I relented, and asked to see my wife.

Although the warden approved the visit, and the captain said it would happen, I left five weeks later, shipped back to Cumberland, without the visit or seeing my wife, or anyone else, for that matter, besides my attorney.

I was a nonviolent white-collar inmate, being housed as though I were a severe threat to staff and the facility. They may have had to isolate me, but there should be other ways to do so besides the extreme measure of solitary confinement. It was playing havoc

with my mind. All that time I'd spent in prison corridors and cell blocks, talking to inmates, dealing with inmates, battling with them, running prisons, building them. Now I was on the floor of one, losing my mind.

At Rikers, we used solitary confinement for inmates who were a threat to staff or other inmates. But to use isolation and solitary on vulnerable inmates, the mentally disturbed or suicidal, for minor institutional infractions, protective custody, or witness protection, is nothing short of inhumane and cruel and unusual punishment. Putting a suicidal inmate in the SHU can be considered aiding and assisting suicide. These uses of solitary confinement are further contradictions of our justice system's mission statements, a refutation of the claim that we intend to help offenders return to society better people.

As correction commissioner, I used to crack the gate and walk the solitary block at Rikers by myself, to inspect and look around. The inmates would see me and come to their barred windows, asking me for stuff, everything from shaving cream to visiting rights. My TEAMS prison management system looked at the things inmates are supposed to receive in order to avoid outbursts. If the inmates are taken care of, you're going to have fewer problems, and less need of solitary. That's where the answer lies.

My mental and emotional strain while in the MCC became evident, especially to my wife and lawyer, who found my letters disturbing and repetitive. I have many of them still, written on faded yellow legal sheets. They are scary to read again. It's so obvious that I'm cracking up, holding on too tightly to things then outside my control. For me personally, the mental punishment was not enough to cause permanent damage or mental illness, but no one will ever be able to convince me that any good comes out of this

———

type of isolation, other than protecting staff, the institution, or society from the most severe threats.

Throwing young inmates in the box does nothing but make them outraged and angry, and can lead to other problems, both inside and outside the institution. That is not what the system is meant for.

In my case, I was a state witness, convicted of federal false statement and tax charges, hardly the justification for extended solitary, and although I understood the need to keep me segregated from the rest of the inmate population, the lack of a reasonable classification alternative that was not so punitive was more than troubling—not only because it was about me, but because the system is failing when it intentionally, recklessly, and blindly subjects prisoners to such conditions, knowing that it has a responsibility not to scar them permanently with long-term mental illness.

As bad as it was for me and the others around me, I must admit, it was made easier by the remarkable staff members of the BOP assigned to the MCC's SHU. The solitary unit is usually the hardest group of inmates to manage. Unlike the staffs of many institutions that cage you and leave you to your own devices, these men and women were responsive and alert. This was the kind of correction work I had encouraged as commissioner, the kind of conduct, behavior, and work ethic that I encouraged in the guards under my command when I ran Rikers.

I guess I had also become used to the BOP staff back at Cumberland, who for the most part spent more time and effort trying not to do their jobs and seemed to go out of their way to ensure that no matter what you needed, you weren't getting it, even when it was mandated by law and policy. I just assumed that the entire BOP operated in the same manner—until I arrived at the MCC.

———

Inmates who exhibited any sort of trouble were addressed immediately, and if the COs couldn't handle it, a lieutenant would show up, and if necessary, they were followed by a doctor and staff from psychological services. I was impressed by most of the staff, and proud of their service. As in any public safety agency, there were staff members who were sometimes unnecessarily insulting or demeaning. The inmate next to me complained about the mice and rats, and a guard basically told him, "Get over it, you're in jail; this is how it's supposed to be." In my cell nearby, I heard this and thought, No, that's not the right answer; the answer is that we're not supposed to be living in rat shit. But most guards were professional, caring, and security-conscious.

For years, in the aftermath of the 9/11 attacks and the global war on terror, I have heard civil liberties groups complain that terror suspects were treated more harshly than other prisoners, but based on what I witnessed personally during my sixty days in the SHU, I'd disagree.

The SHU supervisor, Lieutenant Doctor, and Counselor Sharon Fields visited our wing daily, and checked on each inmate equally. If one of them had an issue or complaint, terror suspect or otherwise, it was addressed in reasonable time, most often immediately.

Every Thursday, the entire executive staff, including the warden, a woman by the name of Suzanna Hastings, and on down, toured and spoke to every prisoner. If you had a complaint that had not been addressed by the unit staff, the warden and her subordinates jumped right on it.

I was impressed and I was thankful.

Although I didn't have many issues, other men did, and not resolving such issues leads only to anger, aggression, depression,

banging on the doors, screaming and yelling, and flooding the tiers. It could put the staff and other inmates in jeopardy. It's just a matter of ensuring that they get what they're supposed to get—nothing more, nothing less. Usually, if that's done, they're fine unless they go over the edge, and that usually happens at night when no one is around and the walls begin to close in on you.

. . .

On the night of November 21, Ms. Towanda Smith, a black CO with a slight British accent, was running the SHU. She was one of the best officers I encountered during my stay there, reminding me of the best professionalism I witnessed during my time at Rikers. I was always relieved when she was working, because the inmates respected and listened to her.

If you had a problem, she handled and resolved it. From my cell, I once heard her apologize to an inmate because he didn't get his insulin medication when he thought he should, which really wasn't her fault, but she took the heat, apologized, and ended what could have been a huge headache, given the inmate's violent background. The fact that he had been housed in the SHU for more than a year didn't help, I'm sure.

On this night, as a young inmate was screaming for Jesus, banging on his door, begging for someone to let him out of his cage, the guy in the cell to my left began crying hysterically—and the entire wing went off. The screaming and banging on the doors were so loud you could hardly think straight. It was deafening.

Then from a distance, through the mayhem, I could hear a female voice faintly singing or humming. It grew louder and louder. It was almost angelic, like a Gregorian chant, and the louder it got, the quieter the prisoners became.

"O Holy Night" began echoing through the wings of the SHU in a powerful and stunning operatic voice, paralyzing the anger and paranoia of the inmates.

It was Ms. Smith, her voice soothing for the moment even the most troubled minds. I was fascinated by her voice, and even more, stunned by what she'd accomplished. Within minutes, the SHU became silent, for which Ms. Smith thanked us. About thirty minutes later, as her shift ended and she was leaving for the night, I heard one inmate after another saying, "Good night, Ms. Smith, see you tomorrow."

My sixty days in the MCC obviously seemed like nothing to some of the men. One had been there for a year, another for two. Many of them knew that they would eventually leave there for another facility with not much better accommodations. The suspected terrorists and most violent inmates would probably leave there for an equivalent cell for the rest of their lives. The BOP's online prisoner locater might as well list their "out" or release date as DECEASED. That puts everything into perspective.

For me, those months were a learning experience I hated, but equally appreciated. The experience gave me more admiration and respect for the men and women who day in and day out guard those gates and secure our country's jails and prisons. It also once again opened my eyes in a way that I'd never experienced as a law enforcement and prison administrator.

Policies on solitary confinement must be seriously looked at and constantly evaluated. Misused or abused, it can be torturous, inhumane, and mentally devastating. It can contradict the very essence of "Good Correctional Practice" and our laws that are supposed to protect Americans from cruel and unusual punishment. Voices from across the political and ideological spectrum are rais-

ing this cry. Much of our current, accepted practice is simply cruel and inhumane. Pretrial inmates can easily be manipulated into confessions, and/or pleading guilty with promises or suggestions of being released from the box. You're willing to do anything to be freed from the isolation that is mentally and emotionally breaking you down every minute you're there. For a judge to entertain a plea or motion from any defendant who is secluded in the hole, or worse, for a prosecutor to put anything like that before the court, raises serious questions of fair and impartial treatment. Of course, police get accused of the same kind of practice. As a cop I leaned on evidence. Even while in the DEA, I didn't use those games. You don't have to when you have evidence and the law is on your side.

I'm sure that most authorities have no clue how devastating and mind-altering solitary confinement can be. Common sense calls for us to address this. I say this today, but would I have said or thought it ten, fifteen, or twenty years ago? Probably not.

Every prosecutor, judge, correction officer, and jail and prison official should have to spend seventy-two hours in the hole to see what it's like. Knowing what I know now, if I still ran Rikers today I would make it a mandatory training exercise so that the COs could understand how important their jobs are when it comes to caring for and controlling those held in the SHU. There must be psychological and specialized training for those who work in solitary confinement units. The wrong staff assigned to a unit like that can be destructive and extremely dangerous.

There is a definite need for solitary confinement, in securing an institution's most violent prisoners, and our greatest threats to society and country. However, solitary should be prevented at all costs for pretrial or suicidal prisoners, protective custody or witness protection, juveniles, or as a punishment for minor infrac-

tions. I've witnessed and felt firsthand how it can cause unnecessary damage and destruction, in mental and emotional breakdowns, creating more trouble for society in general.

I've learned that the human mind can grow accustomed to and live through anything, but does society want to have to deal with people who have been through this type of treatment unnecessarily, after they've been released? We'd be fools to say yes.

. . .

I lay on my cell bed shivering from the bitter cold, downtown in the city I once helped run. I could smell something burning. Probably a fire started by an inmate in another cell. Paper, clothing, and metal burning. I knew the smell well.

Less than half a mile away was Ground Zero, where ten years before I helped lead the rescue, response, and investigation of one the deadliest terror attacks in history. It was the same smell, just from a very different source.

———

7

A Supermax for the King

A few years before becoming an inmate, I built a prison.

In 2005 His Majesty King Abdullah II of Jordan asked if I would assist him with several national security projects in his country, including designing and building a national crisis-management headquarters.

I'd met the king two years before, during my stint in Iraq as the interim interior minister in the early days of the war. From Baghdad, Ambassador Paul Bremer sent me and a group of other ministry heads to Amman, Jordan, to see if King Abdullah might help us with resources. In advance of this trip I prepared an outline of some of the things I thought the Jordanian government could help us with. In Amman we met with Jim Putt, the CIA's deputy head of station.

Around a long rectangular table, Jim and I spoke for a bit, then a door to the conference room opened and in walked His Majesty King Abdullah. He was shorter than I expected, stocky and well built, with a bit of a cocky swagger to him. He was in his late forties and spoke softly with a slight British accent. He greeted everyone nicely, then we went around the table and each visitor

introduced himself and explained what his role was in the Coalition Provisional Authority. I noticed that not one of these senior advisors was telling the king exactly how he could be of help to them, what they might need. I was slightly dumbfounded, thinking, What the fuck are we here for then if we're not telling him what we need? I felt as if we were wasting his time.

So when it was my turn to introduce myself, I decided to give my outline a shot. I brought it out, gave a copy to the king and one to Jim. Two pages of bullet points.

His Majesty studied it for a moment, looked up, and said, "This is exactly what we need." He said it would be helpful if the others followed my lead and put together lists of specific needs, which would give him a better idea of how he might help the mission in Iraq. With that the king stood, then we all did, and he walked out the door. Jim leaned over to me. "Great job," he said.

Over a drink later that evening, Jim told me that the king had asked him to work with me and his general director of the Public Security Directorate, to assist me however possible. Jim said that the commander of the PSD was Lieutenant General Tahseen Shurdom, and that the guy ate nails for breakfast.

"If Tahseen likes you," Jim told me, "your relationship with them will work. If he doesn't, he'll tell you to go fuck yourself and you'll never hear from them again."

I appreciated that. "I think we'll get along fine then," I said.

I liked Jim Putt, I liked the king, and I liked Jordan. I definitely wanted to work with them more closely.

Fast-forward two years. I got a call at my house from my old friend Charlie, now station chief in Jordan. "My friend here would like to see you," he told me. "You think it's possible for you to come see him tomorrow?"

I jumped on a Royal Jordanian flight to Amman the next evening, and met with His Majesty the following afternoon. Charlie and I sat with King Abdullah II privately as he explained that he wanted me to build him, from the ground up, a national crisis-management center.

By that point I had been working on national security projects for three years, with Rudy Giuliani and then on my own with The Kerik Group.

I was passionate about the work, and the Jordan possibility in particular. To me it was less like a job and more like a mission. I didn't get to contribute to the good fight as U.S. homeland security secretary, but I felt that the Jordan project was still a part of our national security, in our new-age battle against terrorism and Al Qaeda.

Jordan was and still is one of our closest allies in the Middle East, and they have lived with terrorism up close and personal. His Majesty was asking me to be part of protecting the peace and fighting against violent forces. I was ready and willing.

So our first project was to design and build this crisis-management center, a facility unlike any other in the Middle East, probably the first of its kind. Nobody knew what we were doing—except that there was this massive hole in the ground on the outskirts of Amman. It was about half the size of a football field, and about a hundred and fifty feet deep.

When I left the Jordan projects due to my legal issues, the crisis-management center was about 40 percent done. I'm sure it's fully operational today, and I'm proud of our work. Knowing this was my only income at the time, federal prosecutors made sure that I surrendered my passport, preventing me from continuing my work in Jordan, in turn substantially diminishing my ability to pay for my legal defense.

In 2006, about a year into working on the crisis-management center for King Abdullah, I got a call from his younger brother, Prince Ali, who was the commander of the Royal Guard, the Jordanian equivalent of the U.S. Secret Service. At that moment I was back in the States, as I used to frequently travel back and forth between New York and Amman. In fact, I flew into the Middle East forty-three times during the three years that I worked for the king.

When Prince Ali called, I was in Atlantic City attending an annual exhibition of police and correction equipment companies. Ali's voice was tense.

"We've had a serious riot in one of our prisons," he said grimly. "We'd like your help with this."

At Qafqafa, which at the time was the third-largest prison in Jordan, inmates had rioted, taking several policemen hostage and using smuggled cell phones to contact other prisons in Jordan, friends, and the media, including Al Jazeera, which widely broadcast the rebelling inmates' international call for Muslim solidarity.

Of course this was an embarrassment for King Abdullah and his government. Prince Ali said His Majesty wanted to see me to discuss the matter.

"I'm on my way," I told him.

Three weeks before that call I'd had dinner with the king and his two younger brothers, Faisal and Ali, in his modest but elegant home in Amman. We had come around to discussing how radical extremists were recruiting within Jordan's prisons. I told His Majesty that it was only a matter of time before the prisons erupted in violence. The riot happened three weeks later.

Now King Abdullah asked me to take on, in addition to building the crisis-management center, an assessment of Jordan's eleven

prisons. He wanted me to make recommendations to ensure that the country's penal facilities were safer and more secure and that they met with international standards of human rights.

The king publicly announced Jordan's worthy goal and my new role in it. "We're struggling to make our prisons tighter and more effectively guarded, while also improving on our past record in terms of compliance with minimal human-rights standards," he told reporters. "When we win credit from international monitors for having achieved these goals, it's going to be a tribute to Bernie Kerik."

King Abdullah was adamant about bringing Jordan's system into the twenty-first century in terms of civil and human rights. He was westernized. His mother, Princess Muna, the second wife of the late King Hussein, was British. Abdullah attended Oxford. So his general sensibility was progressive and modern.

As we geared up to undertake this sweeping assessment of their prison system, the king asked me to meet with Ahmad Obeidat, director of Jordan's National Center for Human Rights, to let him know that I had been retained by His Majesty to conduct an operational review of the Public Security Directorate's Department of Correction and Rehabilitation. A former prime minister, Obeidat was a kind man in his sixties. I explained to him that the purpose of our review was to identify operational strengths and weaknesses and barriers to efficiency, and to provide the kingdom with recommendations on how to restructure and modernize its correctional system.

Obeidat was excited to hear what the king was doing and that I would be including in my recommendations a review of the findings and concerns highlighted in recent reports on Jordan by the Red Cross, Human Rights Watch, and Amnesty International.

———

For my assessment team I recruited some of the standouts from the NYC Department of Correction when we led our historic turnaround in the late nineties—including a brilliant woman by the name of Debbie Kurtz, a former deputy commissioner who oversaw training for Rikers Island, and retired captain Jim Grillo, an extremely experienced and knowledgeable officer who oversaw training and logistics for the DOC's Emergency Services Unit.

Over the next year, Kurtz, Grillo, and a few others conducted numerous site inspections of the eleven prisons located throughout the kingdom, examining the system using the standards outlined by the United Nations for the treatment of prisoners, criteria used to examine prisons in the United States, and the correction principles we employed during our turnaround of the New York City jail system.

Even before I hired my team, I toured three or four facilities myself to get a sense of how big a job this would be.

In an interview for the movie *Zero Dark Thirty*, Jessica Chastain, who played a relentless CIA officer searching for Osama bin Laden, said that she felt uncomfortable watching the movie's scenes of interrogation, filmed in part in a prison on the outskirts of Amman.

I saw those cells up close. My overall takeaway at that time: "This ain't America." In many of those prisons you had thirty guys living in a room the size of my home gym, with a dirt floor with a hole in the corner where you had to shit and piss. Of course, the Middle East in general has long had a horrendous human rights record.

To anybody who says that other countries have better prison systems than the United States, I'd say, "Depends on where you're talking about." Not a place like Jordan. Not back then.

We inspected Qafqafa Prison, the scene of the riot, which had

Abdullah and his advisors aware of many other failings in their system:

- Doors to the visiting areas were left open.

- Screening of people coming and going through the front gates was lax.

- Digital cameras for identifying inmates were working in only three of the eleven facilities.

- The box trucks used for transporting inmates had poor ventilation and easily overheated in the 120-degree heat.

- Every facility except the women's prison at Jweidah needed serious cleaning and maintenance work.

- Department-wide they needed better communication of unusual events, fights, escape attempts, uses of force—communication like we had at our TEAMS meetings in New York City.

On one inspection I noted in the cafeteria that the tables were made out of marble or slate. I screamed at the Jordanians and everyone else there. "I could break off a piece of this fucking table and beat you to death with it!"

The remote desert prison of Jafr was in nasty shape and had a reputation for torture. I told the king that it was a human rights nightmare and should be closed immediately. Doing so would signal to human rights groups and the world that Jordan was serious

not been disturbed since the incident. In the housing area where the trouble had started we found that inmates had fashioned the long metal tubes the beds were made of into weapons, using these to injure officers during the melee. During this same inspection we found one Jordanian guard sleeping in a stairwell leading to the roof because of the heat in his living quarters.

We found another guard asleep in an unlocked room right next to the entrance to a cell block, his uniform placed on the chair next to him.

We determined that it was a lack of essentials, minimum standards, that had led to the inmates' violence at Qafqafa. We duly reported this simple yet crucial finding to the king—something I had seen before, at Rikers, even all the way back to Passaic County jail. Simple fairness by the authorities, or the lack thereof, or the perception of the lack, can spell the difference.

We heard that years earlier, if there was agitation brewing, the director of Jordan's prisons would go to the hardware store, buy garden hoses, cut them into strips, give them to his COs, and then order them to go into the prison blocks and beat the hell out of everybody.

Jordan's General Intelligence Department would take certain prisoners out of jail for questioning and would mess them up, and then leave them with no medical attention. We found inmates in cells by themselves, seemingly abandoned. In one of the prisons we found an inmate who had been badly beaten and hadn't been given any medical treatment.

When I reported this stuff to His Majesty, he was furious and immediately called the commanding general of the Public Security Directorate and ordered him to ensure that things like this did not happen again. In our final report, our assessment team made King

Abdullah and his advisors aware of many other failings in their system:

- Doors to the visiting areas were left open.

- Screening of people coming and going through the front gates was lax.

- Digital cameras for identifying inmates were working in only three of the eleven facilities.

- The box trucks used for transporting inmates had poor ventilation and easily overheated in the 120-degree heat.

- Every facility except the women's prison at Jweidah needed serious cleaning and maintenance work.

- Department-wide they needed better communication of unusual events, fights, escape attempts, uses of force—communication like we had at our TEAMS meetings in New York City.

On one inspection I noted in the cafeteria that the tables were made out of marble or slate. I screamed at the Jordanians and everyone else there. "I could break off a piece of this fucking table and beat you to death with it!"

The remote desert prison of Jafr was in nasty shape and had a reputation for torture. I told the king that it was a human rights nightmare and should be closed immediately. Doing so would signal to human rights groups and the world that Jordan was serious

not been disturbed since the incident. In the housing area where the trouble had started we found that inmates had fashioned the long metal tubes the beds were made of into weapons, using these to injure officers during the melee. During this same inspection we found one Jordanian guard sleeping in a stairwell leading to the roof because of the heat in his living quarters.

We found another guard asleep in an unlocked room right next to the entrance to a cell block, his uniform placed on the chair next to him.

We determined that it was a lack of essentials, minimum standards, that had led to the inmates' violence at Qafqafa. We duly reported this simple yet crucial finding to the king—something I had seen before, at Rikers, even all the way back to Passaic County jail. Simple fairness by the authorities, or the lack thereof, or the perception of the lack, can spell the difference.

We heard that years earlier, if there was agitation brewing, the director of Jordan's prisons would go to the hardware store, buy garden hoses, cut them into strips, give them to his COs, and then order them to go into the prison blocks and beat the hell out of everybody.

Jordan's General Intelligence Department would take certain prisoners out of jail for questioning and would mess them up, and then leave them with no medical attention. We found inmates in cells by themselves, seemingly abandoned. In one of the prisons we found an inmate who had been badly beaten and hadn't been given any medical treatment.

When I reported this stuff to His Majesty, he was furious and immediately called the commanding general of the Public Security Directorate and ordered him to ensure that things like this did not happen again. In our final report, our assessment team made King

about reform. A few months later, King Abdullah took my recommendation and closed Jafr Prison.

Another one of my recommendations was to build a super-maximum-security facility near Amman to hold radical militants such as members of Al Qaeda. Jordan is in the eye of the storm in the Middle East. I used to tease King Abdullah, "You live in a really bad neighborhood." Iraq, Syria, Iran. It wasn't as if he could pick up his country and move. We both had seen the threat up close. Fighting it linked us.

By putting radicals and the worst and most violent inmates in their own facility you eliminate the possibility of their recruiting nonextremists into their groups. Later, I'd see this prison process of negative assimilation—guys getting worse in all kinds of ways, whether by radicalization or by gang initiation—in U.S. federal prison.

One of the most notorious terrorists since 9/11 was Abu Musab al-Zarqawi. A Jordanian from Zarka, he was turned radical and bloodthirsty by Islamist extremists in Jordanian prison. Besides his disgusting videotaped murder of American Nick Berg, Zarqawi had organized the hotel bombings in Amman that I witnessed. He was the most wanted Al Qaeda terrorist in Iraq, until U.S. forces finally caught up with him and killed him in 2006.

The supermax was going to have roughly 250 beds. I also set about training the Jordanian police who were going to work there. Some early reports speculated that this was in fact a CIA Al Qaeda ghost prison. But that was wrong.

I'm asked now about the concept of super-maximum-security facilities—is it humane? Is the isolation cruel or unusual? Is such treatment necessary? As someone advocating wide reforms to the system, how can you support the idea of the supermax?

———

I still think such facilities are appropriate and useful for the most violent and dangerous prisoners. And they can still be designed and managed within standards. I have no disagreement with the use of solitary confinement or the kind of custody in a supermax, as long as it's used for the right purpose, in the right instances—for example, in the case of a threat to national security. You don't want prisoners who are threats to national security to have access to intelligence, materials, or weapons of any kind. I don't think that many would disagree with this.

Even then, there are standards and policies you must abide by.

In the supermax outside Amman we built recreational pens at the back of each cell so prisoners could have more movement. Adequate showers. Reading material.

Nearly every recommendation I made to the king about his prison system, including those regarding prisoners' rights, he signed off on and set about carrying out. There were more than 130 such recommendations by the end, on everything from training and equipment to infrastructure and design. He never once disagreed with me.

It's important to note that my work for King Abdullah and Jordan was going on while I went through the Bronx case and then the federal investigation began. I was serving a positive role in Jordan while being indicted, prosecuted, and publicly shamed back home. But the king and his family never wavered in their faith in my ability, their trust in my loyalty to them, or their belief that I would give them my honest opinions and thoughts. It was as it had been in the past with Rudy Giuliani—having the buy-in and support of your higher-ups is invaluable. As had been the case with Rudy and the correction and police departments I ran for him, the king had hired me for a job and then given me the resources to get it done.

———

Once I was sitting with King Abdullah in the Four Seasons Hotel in Washington, D.C., when a reporter asked him, "Why go with Kerik when he's having such legal trouble and scandal back home?" The king repeated what he had said on several other occasions: "Aside from his success in crisis and prison management, I know Bernie will tell me what I *need* to hear, not just what I *want* to hear." He said that in his position he needed people like me around.

In fact, I told him a lot of bad news, things he may not have wanted to hear regarding his country's prison system and its security. The fact that the king stood by me the way he did during that time, as my life crumbled back home under the glare of the law, meant a lot to me. And I remain proud of the work I did in Jordan, though I know the country is still questioned on its record of human rights and the treatment of suspects and prisoners. But I also know that nowhere in the Middle East is there a head of state more concerned with international human rights than King Abdullah II.

I'm sure that I'd still be there today, working on His Majesty's national security projects, were it not for my federal conviction and incarceration. It was important work, work I was good at. Unfortunately, for now those days are pretty much over—part of the collateral life sentence every convicted felon lives with.

8

———

Terror

"I am not Osama bin Laden!" screamed Mark Mrad, a sixty-six-year-old Lebanese American, as he recounted to me in broken English how federal agents had terrified him and his wife when they stormed into his home at six in the morning. That's how he ended up with me in Cumberland. A little overweight, with thinning hair, Mrad walked with a slight hunch from a bad lower back. His blood pressure was off the charts, and his blood sugar was just as high. He was soft-spoken, with a pleasant smile, but the more he talked about his case, the more outraged he became.

Mrad had been uncomfortable in his dormitory in Cumberland, where everyone around him was a drug offender, among them some of the rougher guys in the camp. So I went to our counselor at the time and requested that Mrad be transferred to my wing, a much quieter environment. We became friends and he told me his story.

Armed as if they were taking down the world's most wanted terrorists, the agents had screamed at Mrad's wife as she stood at

———

the top of the second-floor stairs in their Vienna, Virginia, home. Mrad told his wife to calm down, then noticed red laser dots on her forehead and chest from the guns the agents had trained on her.

Mrad had pled guilty to one count of attempted money laundering in Eastern District Court in Alexandria and was sentenced to fourteen months in federal prison.

After getting to know him in the first few weeks he was there, I found it difficult to believe the newspaper reports that said Mrad had been part of a federal sting operation and had been sending money to a terrorist group in Beirut.

Curious about his case, I asked him if I could see the complaint filed against him and was surprised by what I found, and disappointed by the actions the government had taken against him.

Fighting individuals intent on killing Americans and damaging our country, absolutely. I'm all for it. Protecting the country from terror threats, certainly. But frivolous and misguided prosecutions of suspects—no. Go find some real terrorists. They're out there.

The FBI said they had an informant who had been reporting information "about Mrad" for six years.

Their informant had been convicted of Social Security fraud and sentenced to probation, and then worked for the FBI for financial payments that he would receive upon completion of investigations that resulted in convictions. The FBI also assisted that informant in obtaining his green card, as a reward, I suppose, for his work for the government.

From a letter to the government written by Mrad's attorney, I learned that the informant had first tried to sell Mrad a firearm, which he declined to buy. The informant also suggested that he and Mrad use a bogus Social Security card that the informant had

obtained in order to open a credit card account as well as purchase iPhones for resale. But again, Mrad showed no interest in the proposed illegal schemes.

Finally, the informant was able to convince Mrad to assist him in sending what the informant said was one hundred thousand dollars, bundled up, to Lebanon. The money would be hidden in a car and shipped to Beirut. During the course of a conversation with Mrad after they had put the money in the car, the informant suggested to him that the money could be going to some terror group.

The complaint was loaded with the words *Hamas* and *Hezbollah*, terror organizations, which of course resulted in bold newspaper headlines, including "Virginia Man Charged with Smuggling Cash to Hezbollah."

What the government failed to mention, and the press didn't know, was that in reality Mrad had known the informant for five or six years, and treated the young man as if he were his own son. When the man needed money, Mrad helped him find a job. When he said he was separating from his wife and needed a place to stay, Mrad even offered him his own house.

"He was like my own son," Mrad told me with tears in his eyes as we walked in circles around the massive gymnasium. His words trembled with emotion. I was forcing him to exercise daily, and on that day I was pushing him to the limit.

In his broken English, he said, "I would give him the shirt from my back."

Threatened with a twenty-year sentence, Mrad accepted a negotiated plea agreement under which he was sentenced to fourteen months in prison, fined fifteen thousand dollars, and had to forfeit five thousand dollars. He also used his retirement fund to pay for his defense.

———

Allowing someone to send cash out of the country unreported was wrong, and he should have been held accountable. But was prison necessary?

I don't think so.

Mark Mrad learned the lesson from his mistake when those FBI agents stormed his house, when he lost his business and income, and nearly lost his home. But none of that bothered him as much as what the press said about him, implying that he was working for Hamas and Hezbollah, the two Muslim radical extremist groups that have destroyed Lebanon and that region over the past three decades.

The reality was that Mark Mrad was Christian Orthodox and—another glaring omission in the government's case against him—had in fact served in the Lebanese government for years, fighting terror groups like Hamas and Hezbollah, and foreign fighters from Syria. He was not someone likely to be siding with Hamas, Hezbollah, or any Muslim extremist group, and the most basic of investigations would have revealed this.

Here's a guy whom the U.S. government put in prison using an FBI informant who got paid based on convictions, who came up with a scheme, used the FBI's money for his plan, and then convinced an old man who loved him like a son to assist him in sending the fake money to Lebanon. According to Mrad, the informant had told him that he was separating from his wife, and didn't want her to have access to his money, and that's why he was sending it back to Lebanon. Mrad said he knew what he was doing was wrong, but he thought he was helping his friend.

What's worse about the case is that it wasn't until the money had been placed in the car, and the car had been shipped overseas, that the informant started talking about militant groups, but the

informant spun it in a way that gave the appearance to the FBI that this had been Mrad's intent. I don't believe it was.

In fact, the charges, to me, seemed preposterous in light of his background. He and I talked several times about Iraq and terrorism and related issues, and it seemed clear that he despised Al Qaeda, despised radical Islamic extremists, and loved more than his own native Lebanon the country that had now put him in federal prison for fourteen months.

I've witnessed radical extremism up close and personally, both here at home and in the Middle East. As I stared at Mrad lying on his bed, reading the blue Bible his daughter had sent him, my thoughts drifted back into the stew of my past—protecting New York City; the Iraq War; the men and women I've known over the years, soldiers, police, security; the continuing legal, military, and ideological fight—my prison mate brought it all back to me. Nine-eleven. Those numbers, that day. Of course the attacks of September 11, 2001, are indelibly marked in my psyche and memory.

My trial had also brought those events back. The government had made it a point, a motion even, that neither I nor my lawyers could speak about my leadership of the NYPD in the aftermath of September 11, not even as part of the ledger in defense of my character, my public service as mitigation at sentencing. "It doesn't serve any purpose in this case to say anything about nine-eleven," Judge Robinson said, agreeing with the prosecution. "It doesn't; it's not relevant in this case, and we are not going to get into a fight about what he did or didn't do, or what he was supposedly— what he is taking credit for doing that other people argue he really didn't do. We are not going to get into that."

Judge Robinson had made himself clear. And yet at my sentencing, contradicting himself and the motion, he said to the

courtroom and the press, "The fact that Mr. Kerik would use that event," referring to 9/11, "for personal gain and aggrandizement is a dark place in the soul for me." So September 11, and all that surrounded it for me, wasn't relevant, except where the judge could use it to try to publicly disgrace me further and sentence me beyond what the prosecution requested. This is how it went.

I do realize that Robinson's words echoed a criticism, a feeling, that has existed since that tragic event more than ten years ago: that the Bush administration, Mayor Giuliani, I, and others in a position to do so somehow rode the tragedy for political and personal gain. I understand the Left saying this. I get it. This is clearly a political view. But I do not understand a federal judge saying it, politicizing the courtroom, even after ordering that the event in question had no relevance to the case.

People can say that I became famous because of 9/11. I became "America's Top Cop," cultivated a political profile, wrote books, became a security consultant. But I'd give anything for that day not to have happened. I wish it hadn't. But it did. And I happened to be there at the time. I was there, and I did the best I could do under the circumstances. It's all any of us did.

. . .

Within minutes after the attacks on that morning, the NYPD was placed on Condition Omega, the city's highest state of alert, with existing duty charts suspended and uniformed personnel working twelve-hour tours of duty, with all days off suspended. The NYPD Command and Control Center was operational twenty-four hours a day and lower Manhattan, south of 14th Street from the Hudson to the East River, was frozen, accessible only to emergency personnel. Commercial enterprise was suspended. Employees evacuated.

Southern Manhattan was a war zone. We can see now that Ground Zero was in fact the most significant battleground in the modern war against radical Islam, which will last for decades to come.

On September 14, 2001, President George W. Bush visited Ground Zero and made it clear that there would be justice for those who attacked America. The next day we buried the Fire Department's first deputy commissioner, William Feehan, their chief of department, Peter Ganci, and the beloved FDNY chaplain, Reverend Mychal Judge.

On Monday, September 17, Rudy, Governor Pataki, a number of the city's first responders, and I attended the reopening of the New York Stock Exchange with Dick Grasso, the chairman. That night, Edward Cardinal Egan presided over a memorial service for the fallen and missing uniformed officers and rescue workers at St. Patrick's Cathedral.

The next day I stood next to Governor Pataki as he signed legislation into law, adding five new sections to the New York State Penal Law and one to the New York State Criminal Procedure Law, to address terrorist-related activity. Today, this brings up all kinds of thoughts for me about civil liberties versus homeland security; extrajudicial rendition; removal of due process in the name of antiterrorism; torture or enhanced interrogation; and holding suspects without charge indefinitely. The search for balance in justice and security never ends. We must be armed, but well trained. We must be ready to attack and defend, but we must be smart, prudent, and selective. We must be disciplined and strong, but also humane.

At the time I had no objection to the Patriot Act, and don't if it's carried out with the intent and purpose for which it was

———

designed. But we've seen many instances in which it hasn't been. Does it have the right oversight? That part of it is problematic for me. The solution—there must be more accountability for U.S. prosecutors, across the board, in particular in cases involving the Patriot Act and similar laws. The oversight should be more than just the inspector general, because he comes in and looks at things periodically. He may see violations after the fact, but if somebody's already been violated, what good is that? There has to be more accountability to ensure you don't have abuse, because the deprivation of freedom is profound for any man.

It's hard for me to walk a fine line between the two: I want to eliminate terrorists or bring them to justice, but we cannot violate the law to prosecute and punish them. Then we're no better than they are.

In the wake of the attacks, these larger thoughts were still distant.

We held a prayer service at Yankee Stadium for next of kin, families, and relatives of all those killed or missing. It seemed as if every day until I left office on December 31 we attended a funeral, memorial mass, or wake.

The week following September 11 was the most emotional and draining one for me while I was in office. I attended wakes and memorial services for my cops: Police Officer Vincent Danz of the Emergency Service Unit (ESU); Police Officer Glenn Pettit of the Police Academy's Video Production; Police Officer Santos Valentin of ESU; Police Officer Ronald Kloepfer of ESU; Police Officer Thomas Langone of ESU; Police Officer John W. Perry of the Fortieth Precinct. . . .

Most of America watched from the sidelines in shock, fear, and anger. Many were unaware of the magnitude of the response and

the work that was being done to rescue the injured, recover the dead, secure the crime scene and investigate, and ensure that New Yorkers would be as safe and secure as possible.

On September 20, I sat two rows behind First Lady Laura Bush as the president addressed a joint session of Congress. He rallied the nation and promised a swift and strong response to Al Qaeda and those responsible. It was one of the most memorable days of my life.

Although I didn't know much about President Bush at the time, in the nine days since the attack on the World Trade Center, I'd watched his response and listened to his message. I still believe his response was just what it should have been. A few days earlier, in a secluded area behind blue curtains at the Jacob Javits Center, I watched President Bush spend hours speaking to, thanking, and holding hundreds of loved ones of those missing in the attacks on the World Trade Center—mothers and fathers, brothers and sisters, relatives and friends—one by one, with compassion and sincerity.

America and our political leadership stood behind him that evening, though their support over time would deteriorate until his poll numbers reached historical lows as he was about to leave office. But I believe that besides his leadership in the aftermath of 9/11, he accomplished something else, one of the most important missions of his time. In the seven years President Bush was in office after the attacks, we were not attacked again on U.S. soil. Like him or not, that was to his credit. Over time his critics have tried to take that away from him, but for me and those who were there, the images are deeply ingrained in our memory, and I appreciate more than ever his response and commitment to keeping us safe.

On the morning of September 26, I put together a meeting of

———

high-level representatives of federal, state, and local law enforcement agencies to establish the New York Metropolitan Committee on Counter Terrorism. As we would learn over time, there were major flaws in our intelligence networks and the ability of local, state, and federal authorities to communicate. The purpose of the committee was to review existing security measures, technology, information-exchange protocols, and levels of cooperation among the participating agencies and develop recommendations for improving them. These were federal and national issues, not just local, but I wanted to make sure that if there was anything we could do from the city's perspective, it got done.

Soon after, I testified in Washington, D.C., before the United States Senate and the Judiciary Subcommittee on Administrative Oversight and the Courts, regarding an amendment to the Patriot Act. I wanted to make sure the Senate knew and understood the importance of passing Senate Bill No. 1615, which would give federal law enforcement agencies the discretion to share terrorist-related intelligence and information with local and state law enforcement officials.

Rescue and recovery was an enormous task—and then there were so many other matters to deal with: protests by various ethnic and national groups; hundreds of hate crime incidents; bomb threats; reports of suspicious packages; 911 calls; the anthrax attacks and scares that followed. Then American Airlines Flight 587 took off from JKF destined for Santo Domingo in the Dominican Republic and crashed in Rockaway just after takeoff, killing 251 passengers, nine crew members, and five people on the ground.

Dignitaries came to Ground Zero a month after the attack and were shocked to see fires still burning under the rubble. We explained to them that these small fires would flare up as a result

of pockets of air, voids, underground. Those fires lasted for more than two months.

On Tuesday, October 30, I attended the funeral service for Detective Joseph Vigiano, at Our Lady of Mt. Carmel Church in Patchogue, Long Island. Joe Vigiano was a highly decorated cop who was killed on September 11 and whom I had the honor of meeting and knowing personally. At his service, I spoke to his three sons and told them that Joe was my hero, and I meant every word of what I said. This was a man who had been involved in two separate gun battles during which he was shot a total of five times and yet still lived to talk about it. Then he volunteered for an assignment in the department's elite Emergency Service Unit, one of the most dangerous jobs in the NYPD. He was a great cop and a great father to his three sons. His wife and parents were pillars of strength for me, more than I was for them, I think. Joe's mom and dad suffered not only the loss of Joe, but the loss of their son John as well, a New York City firefighter who also died at the Towers. In my meetings and contacts with them, I was awed by their strength and faith throughout those difficult days.

Looking back at all the work and the things that got done, I see that the men and women of the NYPD, FDNY, and PAPD did much that went largely unnoticed. Their service and dedication in the face of death, devastation, and destruction were inspiring beyond words. I wanted to memorialize their service to the city and the sacrifices they made. All too often in public service, first responders such as cops, firefighters, and EMS workers are taken for granted. They go out every day and put their lives on the line. People say, "That's their job. That's what they get paid to do." That's partially right. These responders do get paid, but do they get paid what they are worth? Sports figures make millions of dollars a year

to play a game. Their lives are never in jeopardy. They don't rescue anyone. Or think of the risks for an attorney, prosecutor, or judge compared to those faced by a cop, firefighter, or correction officer every day. Our society's values are out of proportion. Although that's probably never going to change, I think people should be reminded of what our public servants are worth.

After 9/11 I wanted to ensure that every cop who worked for the NYPD on that day was recognized. So I designed a breast bar medal to be worn on the uniform. Most of the medals worn in the NYPD are green and white, or green, white, and blue. The three highest awards are the Medal for Valor (a solid blue bar); the Combat Cross (a solid green bar); and the Medal of Honor (a green bar with twelve gold stars in it). In 1993 I was awarded the Medal for Valor for my involvement in a gun battle in which my partner, Hector Santiago, was shot and wounded.

I made the new medal a solid black bar with the letters WTC in gold. I ordered for it to be worn as the highest medal on the uniform, above the cop's shield or badge, to honor the historic sacrifices made that day in our department.

Since the late 1800s, the New York City Police Department has honored its men and women once a year in an annual Medal Day ceremony held at police headquarters.

The 2001 Medal Day Ceremony had been planned for September 26, but in the aftermath of the attacks, I postponed it. In November I told my staff that I wanted to move forward with the award ceremony and in addition to the awards that were already scheduled, I wanted to honor the twenty-three police officers who died on September 11. Under normal circumstances, they would have been posthumously honored at the following year's ceremony, but the circumstances of their death were far from normal,

and since the attack took place on my watch, I wanted to be the one to bestow on the families the department's highest honor.

We held the ceremony in early December at Carnegie Hall. One of the most poignant moments of that event came when Chief of Department Joe Esposito called the name of Moira Smith, to receive the Medal of Honor posthumously. She was the only female NYPD officer to die on September 11. On the day of the ceremony, her husband, James, who was also a member of the department, walked across the stage with their two-year-old daughter, Patricia. Mayor Giuliani put the medal over Patricia's neck as thousands of moved spectators watched. It was heartbreaking to think that Patricia would never know her courageous mom.

The attacks, the work, the recovery, the emotions—all of it was overwhelming.

. . .

The turmoil of the attacks had also churned up a piece of my past that I'd thought was lost.

In November a certain Ms. Lee called my office several times, saying that she was a close personal friend of mine and wanted to speak with me. My personal assistant, Janet, mentioned that the caller had a Korean accent. This hit me in the forehead like a brick.

My God, it can't be, I thought. I hadn't heard her voice for more than twenty-four years, but when Ms. Lee and I finally spoke on the phone, it was as if it had been just yesterday.

"How's the baby?" I asked her. Lee laughed.

"She's fine, but she's not a baby anymore," she said. "She's twenty-six, married, and lives in Georgia."

In the fall of 1975, when I was in the U.S. Army and stationed in South Korea, Lee and I had a child together, a daughter, Lisa Marie.

Right after Lee had the baby, I was transferred back to Fort Bragg, North Carolina, and over time she met and married another American soldier. The three of them moved to the United States in the early eighties. I had searched for Lisa Marie over the years, feeling that I'd been stupid and immature not to stay a part of her life. Lee told me that her husband had officially adopted Lisa and that she knew her biological father was American, but didn't know my name or who I was. I told Lee that I wanted to speak with Lisa Marie.

Lisa Marie and I finally spoke on the phone, a three-hour call. I was overwhelmed with emotion. At that moment, there seemed to be no difference in the love I felt for Lisa and the love I have for Joe, Celine, and Angelina. I tried to pack twenty-six years into that first phone call. I had one objective now, and that was not to make the same mistake twice in my life. Now that we had found each other, I wanted to make sure we would never be separated again, so I began making arrangements for us to meet in New York. I had Lisa Marie fly into Newark Airport and had her picked up and brought to my office, where we sat for hours talking. She was beautiful, with long black hair and freckles over her nose, which I was sure did not come from her mom. Over the next three days, I had Lisa Marie stay in the Plaza Hotel across from Central Park and every spare moment I could find I went to see her or would have her meet me for lunch or dinner.

By the time she left to head back to Georgia, there was no doubting that she was my daughter. There were probably a dozen things that we did the same way: our favorite foods, the way we picked at them. Lisa Marie met my son, Joe, and they have grown close. Today, Lisa's husband, Josh, is a fitness trainer and he has trained both Joe and me long distance. Lisa contributes with advice on diets, meals, and routines.

It would be impossible to make up for the twenty-six years I was absent in Lisa's life, but now, in the wake and turmoil of the horrific attacks, this gem had been returned to me. I had found a piece of my heart that I thought was lost forever.

. . .

December 31, 2001, was my last day in the NYPD. There were people in and out of my office all morning long. In a long-running tradition in the department, I drafted a letter to the incoming police commissioner, sealed it in an envelope, and placed it on the inkwell that sat on my desk.

Dear Ray,

On September 24, 1993, I stood before you, a detective, and bowed my head as you placed the medal of valor around my neck. You were a man who represented to me the tradition, honor and integrity of the greatest police department in the world. I was overwhelmed with pride and in awe of the honor that you bestowed upon me.

I have since learned many hard and painful lessons, and, in particular, in the last few months of my service as the 40th police commissioner of the City of New York. The most important lesson, perhaps, is that I have been humbled by the sacrifice and heroism enacted by our finest on September 11, 2001. The measure of a man, our predecessor Theodore Roosevelt once said, is that he exhibit the toughest and most tender qualities in all of his actions. I only hope and pray that I have met that measure of a man during both our darkest and greatest hour.

As I now turn the Tiffany shield over to you, I wish you the courage and conviction to lead the NYPD into the uncertain future with honor and dignity, and I have faith that you will, with all of

*your manly virtues, serve and protect the greatest city in the world,
as have the 38 others before us.*

It was an honor to serve you and the people of this great city.

My very best wishes for a victorious administration.

BERNARD B. KERIK

Then it came time for me to walk out of police headquarters for the last time as commissioner. I followed the tradition. My immediate staff surrounded me in my office; Joe Dunne and John Picciano escorted me downstairs in the elevator with Janet Fitzpatrick, while Chief Esposito greeted me on the first floor with the uniformed executive staff. To my surprise, Hala was there as well, with tears in her eyes, holding Celine in her arms. The uniformed union leaders were there to say good-bye and there were hundreds of cops who came from all over the city to be there. They lined both sides of the hallway of the first floor and then both sides of the walkway from headquarters to Centre Street, separating us from City Hall.

As I walked through the line of applauding cops, it was a bittersweet moment. Although we'd been hit and hit hard, I felt that I'd served the city well. My goals had been accomplished: lower crime, better community relations, and higher morale in the rank and file of the department.

I regret not having more time in the position. Mayor Bloomberg asked me to stay on in his incoming administration, but I felt my loyalty was to Rudy, and I'd already promised Hala that I was leaving government.

In some way I'll always be a cop. And September 11 will always be relevant.

———

. . .

One afternoon in Cumberland, I heard yelling from the TV room. I walked down the hall, looked in, and saw Mark Mrad, the Arab American convicted of money laundering on behalf of terror organizations, screaming at the top of his lungs at a black Muslim inmate. There were about two dozen of these black Muslims in Cumberland, many of them jailhouse converts to the faith, which served as a protective crew as much as a religious group. On the TV was a news report about drone attacks carried out by the U.S. against radical Islamist targets, the Taliban. The black inmate was cursing the United States, saying the country was bullshit for killing innocents, for waging war against Islam. "Fuck the U.S.!"

"You're a fool!" Mrad yelled back at him, defending the country's right to go after these enemies. Here was an Arab American charged with funding terrorist groups standing there defending the United States and its response to militant Islam to a black American Muslim cursing the country. I could only shake my head in dismay.

9

Life Lessons

During my final six months in Cumberland, about twenty-five other guys and I, all of whom at one time had served in the U.S. military, began meeting monthly with a Veterans Administration counselor. He was actually a county representative who assisted veterans in counseling and employment and providing them with veterans' program material. When he first came, I thought of the great benefit he could be to many of the men who had nothing to return to and were going to be there awhile. But it wasn't to be. The counselor's intentions were good, but the only real benefit from his monthly visits was obtaining military records for the men, or birth certificates and other documents they weren't able to get on their own. I sadly learned that VA educational and vocational programs and support are available to veterans only *after* they've been discharged from incarceration, which is ass-backward and too late. These men are sitting here, doing nothing, idle time on their hands, when they could be using that time to get an educa-

tion or vocational schooling, but they cannot apply for veterans' assistance until they're ready to leave.

So a young man like David Lynch, a twenty-seven-year-old air force veteran serving ten years on a drug charge, can't apply for anything until he's ready to walk out the door—yet he will spend eight and a half years in Cumberland doing nothing!

Only after prison will the VA give them financial and educational support for a period of time, during which the chances are, they won't be able to find a job, the money won't be enough, and they will be sorely tempted to revert to criminal activity to support themselves and their families.

The VA should be helping these men in prison, long before they leave. The money would be much more wisely and effectively spent up front, on education and vocational programs, while these men are a captive and eager audience—so that these veterans can hit the ground running when they're released.

What incentives toward good behavior and positive work on oneself were available to me? What does the system offer the inmate in terms of basic encouragement?

It is quick to overpunish and uninterested in rewarding good behavior. What would we say about an individual who had these characteristics? Mean? Cruel? Heartless? Mindless? Hypocritical? Stupid?

I couldn't join the drug program, which does give an inmate a sentence reduction.

General policy says that a warden can give an inmate up to twelve months' halfway house or home confinement time—which is encouraged by the federal Second Chance Act—but none of them do. You never see that.

In the vain hopes of sentence reduction and to keep himself

busy, my friend Gary Antonino helped guys with their resumes. He sent his wife emails about other inmates so she could search for jobs they might apply for once they were released. Gary also taught a parenting class and worked in the warehouse. He was the photographer in the visiting room. He volunteered for every job he could.

And yet he got nothing extra. He got the same amount of good time as any inmate with the same sentence who was running around the camp acting like an animal.

I taught a Life Lessons class in the camp library for two years. One hour every Thursday evening. In it I tried to share with other interested inmates insights gained from my life experiences, successes, and failures. I spoke to different groups of flawed, struggling men over those two years about leadership and courage; treasuring family; discipline; turning negatives into positives; and surviving challenges. Many of them listened and took my words in. And to make that effort felt good. It was satisfying to hear their positive responses, to hear guys from the inner city and rough homes tell me, "If I had someone like you talk to me like this on the outside, I could've done something different. Maybe I wouldn't be here."

Cumberland's warden recommended me for nine months of halfway house time, but somewhere between my case manager and the halfway house, it never panned out. In the end I got five months of home confinement off my four-year sentence, to go along with my seven months of good time, which was no more or less than I had coming to me.

I served three years and eleven days.

Two weeks before my release, Courtney, the only CO I felt comfortable speaking with man-to-man in Cumberland, came up to the camp to see me and say good-bye. By then he'd been pro-

moted to case manager and moved down the hill to work in the medium-security facility.

I was sitting on my bed in the cube reading. The guys in the rest of the wing got really quiet, the way they always would when a CO came around. I picked my head up from my book to see what was going on and saw Courtney just standing there in my cube not making a sound, staring at me.

"What the . . . You know you're like some kind of surreptitious snake!" He laughed. He was always slick like that, moving around quietly, always popping up somewhere when we didn't expect it.

One night around 9:00 p.m., I was up, standing by my bed in the cube, when I thought I saw something move outside in the yard. I went over to the window to get a better look, but I saw nothing. I turned around to get onto my bed, glanced back, and practically jumped out of my skin. Courtney's face was pressed up against the window. Scared the fuck out of me. When he saw me jump, he started laughing and then backed away, disappearing into the darkness. He was in the habit of walking around outside the building like that, peering through the windows into the cubes. It was actually a crafty way to see what was happening on the inside.

So two weeks out for me, and Courtney has come to say good-bye, appearing in my cubicle like a phantom from the BOP.

"What's up?" I asked him.

"Let's take a walk."

We strolled outside. Many of the other inmates were wondering who he was, since he had been gone from the camp for more than a year. We stood near the reception center and talked for about twenty minutes.

"You're almost home, Bernie. What are your plans?"

Although we didn't discuss it then, from our many conversa-

tions I'm sure he knew that my goal, once I was back outside and free, was to do all I could to add my voice to the call for national criminal justice reform.

On my last day some of my friends in the wing got up early. Little old Rodrigo from the Bronx, and Joe Burchfield, the former city councilman from Rhode Island. We walked over to have breakfast together—one of my rare appearances in the mess hall. We said our good-byes. They wished me luck. I'd been there for two years with Joe, and three years with Rodrigo. The thought of their staying behind in that nothingness for more years was deeply disturbing. Nothing about that harsh reality seemed to be serving anybody—not society, not the families of these men (Joe had a daughter he loved who was torn apart over her father's long absence); not these men themselves. There is no benefit to anyone, a realization that carries with it a kind of deep despair.

How much do you punish? At what cost do you punish? What are the consequences of this punishment, the consequences of prison? Many in positions of power within the criminal justice system haven't thought enough about these questions.

I walked out of Cumberland with nothing on me. A lot of guys walk out with a laundry bag full of stuff, boxes, papers—I wanted nothing to do with any of it. I didn't want any reminders on my person of where I'd just come from. I'd sent all my things (books, clothes) home in advance.

I'd lost so much weight in Cumberland that Hala had to buy me a whole new wardrobe for when I came back. Once as heavy as 250, 260, I left Cumberland 180 pounds. My waist went from a 38–40 to a 32. Much of that was from eating basically chicken and tuna fish for three years. And thousands of push-ups, burning off the bitterness. My brother, Don, once joked that I was like Paris

Hilton. When I asked him what the hell he was talking about, he said, "Who else makes the cover of the *Daily News* because he lost some weight?" That had happened seven months earlier when a flood of press accompanied my arrival at a Bronx courthouse.

I walked down to the medium facility in my prison sweats and a T-shirt. Inside I took off the sweats, my prison boots, and my T-shirt, and threw them all into a garbage container. I changed into the new clothes Hala had brought me. During my final processing I thought, "Three years of my life wasted and you're giving me a check for twenty dollars for my leftover commissary?" Just surreal. It almost reminded me of Iraq in 2003, where I watched people step over dead bodies, watched people get used to or ignore death, ignore the destruction. I had that same feeling as I was processed out of Cumberland. All of it was telling me, *Life is cheap.*

Nathan Berman and Simon Cohen, two of my closest friends, picked me up the morning of my release. Nathan and Simon had taken me to the airport when I left for Iraq, and they had taken me to Cumberland three years earlier.

After the six-hour ride that Hala and my daughters had made dozens of times on their returns from visiting me, we reached my home in New Jersey. There were reporters and television cameras waiting in the driveway. Inside were family and some of my closest friends. I walked around my house greeting and hugging everyone, talking to my kids. But my emotions were overwhelming. I kept having to hold back tears.

My probation officer arrived about an hour later and attached an electronic monitoring bracelet to my right ankle.

I had five months of home confinement ahead of me, which seemed unnecessary after having already been punished with more than three years in prison. But home confinement was better than

having to go to a halfway house, and it was definitely better than Cumberland.

I'm freed from prison but not permitted to travel freely without notifying my probation officer. There'll be monthly reports, various visits, and monitoring and oversight until the day my probation ends in 2016.

PART II

How It Happened

10

A Few Good Men

It smelled like a slaughterhouse. I was standing in an interrogation room in Saddam Hussein's Abu Ghraib Prison on the outskirts of Baghdad. It was 2003, the early days of the war. A stench of blood and death permeated my senses, my clothes, my being.

I had been in Iraq for about a month when I joined Ambassador L. Paul (Jerry) Bremer III, the U.S. presidential envoy to Iraq, and Sérgio Vieira de Mello, the UN special representative, on an inspection of the prison at Abu Ghraib. The Coalition Provisional Authority was rebuilding it, under the supervision of former New Jersey state judge Donald Campbell.

Campbell had been in search of an acceptable holding center for detainees and sentenced prisoners, someplace other than military facilities, or the small jail-type cells that seemed to be in every government building in Iraq. Campbell recommended to Bremer that they rebuild and reopen Abu Ghraib, a notorious piece of hell on earth where Saddam's executioners had tortured and murdered thousands of men and women over the years.

In one bloodstained room, I saw a ramp that led to a platform with hooks in the ceiling for two rows of nooses. The thought of what had gone on in that room in the previous thirty years was sickening.

Since there were no other facilities large enough, still intact, and capable of holding both pretrial and sentenced prisoners, including those who required maximum-security housing, Bremer reluctantly agreed to reopen Abu Ghraib, but with a mandate that it be rebuilt and brought up to international penal standards—and that the torture chambers be kept intact, preserved as a museum so that future generations of Iraqis would never forget the sadistic leadership of Saddam Hussein.

I thought Bremer's recommendation of preserving the torture chambers for others to see was well intended and the right thing to do but got lost in what turned out to be one of the worst military scandals in our country's history. In 2004 it was revealed that U.S. military personnel and government agents were committing human rights violations upon prisoners, including physical and sexual assaults, rape, sodomy, and murder. The abuses apparently started just a few months after I had left Iraq.

As I later watched that ugly story unfold, I thought back to my days as a military policeman in the U.S. Army and couldn't imagine what these U.S. personnel were thinking, how they thought they could get away with the things they were doing. And where was their supervision? That irked me more than anything, because considering the duration of the abuses and the particular acts that were committed, I cannot fathom how just about everyone in the facility wasn't aware of what was happening.

As sick and demented as were the acts for which the violators were ultimately held accountable, the supervisors up the chain

of command, right to the facility commander, were no less responsible in my eyes. Something like that would never have gone on under my command at Rikers, for example, or in any facility that is minimally managed. Use of force? Certainly, sometimes, in individual cases. But not widespread, organized, habitual violation of human rights. Never. We had regular inspections and walk throughs. The inmates would have told us something. We had reporting mechanisms in place. We collected data. Abominations like this couldn't happen.

As we walked through Abu Ghraib just months before it devolved into savagery, de Mello seemed pleased with the progress being made. UN secretary-general Kofi Annan had asked him to serve as his special representative in Baghdad for four months, and although de Mello appeared extremely serious and no-nonsense, we did find some humor in comparing his present assignment to the one he'd just left, in Geneva, as the high commissioner for human rights. His working conditions there had been a bit different from those in Iraq. A handsome Brazilian, de Mello looked as if he could be modeling in a Ralph Lauren catalogue instead of touring a prison in the middle of a war zone. He seemed thoughtful and easygoing. Although our encounter was brief, I liked him, and I thought it would be good to be working with him over the next several months.

Little did we know how much would change in the next few weeks.

. . .

"You've got to be out of your mind!" my brother, Don, shouted at me. I'd just told him that the White House had asked me to go to Iraq to help reconstitute the Iraqi Ministry of Interior and begin rebuilding the Iraqi Police Force.

In early May 2003, Tony Carbonetti, Rudy Giuliani's former chief of staff, and I took the Amtrak Acela to Washington, D.C., and from Union Station took a taxi to the Pentagon.

We arrived around 10:00 a.m. to find Secretary of Defense Donald Rumsfeld's office bustling. I was introduced to Jamie Durnan, a New Yorker who worked for Deputy Secretary of Defense Paul Wolfowitz and appeared to have the most insight in the office about what was going on in Baghdad.

After a bit of New York small talk, Durnan began explaining that since the fall of Saddam Hussein and the Iraqi government, the Iraqi military and national police had dissolved back into their communities. He said that other than the United States armed forces and their coalition partners, there was no security at all in Iraq. He briefed me on what they believed the Iraqi Interior Ministry's table of organization looked like and said that Rumsfeld and Wolfowitz hoped that I could help them get the ministry back on its feet. He said that they were in the process of identifying the various executives who would run each ministry for the new government until Iraqi cabinet members were identified and put in place by the new governing council.

I listened to everything Durnan said and then told him that I would have to talk to my wife before I made a decision, but I wanted to help. Just as we were prepared to leave, Durnan asked, "Can you guys hold on for a few? Someone would like to see you."

I sat down and picked up a copy of the *New York Times* and began to read an article about the White House planning the announcement of former ambassador L. Paul Bremer III, onetime counterterrorism director for the U.S. State Department during the Reagan administration, as Iraq's day-to-day overseer.

Based on the article, it seemed as though Rumsfeld's guy on the ground in Iraq, Jay Garner, a retired U.S. Army lieutenant general, was about to be ousted by Bremer, a longtime civilian and Foreign Service officer, if the White House had its way. Just as I finished reading the article, I heard someone say, "Good afternoon, Commissioner."

I looked up and there stood Ambassador Bremer, looking more like a university professor than a man heading to war.

Bremer was pleasant but to the point. He thanked me for coming and apologized for not being able to spend more time with us, but he had been in meetings with Rumsfeld, who had just returned from Iraq that morning.

He touched briefly on some of the issues he thought he was about to face with his new assignment and said he was leaving for Baghdad in the next few days and was going to need all the help he could get. He thanked me again for coming and we stood up. I told him that I would do whatever I could to help, shook his hand, and made for the door.

"Thanks again. I'll see you in Baghdad," he said.

I looked at Tony as we entered the hallway and said, "I guess I'm going to Iraq. I need to call my wife."

Over the next few days, I had several conversations with people at the White House and the Pentagon and it really started to look as if this was going to happen.

I was briefing Rudy Giuliani daily because whatever happened would have an impact on our business—I worked with him at Giuliani Partners, our security consulting business—and given that we weren't sure how long I would be gone, we had to strategize. At the time, I was overseeing a criminal justice assessment for Mexico City, and we had a few other projects in the fire. But Rudy

was extremely supportive. "Do what you want to do and we'll take care of things here until you get back," he told me.

I went back to the Pentagon the following Thursday and things were moving at 150 miles per hour. I was there to fill out documents for my background investigation, get shots, a helmet, a vest, and some other equipment. I left that afternoon with nothing other than a military identification card and copies of my employment and insurance papers in the event something happened to me. I found it kind of strange that the documents and shots weren't ready and that they couldn't find a vest or helmet to fit me. We were in the Pentagon, for God's sake!

On the way back to New York that night, I was thinking I needed my fucking head examined. I was making close to a million dollars a year and I was going to leave that for $140,000. But I believed removing Saddam from power was the right thing to do at the time, and I was also motivated by 9/11. Weapons of mass destruction or not, Saddam had murdered and displaced millions of his own countrymen and was funding suicidal terror operations against the state of Israel, operations carried out by the same kind of radical extremists who had attacked us. To me, Saddam was as much an enemy and threat to the United States as they were.

I had lived in Saudi Arabia, working in security, in the late seventies and early eighties. I wasn't unfamiliar with the Middle East or the Muslim world. So going to Iraq didn't bother me. Going to a war zone didn't bother me either. In fact, I was fucking excited. My entire career had been one of living on the edge, being in the heart of the action, dealing with life-and-death situations. This would be no different. I'm not sure exactly why I'm like this, or where it comes from. Like many little boys, I loved to play cops and robbers, games of combat, fantasizing about being the

hero, the good guy who saves the day. Many boys grow up and their childhood games and dreams become nothing more than fond memories. But for me, my son, Joe, and those like us, including many of the men I've worked with over the years, those dreams and waking visions didn't end. We grew into some of the very characters we wanted to be as children, still wanting to play our part in the fight between good and evil.

The only thing that really bothered me was trying to explain to Hala my desire to go, but when it came right down to it, it wasn't even necessary. She knew without my saying a word.

During the next few days, Gary Uher, a friend who worked for the FBI, volunteered to go to Iraq with me as the head of my security detail. I also spoke to Michael Braun, who was the special agent in charge of the Drug Enforcement Administration's office in Detroit.

"I'm going to Iraq and wanted to know if you want to go as my chief of staff," I told him.

"I'm going," he said, and that was that.

The next day, I called Mike and Gary to firm up the details. Since both of them worked for the U.S. Department of Justice, and I knew how bureaucratic that could be, I called Larry Thompson, the deputy U.S. attorney general, to ask him to clear the way for them to be temporarily assigned to me and the U.S. Department of Defense over the next several months. By the time I arrived in Iraq, they were both right behind me.

The next few days flew by like minutes, buying equipment and clothes, dealing with insurance issues, closing out stuff in the office, canceling speeches and meetings—all the time trying to keep Hala away from the television and the news channels, most of which was coverage of the war.

———

On the morning of May 18, my brother, Don, got to my apartment early, and for the both of us it was déjà vu all over again, dating back to 1974, when I left home after joining the U.S. Army's Military Police Corps. I was eighteen and Don seven at the time, and he wound up in the hospital with ulcers. Then in 1978, when he was twelve, I left to go work in Saudi Arabia, and he nearly had a nervous breakdown.

Now standing next to me, he was thirty-seven years old, and as he watched me pack we both felt that familiar stress of separation, danger, and doubt. Perhaps it was the thought of my going to war, or maybe just the fact that we were so much closer now than we were when he was twelve and I was twenty-three. He had become one of my closest friends and confidants, and now the eleven years in age between us meant nothing.

As I finished getting my bags together, I told Don that I had some other things to do so that he would leave. I didn't want either of us getting emotional in front of Hala, who was sitting in the living room with the girls. I knew that any minute my close friends Nathan Berman and Simon Cohen would be walking in the door to take me to the airport. I gave Don a hug and a kiss good-bye before he left.

Nathan and Simon came to pick me up, along with their wives, Liza and Erit, who are two of Hala's closest friends. Rudy called and John Picciano stopped over to say good-bye. I called my son, Joe, and then kissed Hala and the girls good-bye, and made it out the door before they could see me tearing up—not because I was going to Iraq, but because I'd be far away from them, and didn't know for exactly how long it would be.

At JFK, Nathan and Simon walked me to the gate, gave me hugs. Once I got through customs and they were out of sight, my mind went into work mode. I was Baghdad bound.

. . .

"Welcome to a free Iraq," Ambassador Bremer said as he stood up from behind a huge desk to shake my hand. The room he was now occupying in the infamous Republican Guard Palace was said to have once been Saddam Hussein's office. Iraq was free from Saddam, but it was far from safe, and I could see that immediately. The buildings were bombed and burned out. The streets were abandoned. I could feel the fear in the air.

I put some of my stuff away in a small trailer that would be my temporary living quarters and went back into the palace to take a look around. I stopped by the Ministry of Interior (MOI) office where I would be working and met a few men who had gotten there in the weeks prior.

The guy who seemed to be running things was Mike Turner from Georgia, who was the team leader from the U.S. Department of Justice. He was overseeing about twenty police advisors who had arrived in Baghdad two weeks earlier to conduct an assessment of the Ministry of Interior and Iraqi National Police. Before Iraq, he had worked on police training and civilian-police activities in Kosovo and had been the chief of police in Monroe, Georgia.

I also met Carr Trevillian IV, Turner's deputy, who had worked with him in Kosovo, and Sam Juett, who had served as city manager in Monroe, Louisiana, and Monroe, Georgia. Also in the room were Bob Gifford, who worked for the U.S. State Department's Bureau for International Narcotics and Law Enforcement, and a few other men who were hard at work and never looked up. Gifford was supposed to be the guy in charge, but Turner and Trevillian were the doers.

Turner briefed me on the assessment team and explained that

they were there to determine what Iraq's Ministry of Interior had been in the past and what it would take in the future to secure the country. They would be looking at all the agencies that fell within the MOI, including police, customs, borders, and immigration.

Turner said over the next several weeks we would have to outline how and where the police were going to be trained, what that training was going to consist of, and, most important, how we would have to recruit for the service, given that Bremer wanted no one in the senior levels of the Ba'ath Party working for the new government.

Then there was the most critical issue: money. Who was going to pay for this? Would it be the United States, foreign donors, or the Iraqis themselves? Unbeknownst to me at the time, this would become a major problem not only for me and the MOI, but for the entire country. I think I just assumed at the time that eventually the Iraqis would get back up and running, and through the sale of oil repay a lot of what we put into their liberation. But apparently that wasn't a part of the plan.

Once Turner briefed me, I realized that we needed a lot more than the twenty men we had, and given the condition of the country at the time—the looting and lawlessness—I suggested, and Turner agreed, that we get the assessment to Bremer as quickly as possible so that we would know what we were working with, and shooting toward, regarding funding.

The more I learned about the country, the more I realized that the assessment team was stretched extremely thin. We had a few guys up in the north, collecting data and information, as well as guys down south, and the more feedback I got from them, the more I realized that Bremer was not *rebuilding* anything in the country. It all had to be built basically from scratch: the infrastruc-

ture, power stations, water supplies, and the Ministry of Interior building as well. People back home, our political leaders and the media, were complaining and questioning why things were taking so long, but they weren't giving enough weight to how enormous the job was. I believed from what I saw early on that things would get worse before they got better.

Within days after I arrived, I began seeing more stores open, more people on the streets, more cars on the roads. But between the heat and the anxiety of living in what was still a war zone, tensions were high.

Although everything was important, and time was of the essence, fast-tracking border controls and the airport operations, including immigration and passport controls, was critical, so that the country could open to the outside world. In addition to the assessment we were preparing, we were going to have to stand up as many of the former police as possible and begin recruiting new men as well. They would all have to receive training that they had never had before—in everything from human rights to the use of firearms—and would have to deal with a diversity that would include Sunnis, Shiites, Kurds, and, for the first time ever in Iraq, women.

The Iraqi police's idea of a criminal investigation during Saddam's regime was stringing people up by their feet and beating them until they were unconscious. It was going to be a huge task just to change that mind-set.

The standing policy of the Coalition Provisional Authority (CPA) that senior members, or the top three ranks, of the Ba'ath Party had to be purged from government created significant problems for us. This decision was more reasonable, though, than the disbanding of the Iraqi army, maybe our worst mistake and a key

———

failure of our effort in Iraq. There was no way to definitively tell who the senior Ba'athists were; we had only word of mouth to go on. When the coalition forces moved into Iraq, Saddam's commanders destroyed the databases and burned records, and it was nearly impossible to determine who was who once we got settled in. Every time we thought we had a great candidate for a senior position, someone would walk in and tell us that the guy was Saddam's henchman or a mass murderer. As we recruited or brought back former members of the service, the Saddam loyalists and Ba'athists would lie and deny their positions in the former regime. Eventually, we would weed them out, but there was no guarantee to the process.

The pressure on the military commanders to hire local police throughout the country was overwhelming, and they would often overlook some piece of Iraq's recent history. Some of the guys in my team would get into arguments with the military because Bremer's orders didn't give us the discretion to override them. These were all issues that would have to be worked out over time. What had to be dealt with first and foremost was crime. Rape, burglary, carjacking, kidnapping, robbery, and murder had to be dealt with as quickly as possible. We had to get the streets under control. The United States and its coalition partners were still in combat operations, and the Iraqi police were nowhere to be found.

I realized that in addition to all the things that we would have to do to reconstitute the Interior Ministry, the Iraqi police fell under the supervision of the MOI, and the Iraqi citizens knew it. They were coming to our office and to the front gates of the palace in droves, begging for help and protection from former Saddam loyalists. When I asked Gifford, the senior State Department guy on hand, what we were doing to help them, his response

was "That's the military's problem. We've only got about twenty guys here."

Although I didn't like or agree with his answer, it didn't faze me personally until an Iraqi woman came to our office crying, telling us that a group of Iraqi men from the former regime had taken over her home and she and her family had to move out.

She was speaking to one of the police advisors by the name of Nouman Shubbar, an Iraqi American who was a Philadelphia police officer. He'd taken a leave of absence to go to Iraq with the coalition. There was another guy with Shubbar named Jim Steele, a retired U.S. Army colonel, who was assigned to the MOI as well.

I listened as Shubbar translated what this woman was saying, and I could see Steele was about as upset as I was. I looked over at Gifford sitting at the desk, and he just shrugged and said, "Call the military." I immediately felt my gut twist. This woman had already been to the local military commander, who said he didn't have the manpower to assist her, so basically, I thought, she and her family were fucked. When I saw her in tears because they'd been forced to leave their home, there was no way I could let that happen, and Shubbar and Steele felt the same way.

Steele looked at me and said that he and Shubbar would take some Iraqi police from the academy and deal with this. Given that the military was overwhelmed, and that we, the MOI, were responsible for the police, I felt that we had to at least try to help this woman and others like her.

Later that evening, Steele got back to me and said that the woman was back in her home and the intruders had been taken into custody.

I wanted to get a look around Baghdad, so the next morning Shubbar and Steele drove me to the MOI headquarters. It was

bombed out and closed down. We also stopped at a police station and then the police academy, where hundreds of Iraqi cops were milling about, saying that they wanted to come back to work. In reality, they were looking to get paid. They were broke, needed money. Most of them no doubt had families to provide for. It was immediately clear that this was going to be a big problem if it didn't get resolved.

Out of the hundreds of policemen there, I noticed one who appeared to be in charge. He was barking out orders left and right at the other Iraqis. He was Ahmed Kadhim Ibrahim, acting commander of the academy.

Ibrahim was in his mid-forties, with a huge dark black mustache. He spoke in broken English, well enough for me to understand him. Polite and respectful, Ibrahim had worked as a police commander during Saddam's regime. In the mid-nineties, the intelligence services hanged his best friend for speaking out against Saddam. When Ibrahim and his friend's family attempted to remove his body, they were ordered to leave it dangling in the street for three days before they were allowed to take it down.

About two years later, when Ibrahim was the commander of the Baghdad Police Academy, he went out for dinner one night with one of his closest friends. Feeling comfortable after a few drinks, Ibrahim began spouting off about how much he hated Saddam Hussein for what he had done to his friend and his family. The next day when Ibrahim arrived at work four agents from the intelligence service swooped into the academy and took him away. For the next year and a half he was jailed, beaten, and tortured.

So when American coalition forces arrived in Baghdad, Ibrahim was one of the first Iraqis to come forward to assist the Amer-

icans, and assist he did—so much so that he was eventually forced to leave Iraq due to death threats against him and his family.

Shubbar, Steele, and I left the academy and drove through the streets of Baghdad. We drove with the windows down so we could hear what was going on outside and in case we had to return fire if attacked. The entire ride I kept thinking that someone was going to walk up alongside us while we were stuck in traffic and lob a grenade into the vehicle. Given that we stood out like a sore thumb, we automatically felt like a target, sitting at the ready, anxious the entire ride.

Just as we had done in New York City, I ordered our guys to begin collecting crime data daily from the local police so we could monitor what was going on, and with each passing day, the crime numbers rose.

I authorized Steele and Shubbar to pick about fifty Iraqi police from the existing force of about three thousand guys that they felt they could trust, and have members of my security detail train them so that they could go out and respond to calls for help.

My security detail consisted of eight South African contractors who came from conventional and covert units of the pre-1994 South African Defense Force, which included operatives from the Special Forces and the South African Police Special Task Force, a counterterrorism unit.

These men had served as Jay Garner's bodyguards before he left Iraq. I'd first noticed them in the palace's enormous mess hall. They were sitting off to themselves with another small group, an impressive-looking bunch with beards and long hair, armor-plated vests and heavy weapons.

When I asked Steele one day who they were, he said some were South Africans and some were U.S. special operators, Navy SEALs

or Special Forces assigned to a task force looking for Saddam and his sons.

I laughed to myself, thinking, Man, I would not want those guys coming after me.

Once Garner left, Colonel Kim Olsen, Garner's assistant, with help from Steele, had the South Africans' contract assigned to MOI so that they'd be working for us.

There were Loutqie, Loafie, Lyon, Harry, and Adolf, to name a few. The names make them sound like Disney cartoon characters, but these guys were no movie-version commandos; they were real, through and through. (In 2004, a year after I left Iraq, Loutqie and Harry—their real names are Lourens Horn and Harry Carlse—were allegedly involved in a failed coup attempt in Equatorial Guinea, which was supposedly orchestrated by Sir Mark Thatcher, the then-fifty-one-year-old son of the former British prime minister. According to news reports, there was a conspiracy to overthrow Guinean president Teodoro Obiang. Dozens of suspected mercenaries, including Loutqie and Harry, were arrested in Zimbabwe for their role in the plot. They were later acquitted.)

When they worked for me in Iraq, they were professional and polite, but there was no question that they were some of the deadliest men in the country. During my movements outside the palace grounds, Loutqie drove my Suburban and Lyon sat in front of me on the passenger side. Harry could be seen hanging out the back window of the SUV with an AK-47. Adolf drove the backup Suburban and Loafie most times hung out the passenger-side window.

I refused to use an armored SUV, so we had the ability to maneuver quicker and get the windows down if we needed to. We usually drove fast, between fifty and seventy miles per hour, because of improvised explosive devices (IEDs) on the road, which

were usually controlled by timers and a remote cell phone. The faster you were driving, the greater the chance of your getting past the IED's devastating full effect. If a civilian vehicle came close to mine, it was signaled to back away.

When they weren't on the road or in the office with me, they were working out, training, or shooting. To give you an idea of their intensity, Loutqic's leg workout consisted of walking up the fourteen flights of stairs of the Al-Rashid Hotel two or three times with a guy on his back. As dangerous as Baghdad was at the time, I was confident that I couldn't have had a better protective detail. I was thankful for their service to me and the coalition.

Ibrahim assisted in identifying the Iraqis to be trained by Harry and his men, and before you knew it, they were attacking crime in the streets when the military didn't have the manpower or resources to respond. Unlike policing in the United States, where your daily duties are most often routine and extreme violence is limited, this was dangerous and deadly, but someone had to do it or Iraq and its people would pay the price. I had believed in the mission before I arrived, but after personally seeing the mass graves and hearing the horrific stories of Saddam and his reign of terror over his own people, I was more inspired to help.

One afternoon the phone rang in my office and Mike Braun, my chief of staff, who had just arrived in-country, answered. Immediately after he hung up, he stood and began putting on his vest and gun. He looked over at me. "You should get over to the academy," he said. It was Gary Uher who called. Steele's special operations team had just been involved in a gun battle and were on their way to the academy with two dead.

When I pulled into the academy parking lot there was blood leaking from beneath a small car and two dead bodies lying on

stretchers. General Ibrahim, the newly appointed deputy chief of the Baghdad Police, was standing there with a number of Iraqi police officers around him, along with Steele, Shubbar, Uher, and B. J. Turner, a former Special Forces officer for whom I had worked in Saudi Arabia twenty-five years earlier.

Ibrahim explained that while driving back to the Baghdad Police headquarters, he and the team spotted these two men holding the owner of a car at gunpoint, trying to take his vehicle. When they stopped and confronted the two men, a gun battle erupted. This had been the second gun battle of the day for this small team of Iraqi cops who were courageously fighting the lawlessness throughout Baghdad since the U.S. coalition had invaded the country. The first firefight had been just two hours earlier, in a downtown market, where they shot and injured former Saddam regime Ba'athists who were robbing the locals.

As I stood there congratulating Ibrahim and the others on a job well done, I was quickly reminded of how cheap life seemed to be in Iraq. No one cared who these two men were or where they came from. I asked how they got the bodies back to headquarters, given that the gun battle was on the road between the market and the Police Academy. Ibrahim looked at me, surprised, pointing to the trunk of the car that the dead men had attempted to carjack. "In there," he said.

"You drove them back in the trunk of the car?" I asked.

"No, he did," Ibrahim said, pointing to the victim of the attempted carjacking, who was now standing there with a big smile on his face, obviously relieved that he was still alive, with the worst part of his day being that he would have to go home and wash the blood out of the trunk.

It was either leave them where they died or throw them into the trunk of the car to get them back to headquarters. This was a war zone. There was no Emergency Medical Service or Fire Department to call. There was no crime scene or police report.

I've seen more death than most. Although I'm not haunted by it, there's always that moment or two while looking at bodies when you think, That's it? Never to be seen or heard from again. What about their families and friends? You realize quickly that life goes on, and you can only hope that you make a difference while you're alive, because there's no coming back.

As I looked at those two guys lying there, I could hear gunfire and explosions in the distance. I was thinking about how many more would die that afternoon. My thoughts were interrupted as the Iraqi police loaded the bodies into the back of an ambulance while Ibrahim wrote out a couple of lines in Arabic on a blank piece of paper so that the morgue would accept them.

Then it was back to work.

. . .

Just a few weeks before, I'd been sitting on top of the world in my office overlooking Times Square. I went from that to working eighteen hours a day, in a hundred degrees in the shade, in a place where the sound of gunfire is as normal as taxi horns being blown in midtown Manhattan.

We needed help, and we needed it fast.

On June 2, 2003, I submitted a forty-nine-page draft assessment report to Ambassador Bremer, advising him that unless we redesigned and redeveloped the Iraqi police, they would not constitute a suitable, viable, and sustainable police service that could

engender public trust and confidence. I advised him that the police had no real training and structure and were fundamentally unsuited to a new and free Iraq.

I recommended that the CPA or newly formed Iraqi government nullify existing legislation that placed Iraqi police under the military discipline system, which essentially provided them with civil and criminal immunity. In a free and democratic society there must be accountability. Granting immunity to anyone with the power to deprive others of their civil liberties or freedom is an open door to violating civil and human rights.

In the United States, local, state, and federal law enforcement are not immune from civil or criminal prosecution, and they should not be. However, state and federal prosecutors for the most part are. Why? According to legal scholars, it's to ensure that they are not deterred from doing their jobs. But a logical person might say the same could apply to local, state, and federal law enforcement officers. How are they any different? The reality is, they're not. Giving prosecutors immunity creates a slippery slope, as it enables them to engage in misconduct and behavior that clearly violate the civil and constitutional rights of those they investigate. If prosecutors were held to the same standard as local, state, and federal law enforcement, prosecutorial misconduct would be decreasing, not increasing.

I also recommended that the CPA enact legislation for minimum standards, training, continued professional retraining, and appropriate criminal-civil liability certification and decertification for members of the police service.

I believed there had to be accountability in criminal justice, in policing, and in the jails and prisons. For the police in a new and free Iraq to be accepted by their own people, there would have to

be minimum standards, proper police training, and appropriate treatment of the detained and arrested.

I wanted to establish an aggressive Office of Professional Standards, with an investigative and disciplinary process that would ferret out corruption while immediately addressing unprofessional, unethical, or criminal behavior within the service. Without that oversight, there would be no controls, no accountability, and it would wind up being no different from life under Saddam's regime.

The police service had to be restructured to remove the vestiges of Saddam's militarization of the force, including philosophy, rank structure, weapons, uniforms, training, and approach to human rights. Since Saddam's police had sovereign immunity, they were more like savages than police. Physical torture was common, as was murder: ripping out toenails and fingernails, pounding nails through a person's palm, and primitive electrocution, such as wrapping a cord around a guy tied to a chair and then just plugging it into a wall socket. The police had to be taught differently.

We needed to implement a three-week Transition and Integration Program (TIP) for all Iraq Police Service personnel, in addition to a Senior Level Management TIP for all Iraqi police supervisors and management. This training could not compare to that given to modern-day police agencies around the world, but we were under the gun. I figured we would give them the basics first, fast, get them up on their feet, then get them the additional training they needed as time went on.

I wanted an aggressive media and public information campaign, led by reformist Iraqi police leadership. That was a must to rebuild the public's perception and expectations for the new Iraq Police Service. I recommended that they create a law enforcement

criminal intelligence organization that was specifically focused on antiterrorism, drugs, organized crime, and human trafficking investigations. These were just some of the principal recommendations that over the next three months we began implementing, with barely any staff other than some military personnel and a few civilians who began arriving from the United States, the United Kingdom, and other European countries.

It's sad for me to say, but the truth is that in hindsight, viewing Iraq today, it all seems like a waste of time. Ten years later the perception of the Iraqi police is perhaps no different than it was under Saddam. Ten years later, and Iraq is still a shattered zone. It's crushing to consider all the work that was put into the country, the blood, sweat, and resources—seemingly all for nothing.

The twenty-man Assessment Team had grown into a thirty-man Public Safety / Security Advisory Team, with Trevillian as their team leader, after Turner had left the country. On a weekly basis, I was updating Ambassador Bremer on the force strength of the Iraq Police Service, Border Police, Border Guards, Customs Inspectors, and Customs Police.

We received approval of a $120 million budget for the purpose of purchasing equipment, supplies, and goods, and for the refurbishment of MOI facilities countrywide. We were considering standing up an offsite police-training center in Taszár, Hungary (we established one later in Jordan).

I appointed a police chief for Baghdad and a director of internal affairs and obtained preliminary approval by the CPA to separate the vehicle registration and driver's license functions from the Traffic Police and create a new Directorate of Motor Vehicles. The faster we got the bosses in place, the quicker we could begin our recruiting campaign.

———

MOI and the U.S. Army were supporting the Traffic Police with weapons and materials for the purpose of securing their buildings, but progress was incremental. We had the United Nations researching the feasibility of unfreezing the Oil for Food Program funds that had been set aside to pay for one hundred Traffic Police motorcycles that were sitting in storage at the port of Beirut.

We were vetting senior personnel who were being considered for positions, such as the director of the Department of Border Enforcement and the administrator of the Bureau of Nationality and Civil Affairs. We coordinated the first repatriation of Iraqi refugees successfully, through the port of entry at Safwan. They came from a refugee camp in Saudi Arabia. It was amazing to see these people come back to Iraq after years in exile, ignoring the war zone and all the chaos. They just wanted to return to their home country, hoping to live in peace in a world without Saddam Hussein. In the end, depending on when and where they resettled, this hope may or may not have been realized. Today the violence in Iraq continues, and I wonder about those who returned. I wonder now whether they believe they made the right decision.

Steele and Shubbar's special operations team was hard at work responding to one crisis after another. Between June 25 and July 1, the Iraq Police, assisted by MOI advisors and the U.S. Army's Military Police, arrested four insurgents who had kidnapped and murdered a woman in Baghdad; captured General Sabah Mirza, the former chief bodyguard for Saddam Hussein; and arrested General Samir Abdul Wehhab Al-Shaikhly, the former minister of the interior during the Intifada. Then, while looking for a gang of bank robbers in the Karadah area, the police attempted to arrest a suspect in a house who opened fire on them. A gun battle ensued

in which the gang leader was killed and a woman who was with him was wounded.

We were putting together the general guidelines for the police, for the entire country, to be distributed by the military. I submitted the Interior Ministry's requirements for the Congressional Supplemental Request for Resources to Ambassador Bremer, explaining that we had focused on vetting, hiring, training, and deploying Iraqi police forces and other security forces to assist in establishing a secure and permissive environment.

I stressed to Ambassador Bremer that rebuilding the Iraqi police had been a challenge because the existing force was so poorly trained, ineffective, and widely distrusted—but that the creation and training of responsible public safety forces were indispensable to long-term progress in Iraq. Those forces, and the country's whole national security, were dependent on one thing in the near future—money. And it was going to be up to Congress to get us the money we needed to do the job.

Knowing what I know today, I think there's real irony in the fact that Congress spent all that money to create and rebuild Iraq when it refuses to spend money that's needed in our own U.S. prison system—money to teach real life-improvement skills to men who really need it, for example. Not to mention the insane money our country wastes on incarcerating people who could be dealt with, punished, in alternative ways.

Michael R. Gordon, a reporter for the *New York Times*, had just sat down in my office in the Republican Guard Palace, one of many such buildings that Saddam had around the country—a huge waste of gold, marble, and granite—when my cell phone rang. It was Ibrahim calling to tell me that the Jordanian Mission had just been bombed and he was on his way there. I tried not to raise Gordon's suspicions.

———

I stood up to politely excuse myself and I suppose by the look on my face he could see there was a problem. He asked to come with me wherever I was going. Not knowing the details of what had happened yet, I told him that we would speak later and hurried down to Bremer's office, putting on my armored vest as I walked. I told the ambassador that the Jordanian Mission had just been bombed and I was headed there. I spun around as he yelled, "Be careful!"

I was there within ten minutes; you could smell the flesh burning. Eleven people had been killed and more than fifty injured. The force of the bomb blew a car three floors up onto the roof of the building next door.

The attack was assumed to be in retaliation for Jordan's granting refuge to two of Saddam Hussein's daughters, which angered Iraqis.

When Ibrahim arrived, a group of angry Iraqis had stormed the building, smashing everything in sight. He and his men, along with some military police, dispersed the crowd.

I called Ambassador Bremer from the scene. "No way we can investigate something this big," I told him. "We need to call in the FBI." He agreed. From that day on, we were going to need all the help we could get.

Over the next few days as the FBI's investigation was in full force, I went to Bremer and told him that we needed to solidify the Iraqi leadership in MOI, and I had three people in mind. I told him that I decided to make Ahmed Ibrahim the senior deputy minister, which would give him power and authority over the police around the country. I also told him that I had identified the other two deputies as well and wanted to run them by him for his review. He looked at me and said, "As long as General Ahmed Ibrahim approves, it's fine by me."

I told Bremer that Ibrahim was fine with both appointments, but that one of the two might be an issue with the governing council, the police, and Iraqis in general, and that's why I wanted to speak to him about the appointment first. At that point he looked concerned and asked, "Why would he be an issue with anyone?"

"Because he's not a he . . . he's a she," I told him. "It's a woman, and there has never been a woman deputy in the Ministry of the Interior, so it's going to be an issue, but I don't know how much."

I then told Bremer about Hala Shaker Mustafa Saleem, and how she had worked for Interior for more than twenty years, had no loyalties to the Ba'ath Party, and, as I had seen firsthand over the past three months while I tried to re-establish the administrative side of the house, was the one person who knew it all. Every commander or general who needed something done in administrative services went to Hala, but because of her gender, her career was stymied. I told Bremer that she knew the job, knew the players, and had bigger balls than most of the men in the senior ranks, who were scared to death that Saddam Hussein was going to come back to power.

"She deserves the job," I said finally.

Bremer smiled. "Let's do it, then."

I went back to my office and told Mike Braun the good news, and then told Doug Brand, who had recently arrived from the United Kingdom. Brand was a British commander who was sent in as my deputy. He was enormous. He stood about six-seven, weighed three hundred pounds, and wore a British police officer's uniform. He didn't know the Iraqis that well but was learning quickly.

With the three senior Iraqi appointments and a solid chain of command in place in Interior, I felt that the national police,

———

borders, and immigration personnel would begin to feel a sense of camaraderie with their own instead of feeling as if they were working for the coalition, for the Americans and Brits. It would make a big difference in their work ethic, their pride, and their patriotism for this new Iraq. It felt as if things were moving in the right direction.

And suddenly everything came to an abrupt halt. Twelve days after the bombing of the Jordanian Mission, another massive blow struck us—and this time the losses were far greater and were felt around the world.

On the afternoon of August 15, 2003, Jerry, the newly appointed chief of station for the CIA, called me to talk about a recent attack on the oil pipeline near Bayji and Tikrit. I told him that I had ordered an investigation into the incident and then we talked about the 2004 budget numbers that I had submitted to Ambassador Bremer that morning.

Jerry told me that he wanted me to begin discreetly recruiting Iraqi intelligence personnel, and although it might be a sore spot with some, due to the notorious reputation of the intelligence service under Saddam, it was a service that was essential because there was no one better to collect intelligence for Iraq than the Iraqis themselves.

We agreed that this task would have to be done very carefully and have an enormous amount of oversight, because the former Iraqi intelligence service included Saddam's personal assassins, executioners, and interrogators. We had to make sure that the new service was free of the stigma of the past, and that its personnel knew and understood their new positions.

When Jerry and I finished our conversation, he told me he had someone he wanted me to meet. I asked him who it was and

———

he wouldn't say over the phone, so I knew it was work-related. We were all using cell phones at the time that were issued by the U.S. government, but as usual, in any foreign operation, you never know who's listening. At that time it could have been the Iranians, the Kuwaitis, or the Israelis, so we were always careful. I agreed to meet Jerry at my office, and from there we drove to the other side of the Green Zone and pulled up to a house that was secured like a fortress. There were more bodyguards in the driveway than in my twelve-man detail. As we stepped out of our cars we were greeted by a man who took us into the lobby of the house, where we milled around for about fifteen minutes, with security staff watching our every move.

Jerry didn't speak, so I figured I wouldn't either. Suddenly a door opened and a nicely dressed man walked in with a scent of cologne. He greeted Jerry in Arabic.

Jerry turned to me. "Mr. Kerik, this is Nuri al-Badran. He is going to be the new Iraqi minister of the interior."

I shook his hand and said hello. My mind was racing: So this was the secret and the reason for all the security! Evidently, the newly appointed governing council had identified its post-Saddam cabinet and al-Badran would be officially announced soon. This was great news for the Iraqi people, and for me, as it meant I was closer to going home than I had anticipated.

When I first accepted the Iraq assignment, no one knew how long I would be there. I guessed that it could be up to six months, so al-Badran's coming on board was good news for me. I had been in-country just over three months, and as we spoke, I figured I'd stay on for as long as he thought it was necessary. By the next afternoon, I realized that wouldn't be very long at all.

Jerry and I spoke with the new minister for about thirty min-

utes and I agreed to meet with him the next morning. I told him that I would have a briefing book prepared for him so that he could see the progress that had been made. I also mentioned my submission of the 2004 budget to Ambassador Bremer. Al-Badran was immediately interested in this. I also told him about the recent appointments of Ibrahim, Hala, and the other deputy minister, whom he said he wanted to meet as well, and with that, I said good-bye. Jerry stayed behind to speak further with him.

I met al-Badran again the next day for about an hour privately at his home, surrounded by dozens of security guards. By the time we finished our conversation I had a number of concerns.

I learned that he was born in Basra and was the son of a Shia tribal chief and had been Iraq's ambassador to Russia before a fall-out with Saddam Hussein in 1990 over the invasion of Kuwait. Al-Badran fled to London and joined the exiled opposition group the Iraqi National Accord. That was perhaps one of the first sore points with me, that he had a British passport, which meant when shit got rough, he had a place to run to, unlike someone like Ibrahim, who had stayed in Iraq, resisted Saddam internally, and assisted the coalition in freeing the country from the outset with blood, sweat, and guts. I was also concerned about al-Badran's being a Shia, which would not sit well with the 80 percent of the Interior Ministry who were Sunni and fearful that a Shia leader would re-taliate against them for Saddam's horrible acts of violence against the Shia population during his reign of terror.

The other thing that bothered me was that when I explained what we had done to rid the government of the senior members of the Ba'ath Party, as Bremer had ordered, al-Badran appeared to get upset and said abruptly, "That will all change."

My stomach knotted. All this fucking work to get rid of these

guys who were Saddam's henchmen and assassins and all the Iraqis like Ibrahim who had put their lives on the line would be in jeopardy if this new minister and others decided to begin bringing Saddam's regime members back.

Then al-Badran went off in another direction. He wanted to know all about the Ministry's money. Where was it? Who controlled it and who had the power to release it? I didn't like these questions, I didn't like his position on the Ba'athists, and I didn't like him.

During a meeting later with Bremer, Jerry, and a few others, I realized that there wasn't much we could do about al-Badran. He was the governing council's choice and we were going to have to stand by it.

But al-Badran did help me with one critical decision. Now that he was in place, Doug Brand was on board, and the other senior deputies had been appointed, there was no need for me to remain on-site, in-country. I was going home. Although I was happy that I would get back to Hala and the kids, I was concerned about the Iraqis who worked for me, whose lives would be in jeopardy if al-Badran didn't have their back. There was so much work yet to be done, but with the right leadership, anything was possible.

Unfortunately, Nuri al-Badran was the wrong man for the job.

. . .

At 4:30 p.m. on August 19, Eddie Bahdi, a military aide and captain in the U.S. Army, ran into my office. "I think the UN was just bombed," he said. The United Nations had been using the Canal Hotel as its headquarters in Baghdad ever since the first Gulf War.

Gary Uher and B. J. Turner were walking to our office as I was running out with my security team. "Come with us!" I told them.

As we left the palace grounds and were heading toward the UN headquarters, I could see a lot of smoke in the distance. Whatever had happened was enormous, and I remember being on the phone with Mike Braun as we were pulling up. "Not too close!" he said. "Remember, there could be secondary devices."

We arrived about ten minutes after the bomb had gone off. There were dozens of bloody people walking around in a daze. I was stunned when I saw the building. I had been there just a few days before and had a pretty good idea of its layout. It looked as if the brunt of the explosion had taken out the corner of the building where Sérgio de Mello's office was.

The bomber had driven a tanker truck loaded with live ordnance up to that corner and detonated it. That side of the building collapsed. People were screaming in horror, and the rescue teams could hear people yelling for help from down in the rubble.

Four members of THT 46, a U.S. Army Reserve counterintelligence team, along with Steele and Shubbar, were among the first to arrive at the scene. U.S. Army Chief Warrant Officer John Medina, Staff Sergeant Kurt Keller, Sergeant Mike Avila, and Corporal Steve Finnegan had already begun assisting the injured and escorting them away from the building. General Ibrahim, who by that time was the senior deputy interior minister, had ordered the responding Iraqi police to begin canvassing the area for witnesses and looking for evidence.

As I was walking toward the building, Steele, Shubbar, Finnegan, Keller, Avila, and Medina had climbed up the side of the collapsed portion, digging through the debris, shouting into the wreckage. When Steele saw me, he came down from the pile.

"De Mello's in there with another guy. They're alive," he told me. They were working on getting them out. I felt sick knowing de

Mello was in there. Steele said that the military rescue teams were moving the dead to an inner courtyard of the building.

I walked the length of the back of the building where the suicide bomber had stopped. There were pieces of his vehicle everywhere.

"I found the bomber," Gary said, coming over to me. And there he was. As we walked from where the tanker blew up, there were pieces of the bomber strewn in a straight line that ran out about one hundred yards. First his right foot, then left, then his spinal cord, and then his face, which had been ripped from his skull. It looked like a rubber Halloween mask.

I studied his remains, thinking of how fucking insane you have to be to do something like this, and the more I thought about it, the more concerned I became about the enemies we now face in the United States, who are more than willing to die for their cause. There is no deadlier enemy than one who has nothing to lose, and as Gary later reminded me, the only solace we have today is that we have men and women like Keller, Avila, Finnegan, and Medina who are willing to stand against that evil and fight for the good.

As I walked back toward the smoldering building, I ran into Ibrahim and told him to get someone with a camera to photograph the site and secure the bomber's remains.

Patrick Kennedy, Ambassador Bremer's chief of staff, arrived. I briefed him on what we knew about the vehicle and told him we found the bomber's remains. Over the next hour or so, Kennedy remained on the phone, reporting back to Bremer and calling for resources. Sometime later I saw U.S. Army general Rick Sanchez, Ambassador Bremer, and one of the FBI agents who had worked on the Jordanian Mission bombing.

In addition to Keller, Finnegan, Avila, and Medina, who were

———

on the outside of the building trying to dig inward, there were two army medics working feverishly down in the hole with de Mello and the other trapped man, to get them out, but after more than an hour, given the weight of the concrete beams that pinned them down, there wasn't much they could do except remove the smaller bricks and debris around them. They finally reached a moment when U.S. Army medic Andre Valentine had to make a decision.

They couldn't get de Mello out without getting the other man out first, and the only way to get that man out, he determined, was either to remove the concrete beam he was pinned under or remove his legs. Removing the beam was impossible.

With what Valentine later described as an "old rusty wood saw" and his "trusty paramedic scissors," that was exactly what he did, sawing off one leg at a time until they could extract the man from the hole. When he was done, and was able to get that man out, Valentine and the others focused on de Mello.

About thirty minutes later, as I was walking back toward my truck, Gary and B.J. stopped me to introduce me to Avila, Keller, Medina, and Finnegan, who were covered in sweat and dirt and looked exhausted. Medina had been hit in the head by falling debris as he was attempting to dig out another victim.

By their eyes I could see they were shaken, as anyone would be, but I was amazed by their courage and professionalism. Medina said he had been consoling a man whom he and the others were trying to free, but that man had just died, and before I could ask, Steele said, "It was de Mello."

I was stunned and deeply saddened by this loss, one I knew would be felt around the world by those who knew and admired him.

The sights, sounds, and smells of the bombed-out UN building

took me back to New York City on September 11. Again I was witnessing the best and worst in humanity: a homicidal suicide bomber killing innocent people, and the courage and dedication of Medina, Finnegan, Keller, Avila, and the others who responded that day.

I thanked them for being there, for their bravery and service to the country. Standing no more than a hundred yards from the building, surrounded by cars that had exploded during the blast, I told them how much it reminded me of 9/11. As I was speaking, Finnegan broke in. "Boss, we worked for you back then."

What I didn't know was that Medina was a detective and Finnegan a captain in the NYPD. Keller was a cop in Boonton, New Jersey, and Avila was on the police force in San Antonio, Texas. These men didn't have to be there, but they volunteered to serve their country, in addition to the work they did at home. For Medina and Finnegan, too, it was 9/11 all over again.

I saw Bremer speaking to Kennedy nearby. They both looked devastated. I knew from the brief time I had spent with Bremer and de Mello that Bremer admired and respected his colleague, and that de Mello's death would pain him deeply. I also knew that he had to be thinking the same thing I was: If they got to de Mello, then I could be next.

. . .

Sitting here in my office at home in New Jersey ten years later, a Bureau of Prisons electronic bracelet on my ankle, I think about that day in Baghdad, the days that came after, the ones that led up to it. I've often thought of de Mello.

Writing this book has taken me back in time, and one evening while doing so I felt compelled to thank the men I met that diffi-

cult day in 2003. I called the Boonton Police Department looking for Staff Sergeant Kurt A. Keller. An on-duty sergeant told me I'd have to call back on Monday, but before I did, I found an article on the Internet on Keller's being honored for his service in the military. I found it strange that it read like a memorial.

On Monday I called the Boonton Police Department and this time spoke to Boonton's chief of police, David J. Mayhood. I told him I was looking for Sergeant Keller. I explained that I'd met him at the UN bombing in Iraq all those years ago and just wanted to thank him for being there, for his service to our country. The chief sounded uneasy as he told me that Keller had been a great cop, a good man, and a close personal friend.

"He did three tours in the Middle East and saw some really bad things," Chief Mayhood told me. "I suppose the stress really got to him."

My stomach turned and the chief got quiet. Then he confirmed my fear: Keller was dead. On November 14, 2006, three years after I met him in the chaos of Baghdad, Keller had taken his own life.

That night I spoke to his wife, Meghan Keller. She told me that at times he could be wound very tight, but that he was a good cop and a loving husband. Meghan choked up and said she missed him dearly. The following day I received a call from Finnegan and then Medina, both of whom had gotten my number from Meghan. It had been more than ten years since we last saw each other that dark day in Baghdad, and I was still as proud of them as I was then. When they spoke of Kurt Keller I could hear the love and admiration they both had for him.

These men, all of them, are America's greatest asset. Patriots willing to fight for and defend our country's freedom. It has been

a privilege and an honor to work with them, one I will never forget.

In the end, Kurt Keller's life ended much sooner than it should have, and to me, the only thing worse than his death is that had he held on for just six more months, Elsa Keller, the daughter he never got to see and hold, would have met the hero that I did on that fateful day in August 2003. May he and de Mello rest in peace, and may God bless the families they left behind.

11

The Rise before the Fall

My body tensed as I sat across from Rudy Giuliani at our morning executive staff meeting. We were in our Manhattan office overlooking Times Square. Have you ever had to keep a secret from someone you respected, loved, and admired, and who under most circumstances would be the first person you would go to with that secret?

Keeping my secret from Rudy, my former boss, partner, friend, and the godfather to my two little girls, was killing me.

The 2004 presidential election was over. George W. Bush had been re-elected.

The Saturday after the re-election I had spoken to Tony Carbonetti, Rudy's chief of staff, and told him I was interested in Tom Ridge's job if Ridge decided to leave the administration. I wanted to take on the challenge of doing a job I love doing—protection, national security, policing—and I knew I could do it well. Ridge, the former governor of Pennsylvania, had been chosen by President Bush to merge twenty-two federal agencies into the U.S. Depart-

ment of Homeland Security in the aftermath of 9/11, and there were rumors that he was now considering stepping down. I knew it was a huge agency with an enormous amount of responsibility, but I also felt my prior accomplishments in the NYPD and Correction Department spoke for themselves, and if I carried that management style and accountability into DHS, I believed it could be one of the best-run and most successful agencies in the U.S. government.

I asked Tony to speak to Rudy, so that he might relay my interest if he spoke to the president. But this conversation with Carbonetti proved unnecessary, because at the beginning of the following week, I received an email from Dina Powell, President Bush's executive appointments secretary. Dina wanted me to call her at a certain number, at a certain time, and didn't want me to mention the call to anyone. I stared at the email for a second, and then had John Picciano, my chief of staff, look at it.

"Don't say anything to anyone until we figure out what it is," John said. "You know it's Ridge's job, right?" We'll see what Dina has to say, I thought.

I had known Dina since November 2001 when she called me about possibly taking command of the newly created Transportation Safety Administration. I was still police commissioner at the time but had made it known that I was leaving at the end of the year when Rudy finished his term as mayor, so Dina called, asking me if I would be interested in taking on the new agency.

At the time, I had already promised Hala no more government jobs for a while, and I wanted to test out the private sector. Rudy was putting together his consulting company and I knew I would be in the mix, so I didn't want to consider another government job just then. I thanked Dina for her call and the president's offer but had to decline.

———

Just over a year later, she called again, this time with another job offer from the White House. The administrator for the Drug Enforcement Administration (DEA) had stepped down and they were looking for a replacement. Dina asked if I was interested. I was, I really wanted to accept this, but Hala and I had just bought a house in New Jersey with a million-dollar mortgage and there was no way I could afford a move back to government.

I felt I had worked hard for close to thirty years and now I was finally in a position where I began to feel financially secure. But I still would have loved to take that job, heading the DEA. I had worked for the DEA from 1990 to 1994, as a detective assigned to the New York Drug Enforcement Task Force, overseeing one of the largest and most successful drug investigations in the history of New York at the time. The investigation started on the streets of Jackson Heights, Queens, and took us into the jungles of Guatemala, Costa Rica, Ecuador, and Brazil, resulting in the seizure of tons of cocaine and millions in drug proceeds. It was a case full of international intrigue, drugs, money, murder, and good guys against bad. I loved every minute of it.

The DEA is one of the greatest law enforcement organizations in our country, so turning the job down, for me, was a killer. Now here we were again, Dina contacting me, something possibly big at stake.

I called her as directed, and as soon as she answered I could tell this was business. No personal small talk or family pleasantries. She was right to the point and stone serious. She told me she was sending me a piece of paper with some questions on it. She wanted me to answer the questions, and not to date it or put my name on it, and she didn't want me to show it to anyone. She told me that no one was to know we spoke, including and specifically Rudy Giuliani. "NO ONE," she said, "except for Hala."

The press began reporting that possible changes in the president's cabinet were imminent. Colin Powell was stepping down, along with John Ashcroft and Tom Ridge.

It was becoming clear to me that I was on the short list to replace Ridge as secretary of Homeland Security and was now being vetted. As honored and excited as I was about being considered, I was equally nervous and anxious about the vetting process and its strain on my family. Rudy commented on the new openings and possible replacements at one of our morning staff meetings. I didn't say a word about Dina's phone call and questions. It was gnawing at me because I felt an obligation out of my loyalty to him to tell him, but I had been ordered not to. I didn't know if this was a test or not, so I just kept my mouth shut.

In the meantime, I carried on my daily meeting and travel schedule, all the while answering questions from White House staff.

In mid-November, Hala and I traveled to Los Angeles to the International Chiefs of Police Conference, and from there we were going to Hawaii for a four-day vacation. When I told Dina, she said, "Absolutely not. You cannot go so far, in case we need you." So Hala and I decided to travel to Tampa, Florida, to see her brother and his family.

By the time I got back, the interaction with the White House was overwhelming—daily calls, emails, messages, requests for personal documents.

I felt I had to tell Rudy. But Tony, not knowing that I was already being vetted, had followed through on my request. He came into my office one afternoon and told me, "Rudy spoke to the president about you. He recommended you for Ridge's job."

It was as if he had taken a huge boulder off my back. I broke the

news to him and explained what had been going on, that I'd been speaking to the White House for nearly two weeks. He appeared a bit surprised to hear it, but not about my being told to keep Rudy out of the loop.

"It's all good," he said.

When I later talked to Rudy, he was completely supportive and, for reasons I didn't understand at the time, listed a number of people—Washington attorneys and advisors—whom I was going to have to meet with during the vetting process, before my confirmation hearings. At the time, I was relatively naïve about Washington, national politics, and the confirmation process, but Rudy knew the system, knew it well.

Over the past eight years, there have been thousands of articles slamming Rudy Giuliani for recommending me to the White House, asserting that my failed nomination tarnished him. (This reached its culmination in 2007 with *Time* magazine's headline "Rudy Giuliani's Kerik Problem.") But it shouldn't be seen that way.

Yes, he may have spoken to the president on my behalf, thereby increasing my chances of being nominated, but I was being considered and vetted for the position before Rudy spoke to the president, so to blame him and beat him up for my mistakes and failed nomination is unfair. As I would soon learn, the president had his own reasons, independent of Rudy's recommendation, for choosing me.

It pained me to see the press badgering Rudy. He finally stated publicly that recommending me to the White House was a mistake. Whether Rudy truly believed that or not, his words and the headlines that resulted from them left me vulnerable to the press and in the court of public opinion—and, I believe, emboldened

the headline-seeking prosecutors who would soon use Rudy's words against me.

For as much as I disagree with President Obama and what he's done in office, the one thing that I have admired is that he hasn't thrown any of his failed presidential appointments under the bus, no matter how bad they looked or truly were.

There was former Senate majority leader Tom Daschle, President Obama's pick for health and human services secretary, who withdrew his nomination amidst a scandal involving unpaid taxes; Adolfo Carrión Jr., the former Bronx borough president, who never paid for the architect involved in renovating his home— a misdeed that was also a large piece of the prosecution against me—until after it was discovered when he'd been appointed director of the White House Office of Urban Affairs; and there was Treasury Secretary Timothy Geithner, who failed to pay some of his taxes over a four-year period but was approved to head a department that includes the Internal Revenue Service. CNBC *Mad Money* host Jim Cramer told his viewing audience that had he been in Geithner's shoes he'd face criminal prosecution. His point is true. The laws and punishments are often that selectively applied.

In my case I would be charged criminally for my failure to pay payroll tax for our family nanny. I didn't get off easy, as others did, but this isn't the main point. The danger and imbalance are in that selectivity of criminal prosecution, and that danger is not just in corruption cases involving public figures; it can be seen in many other areas of the law.

One thing my rise and fall has taught me about friendships, loyalty, and politics is that when it comes to scandal, right or wrong, justified or not, many self-professed friends and most politicians cower at the first sign of trouble. And although for the most part

you live and learn, there will be some surprises when the smoke clears. For me, I've learned that those standing at your side through challenges are the friends you may have for the rest of your life, and I thank God for them.

. . .

Just before leaving office in early 2001, President William J. Clinton presented posthumously the Congressional Medal of Honor, our nation's highest military award, to the family of a lieutenant colonel for his acts of valor in combat on July 1, 1898. That lieutenant colonel was Theodore Roosevelt, who led his First U.S. Volunteer Cavalry, known as the "Rough Riders," and other troops in two dramatic charges against entrenched Spanish positions in the battle to capture San Juan Heights, near Santiago, Cuba, during the Spanish-American War.

Four years after Roosevelt's proud family received that award on his behalf, I stood in the Roosevelt Room of the White House staring at Teddy's Medal of Honor hanging in a glass case. I thought of the history behind it and the man who earned it. "The president will see you in five minutes," Dina said from the door. "Just stay here until I come and get you."

My mind raced as I wondered if I was making the right decision by accepting the position. I'd be secretary of the Department of Homeland Security. Hala was against my coming to the White House and even considering it, and what most people don't know is that I initially turned down the job, but after speaking to Dina and Andy Card, the president's chief of staff, I changed my mind, as Hala thought I might. She knew I wouldn't say no to the president. We had just moved into our new home in Franklin Lakes, New Jersey, and Hala knew my decision would have a major im-

pact on her and the kids. She kept reminding me that all her family was in New Jersey and I was about to uproot her and the kids to go to Washington, D.C., where she wouldn't know anyone and I would work from six in the morning until at least midnight every night and she and the kids would be all alone and never see me. I tried to calm her fears, but it wasn't working. She hated the political arena and the press and media, and in this position I would be saturated by all of it.

Standing there in my suit in the Roosevelt Room, I started to sweat, wondering if I was doing the right thing. Dina's voice broke my trance. "The president will see you now. Come with me."

I followed her across the hall to the Oval Office, where President Bush was speaking to Andy Card, his chief of staff. As I entered the room, Dina went one way and Andy went the other. Suddenly I was standing there alone with the president. He looked more relaxed than the last time I'd seen him, at campaign functions before the election. He held out his hand and grabbed mine.

"I'm looking for a secretary of Homeland Security," he said. "You want it?"

The question seemed delivered in slow motion. Although I knew what I was there for and expected exactly this, a flash went through me. I had come a long way from walking a perimeter fence as a military police dog-handler at a nuclear missile base in South Korea in the 1970s, walking a foot post as a cop in Times Square.

As I had previously run large law-and-order organizations, the challenge of taking over Homeland Security didn't dissuade me— but having the president of the United States stand in front of me and ask me to accept the position was overwhelming.

———

"Yes, sir, Mr. President," I fired back, standing in front of him in the middle of the room. The words were out before I knew it.

For nearly a month before that day, I had been researching, observing, and reading about this newly formed department and our national security policies to see how I thought I could make them better and what I would do to enhance the agency that Governor Tom Ridge had helped create and lead. I was prepared for any question the president might ask me. One problem: He didn't ask me anything. Nothing, not a single question. He just wanted to make sure I wanted the job. He signaled for me to follow him over to the couch.

"Part of why I'm picking you is for your success in New York and your service in Iraq," he told me.

He said that he needed someone who could go into the department and "break some china." Tom Ridge had done a great job merging twenty-two federal agencies into one, but now it was time to make them *work* as one. "I think you can do that," President Bush said. The closest thing to dealing with Congress, he joked, was probably dealing with the New York City Council, and I'd seemed to do that pretty well.

"Whatever I can do to make it work I'll do," I said.

With that Andy Card walked in, as if on cue. The president told me that Andy would now speak with me privately. Then Dina walked in and the president asked her, "When are we doing this?"

Dina proposed Monday. "What about Friday?" the president asked.

Dina and Andy looked at each other and agreed that the nomination ceremony would be Friday, December 3, 2004, at 10:00 a.m.

I said good-bye to the president, and Andy and I walked to his

———

office. We sat and talked for five minutes about what would happen over the next few days. He wanted me to meet with several members of the House and Senate. He told me when and how the White House would leak my nomination to the press. Then he told me it was likely to be a rough confirmation process because Alberto Gonzales, the president's counsel, was being nominated for attorney general. The nominations would be happening at the same time.

But Al Gonzales would not be the prime headache for the White House.

I would.

ed a doctor.
ment.
comment.
too trivial
ssing: What
tively prove
d wanted to
twenty-two
White House
ly didn't re-
le, if I had a
idiculous to
plain to the
than twenty
aste of time,

costly vet-
Southers, a
r the Trans-
oo, ran into

reprimand
n as an FBI
oyfriend or
ly became a
f a bad joke.
ed he did it
spected law
background

d Renovations

a dream: a high school dropout
d a lot of good luck rose to the
s in the land. Then in the blink
tional public falls from grace in
ned into a nightmare.

eorge W. Bush nominated me
, in December 2004, the New
ng into my career, accusing me
crime and implying that there
ock transaction I was involved
fice and the White House press
try that came in, some of which
rous.

l from the White House to tell
ory reporting that in the early
Saudi Arabia for the royal fam-

ily's medical facility in Riyadh, I once pushed or slapp
Newsweek was asking if this was true and if I had a com

At first I started laughing, saying that no, I had n
I thought they must be kidding, that the matter wa
compared to so many others that they could be addr
would one argument or altercation in one's past defin
about a person anyway? But they were dead serious an
know if I remembered having a run-in with a doctor
years before. When I said that I didn't remember, the V
staff aide asked if the story could *possibly* be true. I rea
member, but thought to myself, Yes, it's entirely possi
reason to engage the guy aggressively. It seemed too 1
me that someone would be so small-minded as to con
press over a run-in he might have had with me more
years earlier. I thought the matter was an all-around w
money, and resources.

I was reminded of my own painful and ultimatel
ting process when President Obama nominated Errol
thirty-year law enforcement professional, to take ove
portation Safety Administration in 2010. Southers, t
problems during his confirmation process.

Members of Congress raised questions about a
Southers had received twenty-two years before wh
agent he ran a background check on his ex-wife's
had a coworker do it for him. His nomination quick
political lightning rod, which to me was something c
The guy admitted that he made a mistake. He admit
and that it was wrong. He was a highly qualified and re
enforcement executive with close to an impeccable

that should have gained him the position he was nominated for and yet did not, and whose loss was it? Ours, the American people's.

If this is how the members of the House and Senate want to apply their scrutiny, then more than half of them should step down and go find another job, because they certainly wouldn't make it through the process intact. Southers deserved and should have gotten that job, but did not because of politics, nothing more, nothing less. That's not the way it should work.

While the press and media dissected my past, the White House prepared a schedule for me to meet with a number of congressional leaders at the Capitol to seek their support in the confirmation process. This was the part of politics—the flattery, the fakeness, the say-what-people-want-to-hear—that I really didn't like.

I was assigned three young White House staffers who carried with them briefing binders for each member of Congress I was going to meet. My old correction, police, and security friend and colleague John Picciano came with me that day. As we walked the halls of the historic building, one of the staffers would pull out a folder with the name of a representative or senator on it, show it to me, and begin telling me what to say to that person: *He's interested in this particular issue, so you're going to tell him that you're going to do everything to help him and you can't wait to work together with him to secure the country.*

What a crock, I thought. I already knew some of these politicians and knew that they didn't like President Bush, so they weren't going to like me—and I didn't like them either. So, I wasn't going for the dog-and-pony show as laid out. My presentation was going to be a simple truth: *I'm looking forward to the opportunity, I'm going*

to do the best I can, and I intend to keep our country safe. When I told my handlers that this was to be my speech and I was sticking to it, they weren't too happy.

So off we went, walking down the massive halls of the Capitol Building. I was beside myself; it was such a farce. No wonder nothing gets done in D.C., if you've got to walk around bullshitting everyone, people who already know you're bullshitting, and who are just as good at the bullshitting as you are. It was disturbing me, and as usual, the more upset I got, the more profanity spilled out of my mouth, until finally, Picciano pulled me aside.

"Look, Commish, don't take it out on these kids," he told me. "They got a job to do and you're scaring the shit out of them. Please calm down. And don't say 'fuck' in front of them anymore, either. I don't know if you're allowed to say 'fuck' in the Capitol anyway, but every time you do, that lead aide squints like someone stuck him in the ass with a needle or something." Pitch was right, so from that point on I was on my best behavior, hating every minute of it.

With the press scrutiny, the White House staffers, the attorneys, and the preparation team in my office collecting my taxes, speeches, and every public document relating to me dating back more than twenty-five years, my mind was in overdrive. But as I arrived back in New York City, there was one other thing bugging me: Marisol!

Marisol, or Mari, as my two- and four-year-old daughters called her at the time, was about four-feet-ten, with jet-black hair and a gold tooth that sparkled when she smiled. She had been taking care of my daughters since 2002 and looked after them as if they were her own.

Like most American families that employed nannies or domes-

tic servants, I paid Mari in cash. In the early fall of 2004, however, Mari told me that she'd be leaving us to return to her own children in Mexico. At the time I was campaigning like a madman for President Bush, and I anticipated that if Bush were to win re-election, I might be in the running for a position in his administration and didn't want any of my personal affairs to become a negative issue. So I had called my accountant and told him that I wanted to pay the payroll taxes for Mari dating back to 2002. I gave him Mari's Social Security number and address.

But in early December, five days after I was nominated, I found out that this back payroll tax still hadn't been filed, so I immediately spoke to Rudy and a number of the attorneys in our office. Based on their input, I decided that I would have my accountant immediately pay the taxes electronically, amend my filings from 2002 and 2003, and then send these amended returns to Ernst & Young, to ensure we didn't miss anything and that the late penalties were covered. By that night, I felt okay and was relieved that it had been handled. Now if this matter of my nanny became an issue before a confirmation committee, I would be able to explain it.

The next afternoon, however, one of my investigators advised me that Mari's Social Security number traced back to a male, not a female, and it appeared that she had been in the country illegally. Rudy and I convened again with the attorneys in our office, but this time I felt that moving forward into a confirmation could be fatal. The situation with Mari was bad, given that the job I'd be assuming would include overseeing U.S. Customs and Immigration. Her status and my employment of her would be a lightning rod, and would give my critics and opponents a reason to pounce.

I immediately called the White House and spoke to Dina Powell, Alberto Gonzales, the president's counsel, and Andy Card, his chief of staff. They all agreed that if I wanted to move forward with the nomination the president would support me. As I considered these high-stakes options, Gonzales told me that if I did decide to move forward, someone from the Justice Department would have to interview my wife. This sent a chill down my spine.

I was seeing how damaging the vetting process could be and did not want to make Hala go through it as well. I realized that the scrutiny, on the nanny, on my taxes, could very well destroy my thirty-year record of meritorious public service. Despite my ambition to serve in a cabinet post, I began to think that no one with a brain would want to be considered for one. The glare can be vicious, the scrutiny overwhelming. It's a necessary process, of course, vetting those among us who want to serve in positions of power, but it should be done with fairness, common sense, and prudence. But it's usually political, biased, and often tainted. The process is too often a disservice to the nominee and the country, and it prevents the best people from wanting to come forward and serve in these positions.

After my conversation with Gonzales, I made what was one of the most important phone calls of my life—to Andy Card to tell him I was withdrawing my name from consideration. Andy understood where I was coming from. He told me to fax the president a formal letter of withdrawal. We spoke briefly about how and when the White House would notify the press. "But be prepared," Andy said. Although I'd withdrawn, the scrutiny wouldn't end, and it might get worse.

I was mortified and sick. One week from the day I was nominated, I faxed the president at the White House:

———

Dear Mr. President:

It is with deep regret that I inform you that I cannot continue forward in the confirmation process for the position of Secretary of the Department of Homeland Security. While I will always consider your confidence in me to be the honor of a lifetime, I am convinced that, for personal reasons, moving forward would not be in the best interests of your administration, the Department of Homeland Security or the American people. Mr. President, as I stated on the day of my nomination, you have been a strong, effective and inspirational leader in the war for freedom and against terror. Under your watch, our nation has taken swift and bold strides against those who threaten our homeland. I remain firm in my belief that I could have made valuable contributions to the Department and its efforts.

Under the present circumstances, however, I cannot permit matters personal to me to distract from the focus and progress of the Department of Homeland Security and its crucial endeavors. For these reasons, I must ask you to withdraw my nomination. I personally apologize to you for not having focused on this earlier.

With respect,
BERNARD B. KERIK

My withdrawal sent the press and media into a frenzy, as they went searching for Mari, the nanny, and looking into my stock transactions and renovations to an apartment in the Bronx that I had purchased five years earlier but no longer owned. I didn't know that those renovations would lead to my ultimate downfall and disgrace.

As a former police commissioner of New York City, I was used to public scrutiny, but nothing close to this level. After the White House announced my withdrawal, the intensity of the press scrutiny increased hour by hour, and just a few days later the New York City Department of Investigation (DOI) sent a series of questions to my attorney, Joe Tacopina, concerning my former Bronx apartment. Before I knew it, I was under a grand jury investigation in the Bronx.

The primary allegation was that while serving as New York City's correction commissioner five years earlier, I had spoken to New York City officials on behalf of my close friend Frank DiTommaso, who according to the press was connected to organized crime and had been attempting to obtain a city license from the Trade Waste Authority, which oversaw the carting industry. The prosecutors charged that in exchange for my assistance in obtaining the city license, DiTommaso had made substantial renovations to my Bronx apartment without charging me for them.

Frank and I admitted that we were friends and denied any wrongdoing. Frank also denied having ties to organized crime. But the Bronx district attorney and the New York City DOI turned the matter into an eighteen-month-long grand jury investigation, during which they would subpoena and harass my friends, family, colleagues, and just about everyone I knew.

In 1999, Frank and his brother, Peter, owners of Interstate Industrial Corporation, had hired my brother, Don, to work for them. After buying an apartment on West 239th Street in the Riverdale section of the Bronx, I asked Frank for a recommendation for a contractor who could assist me in renovating the apartment. My apartment needed a new kitchen, and work done on the bathrooms and floor. Frank suggested someone who was doing work

for him and his brother at the time. That contractor, knowing I didn't have a lot of money at the time, gave me an estimate of thirty-three thousand dollars for the renovations. He went to work, and I paid the bill.

As he progressed on the work, it did appear that he was putting more into the apartment than I was paying. And I let him. Looking back, maybe I should have forced the issue. I should have stopped him from doing the extra work. This was one of those ethical moments that any person in public office faces repeatedly. Often the public figure, me in this case, doesn't see that even the *perception* of impropriety can be your downfall.

State investigators later claimed that Frank and Peter DiTommaso paid the contractor $165,000 toward the renovations being done on my apartment in exchange for my future help in obtaining city permits for them and their company, Interstate— permits that I had no authority over and that the DiTommasos and Interstate never in fact received.

In their zeal to make their case and help substantiate their crime theory, the prosecutors told the court and the press that on behalf of Interstate I met at Walker's Pub, in lower Manhattan, with two city officials: Ray Casey, a DOI deputy commissioner and the head of the Trade Waste Commission, and Michael Caruso, a DOI deputy commissioner who had been the inspector general for the correction department when I was the correction commissioner. Prosecutors also claimed that I called a deputy commissioner of the DOI, a Dyana Lee, on behalf of Interstate, and that I let an Interstate employee use my office to meet with Trade Waste investigators. Their assertion that I was acting "on behalf of Interstate" in an attempt to assist the DiTommasos in obtaining the licenses they sought was wrong.

———

What the prosecutors failed to tell the court or press was that my meeting at Walker's Pub with Casey and Caruso was at Casey's request, to answer questions about my brother's working for Interstate. It was Casey who wanted to meet with me, because he insisted that Interstate was "mobbed up," and he wanted to know all about Don's working there and what he and I might know about the DiTommasos. The only reason I called Dyana Lee was that Casey had ordered me to do so, to answer any questions she might have about Interstate. I didn't know Dyana Lee, didn't know what she did or what her position was, but the government's statements made it sound as though I had called her on my own in an attempt to assist Interstate.

The government's assertion that I let an Interstate employee use my office conference room to meet with Trade Waste investigators, on behalf of Interstate, or to influence Trade Waste's investigation of Interstate, was a complete mischaracterization of reality.

Casey wanted his investigators to meet with the employee, who was a friend of mine as well as a registered informant for the FBI, and this individual did not want to be seen at the Trade Waste offices, so the meeting was arranged in my office. The two Trade Waste investigators who showed up were later interviewed by the Bronx DA and DOI, and both were adamant that I had not attempted to influence anyone in any way. The prosecutors also refused to make this information public.

As the government laid out its crime theory to the press and court, it left out one other, extremely important detail: *that I offered to assist in their regulatory inquiry of the DiTommasos if necessary.*

So for eighteen torturous months, between December 2004 and June 2006, investigators ripped my life to shreds, harassing and intimidating my friends, family, and colleagues. Rudy Giuliani had even been made to testify before the grand jury, though he

stuck by me. The DA's office threatened me with a sixteen-count felony indictment, but when Tacopina, my lawyer, told them that I would go to trial to defend myself before I would ever plead guilty to a felony, they had to admit that they had found no direct evidence of a quid pro quo between the DiTommasos and me.

They said that I would have to accept responsibility for two ethics violations: one for failing to document a personal loan on a city financial disclosure, a $28,000 loan from a friend that I used for the down payment on the Bronx apartment; and the other for accepting a gift in the form of apartment renovations from Interstate in the amount of $165,000.

I immediately told Tacopina that I would not say that I accepted a gift from Frank DiTommaso or Interstate, because I had no personal knowledge that Interstate actually paid for anything, and I didn't know how the government came up with the figure of $165,000 for the renovations.

Tacopina came back to me and said that the district attorney agreed to change the language in the plea agreement to read "Interstate, or *a subsidiary*," which I understood to mean the contractor. I asked him why Interstate had to be mentioned at all, because I had no knowledge that they had anything to do with the renovations. He said that was the language that the DA wanted. He said that the plea deal would end their witch hunt and give Hala and me the opportunity to move on with our lives.

"They're not felonies," Tacopina told me. "Plead guilty to the two ethics violations, pay a fine and penalties, and it's over." It's important to note that at the time Tacopina was not only a high-profile criminal defense attorney with a strong reputation, but also, I believed, a close personal friend.

So on June 30, 2006, on Tacopina's advice and as the result of

the plea agreement negotiated between him and the Bronx district attorney, I pled guilty in Bronx Supreme Court to two New York City ethics violations.

. . .

The night before we went to court, I asked Tacopina if he had determined how the Bronx DA came up with the $165,000 price tag for the renovations. He said he didn't know. I asked him about how my testimony might affect the DiTommasos. I also asked him if I would owe taxes on this gift that I was going to say I received, and he told me I wouldn't. "The DA is claiming it was a gift, and by federal law, the recipient of the gift doesn't pay the gift tax; the gift giver does," he told me.

During a ten-minute hearing in Bronx Supreme Court, I was ordered to pay a $206,000 fine, plus $15,000 in civil penalties. The assistant district attorney informed the judge that there was no direct evidence of a quid pro quo between the DiTommasos and me.

Before that court hearing, I'd met with Barry Kluger, the Bronx deputy district attorney, who echoed Tacopina's statement: Pleading guilty to the two ethics charges would put an end to it all. I believed him, and I believed Tacopina, but as I walked out of the courtroom that morning with Tacopina and Kenneth Breen, another attorney who had represented me during the investigation, Breen had a stunned look on his face. He had not seen my plea agreement or the plea allocution that Tacopina told me to read in the courtroom.

Breen looked over at Tacopina and said, "A gift! You had him plead guilty to accepting a gift?"

By the look on Breen's face and the grave tone of his voice I could tell this wasn't good.

———

Outside the door of the Bronx Courthouse a few dozen reporters barraged us with questions. There was one in particular that bothered me: Did I owe taxes on the gift that I had just said I accepted?

Tacopina looked at the reporter who'd asked this and said, "That's all been taken care of."

Although I believed that everything had indeed been taken care of, I would later realize that this was not the case. I came to understand that Breen was concerned about the consequences of accepting that plea.

Still, for the moment, as we got into my car and drove off, I felt very much relieved. The investigation was over. I called Hala to let her know I was on my way home.

But what a fool I was. This wasn't the end of my legal battles at all.

Within weeks of that court appearance, I saw news reports on television that Frank and Peter DiTommaso had both been indicted by a Bronx grand jury—Frank with one count of perjury and Peter with one count of perjury and one count of obstruction. I was sick to my stomach. According to the reports, during the secret grand jury investigation against me, both men had testified that they had not paid the contractor for my apartment renovations, so the Bronx district attorney used my guilty plea—in which I said I had accepted a gift from Interstate or a subsidiary—to contradict their testimony and accuse them of perjury.

I couldn't understand how Tacopina hadn't thought of this possibility. I didn't know Peter, but Tacopina knew Frank was my friend. I never wanted to hurt them or their family. I felt horrible.

Then I saw in the news that Michael Caruso, my former colleague and one of the DOI guys I'd met with at Walker's Pub, had

filed a federal civil rights lawsuit against the City of New York for wrongful termination.

He alleged in his complaint that during the Bronx DA's investigation of me, he had been ordered to appear before the grand jury in my case and that right before he testified, Walter Arsenault, the first deputy commissioner of DOI and one of the lead investigators in the Bronx case against me, had essentially told Caruso to testify falsely.

Caruso said that Arsenault wanted him to testify that during our meeting at Walker's Pub I had vouched for one of DiTommaso's employees, thus vouching for, or acting "on behalf of," Interstate and DiTommaso, even though Caruso had already told Arsenault that he could not truthfully testify to that. Caruso maintained that his refusal to give false testimony is what led to his being fired just a few days after his grand jury appearance after twenty-seven years of service to the city.

I was fuming. The Bronx deputy district attorney and DOI spent eighteen months ripping up my personal and professional life, only to have to admit that they had no direct evidence of a quid pro quo between me and Frank DiTommaso or Interstate.

When that wasn't enough, they went after Frank and Peter DiTommaso, and then Caruso.

Bronx deputy DA Kluger had said my guilty plea to the ethics violations would put an end to the investigation. It did not. The plea agreement I had accepted was in fact fuel for a new case the Feds were already building against me. The language in the plea agreement, my pleading guilty to the ethics violations, wasn't really about justice; it was just what they needed to get me further.

———

13

In Jordan

"Prince Ali is on the phone," Hala said, waking me from a deep sleep.

"What? What time is it?"

I was in a daze as she handed me the phone. I looked at the clock next to the bed. Six-thirty in the morning. I had just arrived home from Amman, Jordan, thirteen hours earlier.

During the media frenzy surrounding my failed nomination, I had resigned from the security consulting company that I partnered with Rudy Giuliani and had created my own firm, The Kerik Group. For the past eight months I had had a team of about eight people conducting an operational, threat, and vulnerability assessment of Jordan's national security for His Majesty King Abdullah II. So the first thought I had about this call was that one of the men or women who worked for me in Jordan had possibly gotten hurt or was in some kind of trouble.

"Hello, who is this?" I asked.

"Bernie, it's Ali. I'm with His Majesty. Did you hear about the bombings?"

At that point I sat straight up in bed. Prince Ali and His Majesty had been in Kazakhstan on a state visit, he informed me, when suicide bombers attacked three hotels back home in Amman—the Days Inn, the Grand Hyatt, and the Radisson SAS.

Ali said that he was calling on behalf of His Majesty. They wanted me to come to Amman to assist in any way I could, primarily to act as a surrogate spokesman for the Jordanians, because the international press was already questioning Jordan's security and stability. I told him that I'd just gotten in the night before but could return that evening.

Then I remembered there was no direct flight from New York to Amman that evening. I would have to fly to Chicago to get the Royal Jordanian flight to Amman. Prince Ali said he would work on the tickets and he and His Majesty would see me there.

I hung up the phone and Hala looked at me.

"Do you have to do this? You just got home, and they've already blown up the hotels."

"I'll be fine," I said. "I can't say no to the king. They haven't hit the Four Seasons, so I'm in good shape." The little sarcasm at the end didn't help.

"Yeah, like when you couldn't say no to the president. You see what that got us, right?"

At that point I realized I wasn't going to win the argument, so I didn't say a word. I got up, called Kim Petersen, a former U.S. Army Special Forces officer and head of the Diplomatic Protective Security Service for the State Department, and Debbie Kurtz, who had worked with me as a deputy commissioner in the NYC DOC, and told them that I'd been summoned back to Jordan because of the bombings. I needed their help.

After seeing the Grand Hyatt, I went to the other two locations. The scenes were the same. What I kept thinking, what shocked me most, was that these suicide bombers were killing other Muslims—a reminder to me that *anyone* who lives differently than these militants do, or who has differences of opinion with these sick and demented people, can and will become a target. They operate under different names—Al Qaeda, Hamas, Hezbollah, now the hideous ISIS, ISIL, or Khorasan—but they all represent the hijacking of Islam for the promotion of their twisted jihad. When you're fighting an enemy who *wants* to die, it's going to be very difficult to prevent these kinds of attacks.

It was confirmed within hours that there had been three attackers at the three hotels and that they were Iraqis who had entered Jordan three days earlier. More than a hundred suspects were arrested in the following days. Police found evidence that led to the arrest of an Iraqi woman four days after the attack. She was believed to be a fourth suicide bomber whose explosive belt hadn't detonated. According to intelligence officials, she was the sister of a close aide to Abu Musab al-Zarqawi, the notorious Jordanian militant who at the time was the most wanted terrorist in Iraq.

No one has a better intelligence service in the Middle East than Jordan, with the exception of Israel, perhaps, but these Iraqi terrorists were able to slip through the cracks. It could happen again.

For the next three days, with at most a few hours' sleep per day, I did one interview after another, answering questions about what happened, why, how, and what it meant for Jordan, the region, the United States. CNN, Fox News, MSNBC, BBC, and Al Jazeera all wanted answers. His Majesty wanted to be as transparent as possible, and to make sure it was clear that, despite the attacks, Jordan was safe and sound and open for business.

———

Kim said he would start preparing an intelligence package and email it to me before my flight.

I arrived in Amman just shy of forty-eight hours after the bombings. I dropped my things at the Four Seasons and headed for the three bombed hotels with Ghaith al Tayeb, a captain with the Jordanian General Intelligence Department. Ghaith was my liaison to His Majesty's private office, and coordinated my travel in and around the country. A graduate of the Citadel in South Carolina, he was a professional and talented soldier, one who represented the best of the Jordanian armed forces.

As we were heading toward the hotel, I called Hala to let her know I was all right.

As we got out of the vehicle at the Grand Hyatt, the reality of terror was all around: the damage to the outside of the building, the military presence, the barricades.

"This is fucked up," I said to Ghaith as we entered the lobby. It smelled like death. There were pieces of flesh, blood, and clothing everywhere. Thousands of holes the size of small ball bearings peppered the marble and granite walls and the ceiling, some of them so deep into the stone that you couldn't see the projectile anymore. A bloody child's shoe stuck out from under a piece of rug. My heart dropped as my stomach rose. It was sickening. Two days before, the bomber had ordered orange juice in the hotel's coffee shop, then walked into the ballroom and detonated his weapon. Seven hotel employees died in this blast, along with the Syrian-American movie producer Moustapha Al Akkad and his daughter, Rima.

The bombings were coordinated, occurring just minutes apart at the three hotels, which were within a mile of each other. In all, 60 people were killed, 115 injured.

———

It was nearly the same as what we had gone through in the United States after 9/11, when we had to encourage people to get out of their homes, go to the stores, go on vacation, board airplanes, and do everything in our power to send the bastards who attacked us the message that we were not going to cower or stop our way of life.

The way I looked at it, the extremists who had bombed these hotels in Amman were no different from those who attacked us in New York City. They were one and the same, and if we're going to win the battle against them, we need to stand together as one. That means Christians, Muslims, Hindus, and Jews alike have to act as one in this battle against an ideology of hate. In this case in particular, I thought Muslims themselves had to be extremely vocal in their response, and that's what was going on in the streets of Jordan.

There were protests everywhere condemning the bombings, calling for the arrest of al-Zarqawi, and urging Jordanians and Arabs everywhere to speak out against these terror networks. His Majesty's wife, Queen Rania, was leading the charge, walking in the protests and visiting the surviving victims of the bombings in various Amman hospitals.

I met with Prince Ali and Haitham Mufti, the director of His Majesty's private office, during my visit and we discussed Jordan's critical infrastructure and what had to be done to secure it.

Exactly as we had done in the United States in the aftermath of 9/11, Jordan would have to evaluate its critical infrastructure and soft targets and see what would be needed to secure them. Haitham had already begun working on securing the main hotels and tourist locations, but we would have to take a look at everything—government buildings, religious sites, tourist hot spots,

favorite eateries, busy cafés, market areas—much as they do in Israel. Sticking a magnetometer at front doors wasn't going to be enough.

I told Ali that this was a critical time if the king wanted to obtain international funding and assistance. I explained to him that within six to twelve months people would begin to forget about what happened and interest and sympathy would wane. We saw this after 9/11, and even though it was four years after that horrible day, my emotions surrounding it were still strong. I was motivated further by the bombings that had just happened there in Amman.

Now was the time, while the world was watching. Ali said he was going to speak to the boss and get back to me.

On my way back from Ali's home, I passed all the security on the roads and in front of the hotels and buildings. I thought again about the people who had been killed, the children. My mind drifted to Celine, who at the time was five, and Angelina, three. I hated being away from them. Although they were used to my traveling, I tried to limit my trips to a week at a time. This wasn't so much for them as it was for me. I never had the relationship with my own parents that I have with my children. My mother abandoned me when I was three and a half. She was later murdered. I never got to know her. And I didn't get to truly connect with my father, who suffered from alcoholism, until I was in my thirties. I just couldn't take being away from my kids for very long without it really bugging me.

There were certain rituals I maintained with my daughters before I would leave on trips and things we would do together when I got home—lunches, dinners, movies. For a year I had been traveling back and forth to Amman once a month, but as I became

———

more involved with the national security project, the frequency of my visits to the Middle East increased. I grew close to His Majesty's family, particularly Prince Ali—while back at home the state case against me in the Bronx ground on.

By November 2007, I was traveling to Amman once every two and a half to three weeks, and there were a few times that I was back and forth three times within a month.

The night before I was supposed to fly home I was sitting in the Four Seasons lobby with Ghaith having coffee when one of the young Jordanians came from the front desk to tell me that I had a phone call. They transferred the call to the lounge where I was sitting.

It was His Majesty's protocol office. They said that His Majesty wanted to see me and they would pick me up in thirty minutes from the lobby. So Ghaith and I sat there and finished our coffee.

The front of the hotel looked like a fortress, with magnetometers and barriers that had been placed there after the bombing of the other hotels. Military and security personnel had closed down the street in front of the Four Seasons.

As Ghaith and I were shooting the shit, four police motorcycles rode by, then another two. Then there were two or three marked police cars with their lights on, speeding past the front door toward the end of the block. Ghaith and I looked at each other as the sound of revved-up engines got louder. Suddenly several Mercedes pulled up in a line in front of the Four Seasons' front door. A dozen men jumped out and began running past the barricades toward the hotel entrance. In the middle of this scrum was the driver of the car that had stopped directly in front of the door. He was wearing a suit and tie and ghutra, an Arab headdress. He was moving quickly. When he was nearly upon us, Ghaith exclaimed, "Oh, shit!"

———

"Your Majesty!" I said. "What are you doing here?"

He smiled, nodded to Ghaith. "Didn't they tell you I was picking you up?"

I started laughing as we all headed for the cars. "That's not exactly what they said, but I'll get over it."

"Get in," the king told me as he walked around to the driver's side. Prince Ali got in the back as I climbed into the passenger's seat beside a submachine gun aimed down at the floor. As I closed the door behind me, I nearly lost my grip, because its weight was about five times that of a normal car door, what with all the armor plating inside it.

Our motorcade took off. I couldn't help but admire the king, who was such a down-to-earth guy, as comfortable dealing with some of the most powerful people in the world as he was driving his own car—this in spite of his awareness that he is one of the biggest targets for terrorists in the world.

We passed through the gates of his palace and came to a screeching halt at the front doors. As we got out of the cars and walked into the residence together, the king looked at me, shaking his head. "It's been a rough week," he said. "A really rough week."

Once inside, His Majesty told me that he wanted me to assist in critical infrastructure assessments throughout the country. But he also needed something else, something far more important.

Jordan had always received significant funding and military aid from the United States and the United Kingdom, the bulk of which was spent on defense and security against conventional threats to their country. But their resources were limited when it came to internal security.

For the past four decades, the Hashemite kingdom of Jordan had also played a key leadership role in maintaining peaceful rela-

tions and supporting conflict resolution in this turbulent region. By doing so, however, Jordan is seen as a key U.S. ally, attracting Iraq-based terrorists, some of whom had just proven that they're ready and able to attack the Jordanian populace as well as the country's political and commercial institutions.

His Majesty and I agreed that Jordan could be facing the threat of more frequent and violent terrorist attacks. He needed to focus on an antiterrorism program that would further secure their critical infrastructure.

Unlike other countries in the region that possess an abundance of natural resources, Jordan has no oil or natural gas. Her biggest resource is her people, but she's dependent on her friends in the international community. I recommended that we create a national terrorism response program in the aftermath of the recent terrorist attacks in Amman to highlight the improvements desperately needed. While previous U.S. assistance to Jordan had been generous and substantial, additional assistance would be needed immediately. With this, Jordan could address the escalating threat.

I told His Majesty that my team—Kim Petersen, Debbie Kurtz, and Ken Bergquist, a retired Green Beret U.S. Army brigadier general—and I would work with Haitham to begin putting the program together. We would have to meet with the various ministries and government agency heads to analyze and evaluate their present requirements and needs for the future. Haitham and I later agreed that this would be an emergency aid request, to secure Jordan's critical infrastructure. To thoroughly complete this exercise, we would also have to look at Jordan's existing programs and contracts, systems integration, and border control programs between agencies like the Jordanian General Intelligence Department and the Public Security Directorate. We would also need to

perform an organizational assessment of the kingdom's chain of command, lines of authority, and an internal audit of their policies and procedures. The king was pleased to have me and my team there to help. We were about to get very busy.

· · ·

On Tuesday evening, January 3, 2006, I arrived in Amman for a series of meetings. I had dinner at the Four Seasons as usual, went to sleep, woke up about 7:00 a.m., and went down to breakfast.

As I walked around the breakfast buffet, a man came up to me and said, "Good morning, Mr. Kerik."

At first glance, I thought I recognized him, but wasn't sure from where. He spoke with a thick Arab accent and I just assumed he was Jordanian. I said hello back. He then moved in very close to me and said softly that he was with a friend who wanted to speak to me. "Would it be okay if he came over and spoke to you now?"

I was a bit confused, but because I felt that I somehow knew this man I said, "I'll be sitting right here having my breakfast," and then sat down and waited for him to return.

The man walked out of the restaurant and returned in a few minutes followed by what appeared to be a Christian religious leader, a man dressed from head to toe in black, with a thick gold chain around his neck, an eight-inch gold crucifix hanging from it, and a black cone headdress that looked almost like a helmet. Heads turned in the restaurant as this striking figure approached my table. I didn't know who he was, but he appeared to be some-body of importance.

They stopped at my table and the man who'd accosted me earlier introduced his companion. "This is Archbishop Ibrahim," he said to me, before politely excusing himself and leaving me

alone with this impressive figure. I shook the archbishop's hand and asked him if he would like to join me, all the while feeling a little uncomfortable because I had no idea who he was, where he was from, or what he wanted.

He was polite and spoke in a soft deep voice.

"I am Yohanna Ibrahim, the archbishop of the Syrian Orthodox Church in Aleppo."

I smiled. "My wife is from Syria."

He nodded politely, almost as if he thought I was stupid, as if he already knew where my wife was from. In fact, I would soon come to realize that this man knew far more about me and my wife and her family than I could have imagined. I felt as if this might be a *Candid Camera* skit, somebody just putting me on. Or as if I'd stepped onto the set of *The Bourne Ultimatum*.

"Your Eminence, what can I do for you?" He hesitated for a moment, took a drink from a glass of water. "I am here from Damascus with a message from my leader."

His leader? "A message from your leader?" I repeated. He looked at me again as if I were a little slow. "Yes, I have a message from our president."

"Your president?" I was thinking to myself that I'd never heard of a president of a church.

"Yes, my country's president. I have a message for you from President Bashar Assad."

We were basically whispering, and I leaned over the table so I could get as close to him as possible just to make sure I'd heard what I thought I'd heard.

"You came here from Damascus with a message for me from President Assad of Syria?"

"Yes," he said quietly. "It is a message from my president to your

leader. I bring a message for your president." Now my mind was racing and I was still thinking that this could be some sort of setup. It was too surreal.

"Your Eminence," I said, "you understand that I don't work for the American government or the American embassy. I'm not a contractor or agent for the government in any way. I'm here in a private capacity, working solely for His Majesty the king. Why would you bring a message to me for President Bush?"

"We know that you can get this message to the White House and we do not want to go through the American embassy in Damascus or other diplomatic channels here in the region. It is of great importance, and we know you can do this."

I had to clear my head as I realized that this wasn't a joke and had to be taken very seriously. I excused myself for a moment, stepped away from the table, and walked toward the door of the restaurant. I took out my Jordanian cell phone and called Kim Petersen, whom I was supposed to meet in fifteen minutes.

"Listen, I'm down in the restaurant," I told Kim when he picked up. "Get down here as quickly as you can. I need a witness to something. Bring a pen and paper. I want you to take detailed notes."

"Are you okay?" Kim asked me.

"Just get down here."

As I stood there thinking about what was happening, I remembered that Hala had mentioned earlier that week that her cousin in Syria had recently called her mother in the States asking when I would be back in Jordan. He'd said that he wanted to meet me.

Oh, shit, I thought. That was the guy who brought the archbishop to me. I knew I had seen him before. It was probably at some family gathering in the States, at the house of one of Hala's relatives.

Just then Kim walked into the restaurant and followed me back to the table where Archbishop Ibrahim was waiting. I introduced Kim to the archbishop, explaining that he worked for me in Jordan for His Majesty and that I wanted him to sit in on our meeting.

"I'd like to hear what you have to say," I told Ibrahim, "but there's no guarantee I'll be able to get your message to President Bush. All I can do is try."

Over the next hour, Ibrahim explained how President Assad had determined that the relationship with the United States was "going downhill very quickly" and that he was concerned that it might soon reach a point of no return. Ibrahim pointed out that Assad was aware that the UN investigation into the assassination of Rafiq al-Hariri, a business tycoon and former prime minister of Lebanon, would further imperil relations between Syria and the United States. Al-Hariri was assassinated in Beirut in February 2005 when a massive explosion was detonated as his motorcade drove past the St. George Hotel. The UN investigation had begun pointing toward Syrian government involvement in the attack.

I told Ibrahim that Syria had very little credibility in the West in general, and the United States in particular, and that there had been a pattern of deception in the recent past that would call into question the sincerity of Assad's intentions. I told him that I thought Assad had deceived the United States during the Iraq War, had harbored wanted terrorists, and in large measure was being used as a puppet by ministers who had served his father.

Ibrahim nodded politely throughout, accepting but not agreeing with my characterization. "But Assad wants to create meaningful dialogue with outside interests," he told me. "He cannot rely on those around him. He does not trust them, with the exception of his brother and brother-in-law." He thought that Assad was in fear

———

of many people around him, including his military and intelligence commanders.

Kim asked Ibrahim what his specific instructions were with respect to our meeting.

"I've been dispatched here to Jordan by President Assad to pass on the message that he doesn't want to be perceived as an enemy of the United States," Ibrahim explained. "If it isn't too late, he wants to create a dialogue." Assad wanted a positive and personal dialogue with the United States, although it would have to be sub rosa for obvious reasons. He then reiterated Assad's belief that "things are deteriorating fast"; speed was of the essence.

Given Assad's history, I wasn't sure what to think, but you can't fault the messenger, who in this case was truly only the messenger, so I continued to listen.

Ibrahim said that Assad felt he had a poor relationship with the former ambassador who had recently left Syria, and that any contact with the U.S. embassy at that time would have raised suspicions among those around him. He said that only two other people in Syria were aware of his meeting with me: Assad and the vice president of the Ba'ath Party.

We asked Ibrahim how contact could be made with Assad if not through the U.S. embassy. He said Assad was planning to visit Spain and Switzerland in the coming weeks and that would offer an opportunity for clandestine contact between him and representatives of the U.S. government, if the White House was so inclined.

I warned him that any duplicity on the part of Assad would undoubtedly make things worse between the United States and Syria. Ibrahim agreed. Throughout the conversation, he exhibited a calm but urgent demeanor, repeating several times "how important to our two countries" this matter was.

———

Kim and I cautioned him that none of this should be committed to written notes, and that under no circumstance should there be telephone, facsimile, or email communications on these matters. Kim recommended that any future meeting to discuss Assad's offer should be arranged by coded email using my family as the subject.

When we finished the meeting, Ibrahim said he was heading right back to Syria, a reverse of the five-hour drive he had made that morning for the express purpose of locating me to deliver his message.

At that point I promised him that his message would be delivered to the appropriate people in the White House, who would then relay it to the president.

Once we said our good-byes and the room watched Ibrahim walk out, Kim stood there looking at me with a half-assed smirk on his face. "What the hell was that?" he asked.

We stood there talking about what had just happened. We agreed that in light of the pending report by the United Nations on al-Hariri's assassination, Assad was feeling threatened and had concluded that the only way to save himself—and Syria—was to seek out clandestine assistance from the United States that would enable him to command control of the levers of power in his own government.

Now that I had this message, what the hell was I going to do with it?

"I need to get to the White House," I said.

Kim and I went to our meeting at His Majesty's office in the Royal Court, after which I went back to the Four Seasons. I thought about going to the U.S. embassy to contact the White House but didn't feel like explaining to the ambassador or his deputy what had taken place. Instead I sent a cryptic email to Fran Townsend,

President Bush's deputy national security advisor for combating terrorism. She was aware of the work I was doing in Amman and I knew she would be able to figure out the best way to handle getting the message to the president.

Shortly after emailing her, I received a note back telling me to be at the White House on Monday at 10:00 a.m. to meet with Elliott Abrams, the deputy national security advisor.

I told Kim we were going to have to head back to the United States and asked him to prepare a briefing document outlining my contact with Ibrahim and the message he relayed. We went into overdrive during the next two days to finish up tasks and flew back home on Friday. I went home to New Jersey and surprised Hala and the girls. On Monday morning, Kim and I met right before entering the executive offices of the White House to see Abrams.

Abrams had begun his career in the 1970s working for the U.S. Senate as special counsel and then chief of staff to Senator Daniel Patrick Moynihan. He later served as Ronald Reagan's assistant secretary of state for human rights.

In 1991, Abrams was indicted by the Iran-Contra special prosecutor for giving false testimony before Congress in 1987 about his role in illicitly raising money for the Nicaraguan Contras. In order to avoid a trial and a possible jail term, he pleaded guilty to two lesser offenses of withholding information from Congress. In 1992, President George H. W. Bush pardoned Abrams, along with a number of other Iran-Contra defendants. Now he was President George W. Bush's point man on Middle East policy in the National Security Agency.

Abrams, who had thinning dark hair and wore a shirt and tie with no jacket, listened intently as I explained my contact with Ibrahim in Amman and the message that he relayed from Assad.

———

Abrams barely spoke until I was finished. He believed some of what Ibrahim had said, Abrams told us—for example, that Assad was feeling pressured by the UN investigation and that he probably didn't trust most of the people around him. Abrams said that I was the third messenger from Assad they had received in the past few months, but they didn't trust him at all. Assad lied consistently; his words contradicted his actions. He said the U.S. government had made several attempts to get Assad to assist in capturing former Iraqi commanders who we knew were in Syria. But Assad had ignored those requests.

Trying to play devil's advocate, I suggested that perhaps it was because Assad felt threatened in his own surroundings that he was untruthful in his dealings with us. Abrams quickly dismissed this, saying that Assad had had plenty of opportunities to show good faith and had refused to do so.

I was a bit disturbed by Abrams's position because it almost seemed that it didn't make any difference what Assad said—we just weren't going to speak to him. I thought a personal dialogue, or some sort of dialogue, was better than nothing. Although I didn't necessarily agree with Abrams, I understood his position. I also knew that he had access to a lot more intelligence than I did. Of course, Assad has supported international terrorism. His government was involved in the assassination of al-Hariri. He has harbored our Iraqi enemies from Saddam's regime, but I still thought that if he wanted to tell us something we could at least listen. For the sake of the country, I had done what I needed to do and had delivered the message.

In April 2013, Archbishop Yohanna Ibrahim, the distinguished messenger I met that day in Amman, was kidnapped by armed gunmen in Syria, swept up in the region's turmoil and war. There's been no word on his fate since then.

Abrams barely spoke until I was finished. He believed some of what Ibrahim had said, Abrams told us—for example, that Assad was feeling pressured by the UN investigation and that he probably didn't trust most of the people around him. Abrams said that I was the third messenger from Assad they had received in the past few months, but they didn't trust him at all. Assad lied consistently; his words contradicted his actions. He said the U.S. government had made several attempts to get Assad to assist in capturing former Iraqi commanders who we knew were in Syria. But Assad had ignored those requests.

Trying to play devil's advocate, I suggested that perhaps it was because Assad felt threatened in his own surroundings that he was untruthful in his dealings with us. Abrams quickly dismissed this, saying that Assad had had plenty of opportunities to show good faith and had refused to do so.

I was a bit disturbed by Abrams's position because it almost seemed that it didn't make any difference what Assad said—we just weren't going to speak to him. I thought a personal dialogue, or some sort of dialogue, was better than nothing. Although I didn't necessarily agree with Abrams, I understood his position. I also knew that he had access to a lot more intelligence than I did. Of course, Assad has supported international terrorism. His government was involved in the assassination of al-Hariri. He has harbored our Iraqi enemies from Saddam's regime, but I still thought that if he wanted to tell us something we could at least listen. For the sake of the country, I had done what I needed to do and had delivered the message.

In April 2013, Archbishop Yohanna Ibrahim, the distinguished messenger I met that day in Amman, was kidnapped by armed gunmen in Syria, swept up in the region's turmoil and war. There's been no word on his fate since then.

———

After our meeting with Abrams, Kim and I walked over to the West Wing for lunch with Fran, my contact in the National Security Agency. It felt odd being back at the White House for the first time since declining the nomination—also because the Bronx investigation of me was still active. I wasn't sure how I'd be received. I wondered who I might run into. But it was business as usual.

As we were eating, I heard someone say, "Is there a police commissioner in here?" I looked toward the door and it was Karl Rove, who stopped by for a minute to say hello.

Fran and I talked about my work in Jordan and a bit about Homeland Security and the United States' ability to combat terrorism in the future. When I declined the president's nomination for Homeland Security, I hoped that Fran would take the job. She was no-nonsense and had knowledge, insight, and drive. But she wasn't interested. When I asked her why, she just smiled at me, waving her finger as if to say, *No, no, no*.

I also thought Bill Bratton, the former New York City police commissioner who was then the police chief of Los Angeles (and has since retaken his spot as NYC's top cop), would have been another great choice, but ironically he wasn't interested either. After what I had experienced, I couldn't blame anyone for not wanting to consider a cabinet post, exposing themselves to such withering scrutiny.

• • •

I was caught up in another intrigue while working in Jordan in 2006.

One afternoon that summer I was walking through the lobby of the Four Seasons Hotel in Amman when I heard a familiar voice

call out my name. I turned around and saw May, a forty-something Iraqi woman who had worked for me in Baghdad as a translator back in 2003. She was an energetic worker and supported our efforts at creating a better future for Iraq. May was with some other people at a table, so we exchanged numbers and said we'd catch up later.

Over the next several months we spoke often. Every time I was in Amman we met for coffee. It turned out that she was facing a terrible situation.

Sometime after I left Baghdad in 2003, insurgents kidnapped her only son for ransom in retaliation for her work with me and the CPA. He was held for eight days until May and her husband paid the ransom. Her husband blamed May and her work for the Americans for their troubles and one night took their children, a boy and a girl, and fled to Syria to live with his parents.

I felt horrible and guilty as May told me this. It was because of her work for me that her family had been targeted, as had many of our Iraqi allies. I felt personally responsible for her situation.

In Baghdad, May's car was broken into. In it she found a picture of a Christian saint torn in two, which was a threat to behead her, she said. She wore a veil outside at all times. Fearing for her life at that point, she escaped to Amman through a refugee program. Her sister was already there. She told me that she had not been able to see or speak with her children since her husband took them to Damascus. Her husband wanted nothing to do with her and had convinced their son to do the same. May's daughter, however, a beautiful young lady named Dahlia, missed her mother terribly. Their separation was killing her. In Damascus, the father and his family forbade Dahlia from making her own decisions, holding her

in their home like a hostage. She was not in school. She was not being properly fed or cared for. Dahlia was almost twenty-one. She should have been free to choose her own life, not be a prisoner to her father's family, kept apart from the mother she wanted to be with.

I empathized with what May was going through because I'd lived through that fear of never seeing a child again. Of course her story made me think of my own children, of my oldest daughter, Lisa Marie, whom I didn't see for the first twenty-six years of her life.

As May cried her way through her past, I thought, There must be something I can do for her. I have to do something.

Dahlia's situation was becoming more and more desperate. In the summer of 2007, May told me that she had been meeting in Jordan with representatives of the U.S. State Department and Department of Homeland Security. They had advised her that she would be leaving soon for the United States through the refugee program. She had dreamed of this, but together with Dahlia, not alone. If she was sent alone, she would be completely separated from her daughter. All her attempts at reconciliation with her husband had failed.

The other urgency was that if we didn't get Dahlia out of Syria and into the refugee program in Jordan before she turned twenty-one (as per the program's rules) in early September, just a couple of months away, she and her mother would be separated forever—Dahlia stuck in Amman or Damascus; her mother beginning a new life alone in the United States.

"We have to get Dahlia out of Syria," I told May. There was no other way.

At first I thought about putting together an extraction team

to snatch Dahlia from May's in-laws' house in Damascus, but my friends in U.S. and Jordanian intelligence thought it was too dangerous. Someone could get hurt. Then I suggested that we send someone with May to intimidate her in-laws, or bribe them, or bribe the police to get her out of the house so she could escape to Jordan.

Just then, May hit me with a bigger problem.

"Dahlia has an Iraqi passport, and Jordan will never give her an entrance visa," May said, panicked. "Getting her into Jordan will be impossible."

It was a terrible limitation.

"Don't worry about it," I told her. I didn't have a fucking clue how I was going to pull it off, but I felt compelled to help this desperate mother willing to risk her own safety and life for the love of her daughter. And as I said, I felt I owed her.

One early afternoon in July, May sent me a desperate email from Jordan:

Dear Sir,

I wrote to you earlier a message regarding if you would help me or not. . . . I need to go to Syria soon, it should be within this month. Because my daughter will be 6th September 21 years old, so I need to hurry up and to put her in my file (in Jordan).

I finish the interview with the DHS and medical test. Do you know a person who can escort me to go and bring my daughter with me (let her enter into Jordan)? I have no problem (I have a residency in Jordan). Please answer me.

I thank you so much for your reply in advance.

V/R
May

———

At home in New Jersey, I wrote her back the next morning:

May,

I am trying to get someone that can help you get into Syria and get your daughter out. It is essential that it's done properly or it could really backfire and be problematic for both you and your daughter.

I am coming to Amman on the 16th of this month and will probably have a plan worked out by then. I also want to speak to some people from the CIA and USDOS to see what they think the options are as well. Hang in there.

Regards.

After thinking over a dozen options, I concluded that there was only one way to get Dahlia into Jordan and that would be with the help of the Royal Court and the private office of His Majesty the king.

A week or so after my email to May, I returned to Amman. I placed a call to Prince Ali. I usually went through Ali to speak with the king. I called again the next morning, to no avail. Knowing we were running out of time, I had my driver take me to the royal palace, where I met with one of His Majesty's younger siblings, who listened as I explained May's dilemma. I was directed to speak to Major Ashraf Al Hourani, a senior member of the Royal Guard.

After I spoke to Ashraf, a husky, youthful-looking guy without a mustache (interestingly, a lot of the king's guys didn't wear mustaches, unlike the majority of Jordanian men), he met with May and the plan was set in motion. May would travel to her in-laws in Syria by taxi and offer them money for the release of her daughter.

If that failed, May would summon the police, who we knew would help her if she bribed them.

We waited several weeks for Ashraf to work out the details of getting Dahlia into Jordan without a visa. I was confident it was going to happen but knew the time it would take for Ashraf's request to get through the bureaucracy of Jordan's Interior Affairs. Finally Ashraf told us everything was in place.

"Go now!" I texted May from my desk at home in New Jersey, while Jimmy Grillo, who worked for me, and Ashraf were standing by in Amman.

May made her way from Amman to the Syrian border—she had gotten a Syrian visa—and from there to Damascus. There she prayed and cried in a Christian church. Finally she took a bus to the town of Sidnaya, about forty minutes outside Damascus, where her husband's family lived—where Dahlia was.

As they inched into Sidnaya, May said, memories began surfacing. She'd been there before to visit her husband's family in happier times. In the town center, May saw her uncle walking past, an older, humble man. Not having seen him for seven years, she greeted him.

"Where again is the family house?" May asked him. Her uncle pointed up the street.

Then to the house and inside, and there was Dahlia, sitting on an old couch between her grandmom and her grandmom's sister, who looked like witches. Such joy to see Dahlia. Hugs and kisses and excited talk.

But they weren't going to let Dahlia go. Dahlia's father, May's estranged husband, was then working in Dubai, so negotiations were with the father's brother, Dahlia's uncle, and the rest of the family. May didn't know whether they would spit at her or throw her off the balcony.

"I must take Dahlia with me," she told them. "She wants to be with me. She belongs with her mother."

"We will never give you Dahlia," the uncle said, digging his feet into the floor, "without the permission of her father!"

May had no faith in his reason or flexibility. There looked to be no hope of taking Dahlia away.

May offered to pay their rent if they would just give her Dahlia. They refused.

For the next three and a half hours these negotiations over the fate of this family went on.

As a consolation, the family offered May the chance to stay over with Dahlia for the night. This was a momentary joy for May, but her heart was still heavy with doubt and fear. It seemed unlikely that she would be able to rescue Dahlia like this. What if she failed? She might never get another opportunity. She might never see her daughter again.

May and Dahlia talked all night in Dahlia's room. They looked at pictures and laughed and cried together. They hardly slept.

Negotiations began again early the next morning. Other relatives in the husband's family showed up, including a well-spoken cousin, a doctor. Despite the burden in her heart, May stood firm and told them that they would either allow Dahlia to leave with her, or the police would come to search the house, take possession of Dahlia's passport, and allow her to leave.

The uncle and cousin and mother-in-law kept resisting, saying, "Now is not a good time"; "Only the father can decide, and he is not present to make the decision"; "Jordan will not let Dahlia enter anyway, so it will be foolish."

At one point that afternoon, May was alone with Dahlia in her room.

———

"Pack your things," May told her quietly. "I'm going to kidnap you out of here." All through this May knew that her mission at the end would hinge on my help. She was depending on me. Would Mr. Kerik be able to open that final, all-important door? she kept thinking. Will they let us into Jordan?

Across the world at home, I was sitting in front of my phone and computer at my desk, my heart in my throat.

Dahlia wasn't sure of her mom's plan. Could it work? What if it didn't? Dahlia was still scared of her father. May kept trying to convince her that they had to do this. She started to pack one of Dahlia's bags. Dahlia came over to the bed to help, tears in her eyes.

At that same moment, in another part of the house, the family was on the phone with May's husband in Dubai. They explained to him that May was forcing their hand. If they didn't give over Dahlia willingly, the police would come and make who knows what kind of trouble for everyone. After all, they were Iraqi refugees in Syria, their circumstance also precarious.

Over the phone, May's husband finally gave in. He said Dahlia could leave Syria with her mother. The news spread immediately through the house. May and Dahlia grabbed each other and jumped for joy. The same uncle who had been repeating "I will never give you Dahlia" even arranged for the taxi May and Dahlia took to Damascus. May was so happy she didn't hear a word the cabdriver said. He talked and smoked the whole way, she recalled.

Finally, I received May's long-awaited text message: "Sir, I have Dahlia with me!"

Great relief washed over me. And then my body tensed right up again. One crucial step down, an even bigger one to come.

"I will be heading to Jordan tomorrow afternoon and I will

call you when I will be close to the border. Her name is Dahlia K. Fareed Mansour. Passport No. . . ."

I texted her back: "I will let you know shortly what to do."

An hour later I sent her another: "Sorry for the delay, still waiting for a reply from Interior Affairs."

I was a mess at that point. What if the family changes its mind and goes after May? What if the husband flips? What if Dahlia is stranded at the border? There were a dozen things that could go wrong. I sat coiled.

May and Dahlia were at a monastery in the capital, under the care of the bishop. But they didn't end up spending even one night there. It turned out there was no time to waste. They had to make for the border immediately. The chance was now.

I called Jimmy in Amman and he messaged Ashraf, who was at the Royal Guard compound at the palace. Ashraf then texted May: "Go to the border now. Go to the borders. Did you get my message?"

May and Dahlia flagged a taxi in Damascus bound for the border. The driver almost didn't take them. He was sure that the Jordanians would turn Dahlia away at the border, as she had no visa.

At my desk I could think of nothing else. In my mind I imagined the entire journey. And now they had reached the Jordanian border. Now was the moment of truth. Had the message come down in time to these border agents, the right ones, the ones who would make this decision on May's and Dahlia's life? Had my pleas gotten through?

I texted May: "Remember to show them your identification and where you work."

May showed the guards at the border her paperwork and called me as they went over it.

———

"Is this really going to work?" she asked me, her voice shaking. "Please tell me this is possible. What must I do?"

I calmed her down, told her I had taken care of it.

"Who exactly are you?" the guards eventually asked May and Dahlia incredulously. "We've received hundreds of phone calls on your behalf!"

The message from the royal palace had made it.

They gave Dahlia a two-week visa, which could be extended for three months. It was a miracle. Their taxi driver, hanging around to see how this oddest of fares would play out, couldn't believe they'd done it, that the Jordanians were letting this Iraqi girl into Jordan without a visa. They must really be something special.

At last, my phone buzzed with the best text message of all: "Sir, Dahlia and I are in Amman. We love you!"

That night she and Dahlia reunited with May's mom in Amman. They cried and embraced and looked forward to their new life together, after all hope had seemed lost. May and Dahlia soon made it to the United States and now live here together happily. We've stayed in touch.

I felt enormous gratitude toward the royal family and Ashraf for their help. With their assistance we pulled off this mission of love, the reuniting of a mother and daughter in a land of strife. Syria and Iraq, and the wider Middle East, continue to burn. I have an idea of the human cost, of the individual lives caught up in that desperate region. I have known them, worked with them, seen them up close. I wish I could do more, but reuniting May and her daughter, helping them escape, remains one of the most rewarding things I've ever done.

14

The Feds Close In

In the aftermath of the Bronx plea, I believed that I could move on with my life and get the Bronx ethics charges behind me. But on an early September morning in 2006, just weeks after I pled guilty in the Bronx, my world came crashing down.

Using my Bronx plea to justify their investigation — where I admitted to accepting the renovations—federal prosecutors claimed that I owed taxes on the amount I had received, and that I had attempted to illegally eavesdrop on the husband of Jeanine Pirro, the former Westchester County district attorney, at her request, as she believed her husband was having an affair.

I was devastated. I thought the Bronx plea had taken care of any tax issues, and I was sure I hadn't done anything wrong concerning Jeanine Pirro or her husband. But just hours after the federal investigation was reported in the media, federal prosecutors began subpoenaing my colleagues, employees, accounts, and taxes.

Tacopina and Ken Breen began speaking with prosecutors, who were clearly on a mission, and although they refused to tell

us exactly what they were doing or looking for, the media miraculously appeared to know every move they made. Every time an acquaintance of mine got subpoenaed or the federal agents showed up at someone's house, I heard about it from a reporter before I heard it from the actual people involved.

This went on for close to five months. Then in February federal prosecutors had a meeting with Breen and made him an offer—they wanted me to take a plea to one count of federal tax fraud relating to the apartment renovations in my Bronx plea, and one count of conspiracy to eavesdrop, with the stipulation that I would testify against Jeanine Pirro. In exchange, they would agree to a sentence of one year to eighteen months in federal prison.

I told Breen, "There's no way. I can't. A felony conviction will destroy me."

I didn't think I had committed tax fraud, and I knew I didn't eavesdrop. More so, I was not testifying against Pirro when I didn't think she had done anything wrong.

When I refused their offer, they came with the hammer. They began subpoenaing my vendors, clients, business accounts, credit cards, banking accounts, business emails, and just about anyone I'd spoken with between 1999 and 2006.

Then something extremely odd happened. On March 12, 2007, as part of their investigation of me, they subpoenaed Tacopina's financial records.

I considered Tacopina an extremely close personal friend, like family. He was a stocky guy with classic Italian looks. He was smart, a real charmer. But everything I liked about him turned out to be negative later. Between 2002 and 2006 I had given him a number of birthday and Christmas gifts that could be considered quite expensive. In early 2005, when he was trading in an

older model BMW for a newer one, I even paid the difference between the two as a gift to him, a cost of about twenty-six thousand dollars. Together we'd discussed and been involved in a number of business ventures, and he had represented me pro bono in the Bronx case. I learned that the prosecutors were trying to determine whether I'd paid him anything in cash, payments that might easily go unreported and thus be tax violations. More important, I believe that the prosecutors, knowing that Tacopina was representing me pro bono, just as he had in the Bronx, wanted him off the case so I would have to pay for an attorney. Targeting him, creating a conflict of interest, was one clear way to arrange that.

With this conflict, he could not represent me, so Breen took over and immediately sent the federal prosecutors a letter, notifying them that I intended to preserve the attorney-client work product protections and attorney-client privileges that I'd had with Tacopina. We wanted to make sure that Tacopina maintained my attorney-client privileges with him so that the federal prosecutors could not use him or whatever information he had to help build up a case against me.

For the life of me, I could not understand the zeal with which the government was pursuing its investigation, its attempt to turn me into a villain.

Their methods and distortions shocked me, but what bothered me most about all this was how they were turning me into a monster and criminal in the press. Everything they looked at was being secretly fed to the press in order to convict me in the court of public opinion long before I would get a chance to defend myself in court. By no means am I an angel. There are things in my personal and professional life I could have handled differently—such as being more careful about whom I trust and give my friendship

to, and being more aware of how my decisions can be perceived by the public—but the Feds were taking honest mistakes by me and my accountants and alleging they were crimes.

Their investigation spanned the period from July 2006 to November 2007, a sixteen-month pursuit with a vengeance.

On November 8, 2007, I was charged in a sixteen-count federal indictment that made it seem that I was a member of an enormous criminal enterprise. They charged me with honest services fraud, tax fraud, and false statements relating to my children's nanny, a mortgage application, and the renovations issue that had been resolved in the Bronx case. For those renovations I had already been fined and penalized more than $220,000.

I could not understand how they could prosecute me again for this.

The indictment criminalized minor ethical issues and accounting errors—for example, they charged me in the indictment with one count of tax fraud in 2002 due to my accountant's having missed a twenty-thousand-dollar check or wire transfer and failed to claim it in my tax filings; they charged me in another count with failure to report the use of a car, when they knew that that, too, was another mistake by my accountants. As a member of the advisory board of BMW, I was given the use of one of their luxury vehicles every year, which must be claimed as income. My accountants and I had appropriately claimed this in 2004 and 2006, but had missed it in '05. In the aftermath of withdrawing from the presidential cabinet appointment three years earlier, I had paid the taxes, fines, and penalties on my children's nanny, but the federal prosecutors even charged me with that as well.

As Breen and I read through the indictment on the morning of November 9, he said he had never witnessed this sort of overreach-

ing by U.S. prosecutors. He was furious. There wasn't one thing in the indictment that could not have been handled civilly. Instead, they were going out of their way to make everything criminal. Prosecutors too often overcriminalize, overreach, and overpunish. I do believe that mine was a prime example of an overzealous and selective prosecution, the kind we see increasingly around the country.

Although Breen and I couldn't fully understand why they were pushing so hard, it seemed clear to me that Rudy Giuliani's political aspirations at the time had a lot to do with it. Rudy, my mentor, friend, and longtime boss, had announced that he was considering a run for the White House. The more popular he became, the more the press and media focused on me, motivating the prosecutors, and vice versa. It was an out-of-control locomotive.

. . .

On November 15, I watched that locomotive slam into the scales of justice. I learned exactly to what extent federal prosecutors were going to go to win their case when they revealed that Joe Tacopina, my former lawyer, was on their witness list. I was stunned.

I had just met with Tacopina three days before the indictment came down, and he had told me that the prosecutors were targeting him. He also wanted my help with some investment opportunities involving an Italian football team. Unknown to me, as he was discussing this far-flung business deal with me, he was also meeting with and talking to the prosecutors in my case. He had to have known by that point that I was going to be indicted and that he was going to be a witness on behalf of the government against me. I could not believe it. This man was one of my closest friends. He was my lawyer and confidant!

Within days after we learned Tacopina was on the witness list, prosecutors began targeting my lawyer Ken Breen as well. The prosecutors claimed that while interviewing Tacopina, he had discussed with them my conversations with him during the Bronx investigation, and that Breen may have been a witness to those conversations, too—something prosecutors claimed could have created a conflict, and in addition, could make Breen a witness against me as well.

Breen and I were shocked. We knew they had subpoenaed Tacopina's records, but when did they speak to him in person? Why would he agree to speak to them about anything in my case? Why didn't he tell me or Breen that he was meeting with the Feds? As my former attorney, wasn't he obligated to protect my rights?

For the life of us, we couldn't figure out what was going on, but on the night of January 23, 2008, after we had threatened Tacopina with an ethics complaint, he and his attorney, Michael Ross, met with a team of my lawyers at Breen's direction. By the time that meeting was over, we didn't know much, but we knew enough.

Tacopina had met with federal prosecutors to discuss me and the Bronx case as a "gesture of cooperation," according to Ross. During his meeting with the Feds, Tacopina was given immunity from prosecution, as long as the government believed he was telling the truth. I could only conclude that Tacopina was worried only about protecting his own interests. This subpoenaing by the prosecution of a lawyer for the defense, making that defense lawyer a witness for the prosecution, is extremely rare and, I believe in my case, entirely unethical.

But the prosecution got what they wanted: Denying my counsels' request for discovery, Judge Stephen C. Robinson found that the prosecutors were entitled to interview Tacopina and put him

———

on the stand against me and disqualified Breen as my counsel on the grounds that they might want to put him on the stand as well as a witness to my conversations with Tacopina and Tacopina's conversations with the Bronx DA. The judge denied that my attorney-client privilege was violated by any of this. With Tacopina and Breen now neutralized, the prosecutors knew I would be forced to hire a new legal team, which came at a price tag of $1.5 million. Since Hala and I didn't have the cash on hand, we were forced to mortgage our home for the retainer.

Within twenty-four hours after we filed the mortgage application for the retainer, the prosecutors ran into court and filed a *lis pendens* on our home for $187,000, saying that this was what I owed the government in taxes, fines, and penalties for the Bronx apartment renovations, which they were claiming were worth close to $255,000, nearly double what the Bronx district attorney had alleged. As a result, the mortgage, which had been approved, was now rescinded.

This was nothing more than an underhanded way of preventing me from paying for my defense, the Sixth Amendment constitutional right I thought I was guaranteed. They knew what the mortgage was for, and they knew that I had already spent close to a million dollars in legal fees and was hemorrhaging more money than I was making.

The only thing I had left was a 401(k) retirement fund, which I was forced to cash in to use as a retainer for the new legal team. I hired Barry Berke and Eric Tirschwell, of Kramer Levin Naftalis & Frankel, LLP, a prestigious Manhattan law firm specializing in white-collar crime litigation.

With Tirschwell and Berke at my side, the process began. We attended one pretrial hearing after another, but with each hearing

and passing day I began to believe that we had a much bigger problem than just overreaching federal prosecutors and a distorted indictment.

My judge.

. . .

When you are the target of a criminal investigation, it's a fight for your life. A felony conviction is a life sentence. Perhaps not in the literal sense, but once you're labeled a convicted felon in our country you become something of a pariah until the day you die, regardless of the charge, criminal intent, or your guilt or innocence.

As I sat in the courtroom in White Plains, New York, fighting for my freedom and my life, all I wanted and hoped for was a judge who knew the law, had common sense, and would rein in the prosecutors, who I believed were engaging in misconduct.

Instead, U.S. Federal Judge Stephen C. Robinson stunned me. He used the bench as if it were his own personal comedy club—telling jokes, doing movie commentaries, talking about how much he drank, complaining about his salary, seemingly condoning spousal abuse (he once told my attorneys and the prosecutors, who were arguing, to go home and take it out on their wives; "That's what spouses are for," he said), reciting Shakespeare, and talking about his personal love life and dating failures. At times I thought I was in the Twilight Zone.

Another time Robinson regaled us with a story of his mojito-making skills at a Super Bowl party at his home for his staff and clerks, telling us how much they drank. He bragged how most of his jurors loved him, except the ones he'd dated. I almost spat out the water I was drinking. I could not believe my ears. I also

couldn't believe how the press just sat there listening to his demeaning comments about women without crucifying him.

I tried to appear at ease in the courtroom, but Judge Robinson had me on edge. Worse, I felt that my new lawyers, Berke and Tirschwell, were scared to death of him. One minute Robinson was cracking jokes, and the next he was scowling and threatening. Regardless, I still thought that once we got to trial, we'd be okay. Unfortunately, that day would never come.

Just days before trial, Anthony Modafferi, a friend and attorney from New Jersey, sent an email to the *Washington Times* in which he outlined how he believed New York City investigators had suborned perjury and had pressured and threatened grand jury witnesses in the Bronx case against me, and maintained that the federal prosecutors had suppressed and were continuing to suppress that evidence in my current trial. Modafferi had been looking into my prosecution in the Bronx and was considering filing, on my behalf, a federal civil rights action against the New York City Department of Investigation and the Bronx district attorney.

When the federal prosecutors became aware of the email— the *Washington Times* had called the Bronx DA and DOI wanting to know more about Modafferi's claims; the state prosecutors relayed this to the Feds—they were furious and claimed that sharing my federal trial documents and motions with Modafferi violated a protective order signed by Robinson (such a protective order is standard in cases like mine). They threatened me, Berke and Tirschwell, and even Modafferi with contempt, and claimed my new trial team might now have a conflict in the case as well—the conflict being that they did not notify Modafferi of the protective order and that they did not prevent him from releasing information to the *Washington Times*.

———

As a result, Robinson basically suspended my trial team, saying they had a conflict, and ordered me to obtain *yet another* attorney as an independent counsel—costing me more money, of course.

As ordered, I retained a new attorney recommended by Berke, Michael Bachner, to sit in on the conflict issue. Over the next month, in one hearing after another, the prosecutors attacked me and Modafferi, not only for the email to the newspaper, but also for a series of articles that Modafferi had written in which he called my prosecution selective and political, and questioned why I was being treated far more harshly than Democratic cabinet nominees in President Barack Obama's administration who faced similar, if not worse, allegations.

The prosecutors said that Modafferi's statements and articles were false, defamatory, and inflammatory. But the facts spoke for themselves.

Modafferi had written about U.S. Treasury Secretary Timothy Geithner's failure to pay income tax, and President Barack Obama's chief of staff Rahm Emanuel's free use, for five years, of a Capitol Hill town house owned by a pollster with huge contracts with the Democratic National Committee. He also wrote about Adolfo Carrión, Jr., the former Bronx borough president who had been appointed President Obama's director of urban policy, accepting home renovations—in the Bronx of all places—from a contractor who was one of his campaign contributors; about Nancy Killefer, who withdrew her name from consideration after being nominated for chief performance officer, due to her failure to pay nanny tax; and about former Senate majority leader Tom Daschle's failure to pay more than one hundred thousand dollars in income tax.

In his articles Modafferi asked why I, a Republican who had

———

worked for Giuliani and had supported President George W. Bush, had been the subject of both state and federal investigations, yet not one of the Democrats mentioned above had been subjected to anything close to the same investigative scrutiny by the Justice Department. I understand that "But everybody's doing it" is rarely a winning argument—even if it is in large part true. It's not a good legal defense. But the fact that prosecutions are so often baldly selective does erode the notion of justice. It does something to weaken the whole process, to make it more personal and vengeful in appearance and nature than productive and moral.

Although Modafferi compared me to Democrats, the reality is that no one is supposed to be selectively targeted because of political views or associations, and the laws should be applied consistently and fairly across the board. But they aren't.

Judge Robinson, a former U.S. prosecutor himself, fumed at Modafferi's criticism and assertions. Claiming that the information in Modafferi's email to the *Washington Times* was an attempt to "influence the jury pool," on the morning of October 20, 2009, Robinson revoked my bail and ordered me to be taken into custody.

Within moments I would be in leg shackles and handcuffs.

I couldn't believe what was happening. I had defended, worked, fought, and nearly died for our country many times in the past thirty years and was now being jailed because Modafferi attempted to expose what he believed was government misconduct in my case.

. . .

Earlier that morning at home, as I was about to leave for Westchester and the courthouse, Hala had come into my office with a bottle

of religious oil, placed the oil on her thumb, and drawn the sign of the cross on my forehead. I called out to Celine and Angelina to say good-bye. They answered from their rooms upstairs as they got ready for school. "I'm going—love you!" I yelled, and walked out the door.

Not giving them a kiss good-bye, I felt I'd broken one of my cardinal rules from the time that my son, Joe, was a little boy. I've never wanted to leave the house or let the kids go to bed thinking that I was upset with them. Similarly, I always try to give them a hug and a kiss and tell them I love them as I leave the house, even if I'm just going down the street to the grocery store.

Throughout my career I've heard stories of cops who were killed in the line of duty and never got to say good-bye to their wives or children, and that would haunt forever the family members left behind.

One of the most heroic cops I've ever known was a New York City detective by the name of Joe Vigiano, who was killed on September 11, 2001. Ironically, I had promoted him not long before his death, and at his promotion ceremony he had spoken specifically about how important it is to make sure those close to you know you love them before you leave home.

This truth was never more vividly illustrated for me than in the aftermath of 9/11, as I attended the funerals of so many who died that day. We had one cop who had left his house that morning to go to police headquarters to submit his retirement papers. Upon his arrival, the building was emptying out, everyone racing to the Towers. He went, too. Earlier that morning he probably thought the dangers of his career were over, but tragically he never made it back alive.

That infamous day was the most powerful reminder I've ever

been given that you should never take life for granted and should treat each day as if it's your last. When I left for the White Plains Courthouse that morning, it would be the last time I would see my two little girls for many weeks. Not seeing them to kiss them good-bye, tell them I love them, disturbed me greatly.

Back in the courtroom, I noticed a U.S. marshal standing behind me. I looked toward Michael Bachner on my left and realized there was another marshal behind him. I also knew the press was watching every move, so I just stood up, and as I did, I felt the marshals close in. Although I knew it was their job, I wanted to turn around and say, "Where the fuck do you think I'm going?" But I stayed calm.

Before putting me in shackles and cuffs, one of the marshals asked me to take off my tie. Since I knew the drill, he didn't have to tell me what came next. Tie, cuff links, my gold necklace with a St. Michael's medal on it. On my right wrist was a special bracelet, a memorial band that I commissioned on the first anniversary of 9/11, made of white gold to last forever. NYPD—23—WTC is inscribed on it, along with the unforgettable date. I had worn it every day since I put it on in 2002 in memory of the twenty-three cops who died under my command that day.

Another marshal leaned in and pointed to the American flag pin in my lapel. "Don't forget that," he said. As I took off the bracelet and the flag pin, my anger rose. I looked up and saw the United States seal and flag in the courtroom and was overwhelmed. This is not justice, I thought. In my anger and shock, everything went blank.

The next thing I remember I was sitting in a dark gray jail cell, staring at the wall.

———

15

Losing Rudy

After Rudy Giuliani had left the mayor's office and I'd stepped down from the police department, we created a security consulting firm called Giuliani Kerik, a subsidiary of Rudy's principal company, Giuliani Partners. We had great success and worked on a number of interesting projects: an assessment of Mexico City's criminal justice agencies; a security evaluation of the Peekskill, New York, nuclear power plant; accountability recommendations for the U.S. Department of Justice Organized Crime Drug Enforcement Task Forces Program.

But with the negative press firestorm surrounding my withdrawn nomination for Homeland Security secretary and the Bronx investigation opening on the heels of that, Rudy was getting killed, pulled down in the press because of his mentorship and promotion of and friendship with me.

So I did what I had to do. I resigned from Giuliani Partners at the beginning of 2005.

At first, Tony Carbonetti, Rudy's former chief of staff, told me

that Rudy didn't want me to leave. But I saw no other way out of the guilty-by-association-to-me dynamic that was taking on a life of its own. I called a press conference and publicly announced my resignation.

But things between Rudy and me continued as they had before in terms of our friendship and connection. I had been an integral part of Rudy's mayoral cabinet that led New York City into a renaissance in the 1990s. We had made city history together, done great things. Everything seemed okay.

Every year Rudy hosted a special dinner on September 11 at a downtown steakhouse and invited all the people who were with him on that fateful day in 2001. On that date in 2006, just after the end of the Bronx case against me, Hala and I attended the dinner. We sat with Rudy and talked. He was happy that my case was over and that I'd resolved it as best I could. He gave me a hug. "Hang in there. Everything's gonna be all right," he told me. He said kind words and we laughed and joked together.

A week or two after that night, news broke that I was under federal investigation. I didn't speak to Rudy about it and we didn't talk in the ensuing weeks. I understood why he might want some distance from me at that point. In a sense, the separation was mutual. He wasn't contacting me and I wasn't contacting him. I understood from a legal perspective that if Rudy and I were talking during that time the Feds might start asking me why I was speaking to him, or asking *him* questions about *me*. But I didn't think that this marked a permanent break in our friendship or professional relationship.

A couple of months passed. Come November, Rudy's presidential ambitions were gathering steam. The press and media were gearing up for the 2008 presidential primary two years away, and

Rudy was being talked about as the possible front-runner for the Republican Party. At the end of November there was a poll that ranked Rudy as the most popular out of twenty potential presidential candidates. Barack Obama came in second.

Given that my daughter Celine was only six years old at the time, she had no idea of the difference between a Democrat and a Republican. All she knew was that people were saying that her godfather was going to be the next president of the United States. She was talking about it twenty four hours a day, as if that were the only thing going on in her little world. She had no idea of what this really meant, of course, but she was convinced that Rudy was going to be president.

One afternoon she walked into my office and asked when she was going to get to see her godfather.

"He's very busy campaigning, sweetheart," I said. "Maybe we can see him before Christmas."

I called Carbonetti and told him I wanted to bring Celine and Angelina by to see Rudy before the holidays, as we often did. I was going to be leaving for the Middle East, to continue my work on national security and prison projects in Jordan, but would be back by mid-December. We could stop by the office or his apartment then. Tony told me that he put it on his list of things to speak to Rudy about and would get back to me with a time. I told Celine we would see her godfather when we did our annual two-day holiday stay in New York City when I got back from my trip.

She was ecstatic. "I want to get him a Christmas present!" she said. She already had it picked out. "I want to get him the president's jumping horse."

"President's jumping horse?"

She looked at me as if I were stupid, as only a six-year-old can

do, and said, "You know, the jumping horse that's in the president's office. We should get him that horse."

I still had no idea what she was talking about.

"Daddy, the horse you have in the room. It's just like the one in President Bush's office." With that, her little hand grabbed mine and she walked me into the living room. She pointed at the Remington bronze statue in the corner, a man riding a horse rising up on its hind legs. She was right.

Called *The Bronco Buster*, it was originally sculpted by Frederic Remington in 1895. *The Bronco Buster* was the first in a series of twenty-two statues Remington made. I had bought mine years before. When I was nominated for secretary of Homeland Security, I brought the whole family with me to the Oval Office. Celine was only four then, but she had obviously made note of seeing the same statue there that day.

I was pretty impressed with her choice and her memory for details. I pulled her onto my lap in front of the computer and we surfed the net looking for a *Bronco Buster* to buy Rudy for Christmas.

"Every president should have one of these," I said, as we looked through one site after another. Celine was so excited that it was almost comical to watch. I couldn't have been happier.

I ordered the *Bronco Buster* and had it delivered to my house. I told Celine that she and Angelina should make Rudy a nice card and when the statue arrived, we would put the card inside that box and then send Rudy the gift. We got the bronze within a day or two. Celine made a sweet card. The box was three feet high and weighed a lot, so Jimmy Grillo, a retired correction captain who had worked for me at Rikers and was still a member of my staff at The Kerik Group, delivered it himself to Rudy's apartment.

Celine was very excited and couldn't wait to see her godfather. I promised her that she would get to see him when I got back from my upcoming trip.

I didn't hear from Rudy or Tony while I was gone. On December 15, I flew back from London to JFK. I sent Tony an email right away, as I was waiting for my luggage. I was taking the girls and Hala to New York City for the next two days.

I received no reply. I called Tony's cell, and there was no answer. I sent another email, but I was getting the message.

Rudy didn't want to see me, didn't want to talk.

I didn't have the heart to tell Celine. The only thing I could say that she would accept was that he was busy campaigning for president, and that's what he had to do if he was going to win. She didn't like it, but the American Girl doll store, *The Little Mermaid* on Broadway, Rockefeller Center, and the lights of Manhattan clouded the Rudy subject for at least the time being, and for that I was relieved.

Our little excursion to New York City was great, but in every spare moment, I was working—speaking to Kim, Debbie, or Jimmy about our projects in Jordan and Kuwait. Kim was in Kuwait meeting with the National Security Bureau and setting up a meeting for me with their director in January in London.

It was just days before Christmas and Santa wasn't prepared. Although we had made our trip to the city and put the tree up at home, it didn't quite feel like Christmas. Hala had done her shopping, but I hadn't done any. Since that's what really puts me in the spirit, I took off and went shopping, loaded the car with gifts, and came back to the house. I immediately felt better and over the next few days Hala and I would wrap some gifts every time the girls were upstairs and out of the way. My thoughts occasionally returned to Rudy and the gift we'd sent him.

———

Throughout the holiday, we had a number of packages delivered to the house. Unless you had to sign for them, they would just drop them outside the front door.

One afternoon, Jimmy came into the house through the garage, as he usually did, and walked upstairs into the kitchen. He told me there was a delivery on the front porch, so I asked him if he could bring it in. I continued to do what I was doing in the kitchen. About ten minutes passed and I wondered what was taking him so long. The door was ajar and I called out to Jimmy. No response.

I walked down the stairs, opened the door, and saw Jimmy just standing on the porch looking at the box.

"What are you doing?" I asked him.

He looked upset but didn't say anything.

"What is it? Did you open it?" I asked.

"I don't have to. I recognize the box."

I was now staring at the box, too, and just then it hit me. It was the same box with the Christmas gift we'd given to Rudy. It wasn't a mistake or a failed delivery. Jimmy himself had hand delivered this to Rudy's Manhattan apartment. Someone had sent it back.

I told Jimmy to open it. I wanted to see what was inside. The beautiful bronze with its packing was there, but Celine and Angelina's handmade Christmas card to their godfather was gone. I had Jimmy pull the whole box apart thinking that there might be a note explaining why the gift was returned to us.

Nothing.

I was embarrassed that Jimmy had seen this, and I was scared to have Celine or Hala see it, so I had Jimmy put it out of sight in the garage.

I was stunned. Could it have been Rudy, or maybe his wife,

Judith? Did they do this because of the federal investigation? I wasn't working with Rudy at the time. He wasn't in government, even though he was preparing a run for the presidency. And what's more, he was my daughters' godfather and had exchanged gifts with them every year before this. I just didn't understand it. What bothered me more than anything was that whoever sent it back took the girls' card and didn't have the courtesy to send a note back with the box.

When I walked back into the house, Hala took a look at me and knew something was wrong. She thought that Joe Tacopina had called with bad news about the investigation, but I told her that I just had a headache and wasn't feeling well.

In the days that followed, I made several calls to Rudy's office, trying to figure out who sent the box back—to no avail. I thought it was possible that one of Rudy's assistants, thinking he was doing the right thing, had sent the package back without Rudy's knowing. Possible, but not likely. If Rudy himself had sent it back, or made the decision to do so, I just wanted to know why.

Over the next few weeks, I received other signs that the bronze hadn't been sent back to us in error. Up until that Christmas, Rudy had never missed Celine's or Angelina's birthday or Christmas. He always sent them cards. That year there was no card for either of them, and unfortunately there hasn't been one since.

Later, Tacopina told me that someone in Rudy's camp had mentioned to him that our gift had been sent back because Rudy was in the process of filing his Federal Election Commission financial disclosures for his presidential campaign and didn't want to list it as a gift. If that's true, it's a sad but real demonstration of the impact of politics on relationships—but I still didn't understand why he had abandoned the girls.

———

It has been sad and disappointing to me, the way he cut off our relationship, because that doesn't seem like the man I knew, professionally or personally. He was like family to me, someone I could never have abandoned. At my NYPD retirement dinner in 2001, in front of nearly two thousand people, Rudy said that I was like the brother he never had.

But you live and learn.

Of course, my reputation and standing were being slaughtered by scandals—and by that point, 2006, this had been going on for about two years—that as correction commissioner I had used COs on overtime to work my wedding; the *Times* calling the lucrative selling of my TASER stock questionable; or worst of all, in many people's eyes, that I'd used an apartment near Ground Zero for my own selfish purposes when it was meant for first responders to the attacks.

The reality was, the COs who were on duty at my wedding were members of my security detail. Whether I was getting married or working in my office on Rikers or sunning myself on Jones Beach, they would have been with me, on duty regardless. The stock transaction that the *Times* called questionable wasn't questionable at all. I sold the stock knowing I was being considered for the Homeland Security position and wanting to put money into our home, to lessen our mortgage. If I hadn't, I wouldn't have been able to take the job. I was on the board of TASER at the time, so the rest of the board was aware of the transaction, as was the SEC. It was all done by the book, but if you read those articles, you would have thought for sure that I had done something illegal or unethical in the transaction. As for the apartment in Battery Park, that apartment had never been set aside for first responders working at Ground Zero, as the press had reported. The truth is I had

———

to snatch Dahlia from May's in-laws' house in Damascus, but my friends in U.S. and Jordanian intelligence thought it was too dangerous. Someone could get hurt. Then I suggested that we send someone with May to intimidate her in-laws, or bribe them, or bribe the police to get her out of the house so she could escape to Jordan.

Just then, May hit me with a bigger problem.

"Dahlia has an Iraqi passport, and Jordan will never give her an entrance visa," May said, panicked. "Getting her into Jordan will be impossible."

It was a terrible limitation.

"Don't worry about it," I told her. I didn't have a fucking clue how I was going to pull it off, but I felt compelled to help this desperate mother willing to risk her own safety and life for the love of her daughter. And as I said, I felt I owed her.

One early afternoon in July, May sent me a desperate email from Jordan:

Dear Sir,

I wrote to you earlier a message regarding if you would help me or not. . . . I need to go to Syria soon, it should be within this month. Because my daughter will be 6th September 21 years old, so I need to hurry up and to put her in my file (in Jordan).

I finish the interview with the DHS and medical test. Do you know a person who can escort me to go and bring my daughter with me (let her enter into Jordan)? I have no problem (I have a residency in Jordan). Please answer me.

I thank you so much for your reply in advance.

V/R
May

———

At home in New Jersey, I wrote her back the next morning:

May,

I am trying to get someone that can help you get into Syria and get your daughter out. It is essential that it's done properly or it could really backfire and be problematic for both you and your daughter.

I am coming to Amman on the 16th of this month and will probably have a plan worked out by then. I also want to speak to some people from the CIA and USDOS to see what they think the options are as well. Hang in there.

Regards.

After thinking over a dozen options, I concluded that there was only one way to get Dahlia into Jordan and that would be with the help of the Royal Court and the private office of His Majesty the king.

A week or so after my email to May, I returned to Amman. I placed a call to Prince Ali. I usually went through Ali to speak with the king. I called again the next morning, to no avail. Knowing we were running out of time, I had my driver take me to the royal palace, where I met with one of His Majesty's younger siblings, who listened as I explained May's dilemma. I was directed to speak to Major Ashraf Al Hourani, a senior member of the Royal Guard.

After I spoke to Ashraf, a husky, youthful-looking guy without a mustache (interestingly, a lot of the king's guys didn't wear mustaches, unlike the majority of Jordanian men), he met with May and the plan was set in motion. May would travel to her in-laws in Syria by taxi and offer them money for the release of her daughter.

———

If that failed, May would summon the police, who we knew would help her if she bribed them.

We waited several weeks for Ashraf to work out the details of getting Dahlia into Jordan without a visa. I was confident it was going to happen but knew the time it would take for Ashraf's request to get through the bureaucracy of Jordan's Interior Affairs. Finally Ashraf told us everything was in place.

"Go now!" I texted May from my desk at home in New Jersey, while Jimmy Grillo, who worked for me, and Ashraf were standing by in Amman.

May made her way from Amman to the Syrian border—she had gotten a Syrian visa—and from there to Damascus. There she prayed and cried in a Christian church. Finally she took a bus to the town of Sidnaya, about forty minutes outside Damascus, where her husband's family lived—where Dahlia was.

As they inched into Sidnaya, May said, memories began surfacing. She'd been there before to visit her husband's family in happier times. In the town center, May saw her uncle walking past, an older, humble man. Not having seen him for seven years, she greeted him.

"Where again is the family house?" May asked him. Her uncle pointed up the street.

Then to the house and inside, and there was Dahlia, sitting on an old couch between her grandmom and her grandmom's sister, who looked like witches. Such joy to see Dahlia. Hugs and kisses and excited talk.

But they weren't going to let Dahlia go. Dahlia's father, May's estranged husband, was then working in Dubai, so negotiations were with the father's brother, Dahlia's uncle, and the rest of the family. May didn't know whether they would spit at her or throw her off the balcony.

———

"I must take Dahlia with me," she told them. "She wants to be with me. She belongs with her mother."

"We will never give you Dahlia," the uncle said, digging his feet into the floor, "without the permission of her father!"

May had no faith in his reason or flexibility. There looked to be no hope of taking Dahlia away.

May offered to pay their rent if they would just give her Dahlia. They refused.

For the next three and a half hours these negotiations over the fate of this family went on.

As a consolation, the family offered May the chance to stay over with Dahlia for the night. This was a momentary joy for May, but her heart was still heavy with doubt and fear. It seemed unlikely that she would be able to rescue Dahlia like this. What if she failed? She might never get another opportunity. She might never see her daughter again.

May and Dahlia talked all night in Dahlia's room. They looked at pictures and laughed and cried together. They hardly slept.

Negotiations began again early the next morning. Other relatives in the husband's family showed up, including a well-spoken cousin, a doctor. Despite the burden in her heart, May stood firm and told them that they would either allow Dahlia to leave with her, or the police would come to search the house, take possession of Dahlia's passport, and allow her to leave.

The uncle and cousin and mother-in-law kept resisting, saying, "Now is not a good time"; "Only the father can decide, and he is not present to make the decision"; "Jordan will not let Dahlia enter anyway, so it will be foolish."

At one point that afternoon, May was alone with Dahlia in her room.

———

"Pack your things," May told her quietly. "I'm going to kidnap you out of here." All through this May knew that her mission at the end would hinge on my help. She was depending on me. Would Mr. Kerik be able to open that final, all-important door? she kept thinking. Will they let us into Jordan?

Across the world at home, I was sitting in front of my phone and computer at my desk, my heart in my throat.

Dahlia wasn't sure of her mom's plan. Could it work? What if it didn't? Dahlia was still scared of her father. May kept trying to convince her that they had to do this. She started to pack one of Dahlia's bags. Dahlia came over to the bed to help, tears in her eyes.

At that same moment, in another part of the house, the family was on the phone with May's husband in Dubai. They explained to him that May was forcing their hand. If they didn't give over Dahlia willingly, the police would come and make who knows what kind of trouble for everyone. After all, they were Iraqi refugees in Syria, their circumstance also precarious.

Over the phone, May's husband finally gave in. He said Dahlia could leave Syria with her mother. The news spread immediately through the house. May and Dahlia grabbed each other and jumped for joy. The same uncle who had been repeating "I will never give you Dahlia" even arranged for the taxi May and Dahlia took to Damascus. May was so happy she didn't hear a word the cabdriver said. He talked and smoked the whole way, she recalled.

Finally, I received May's long-awaited text message: "Sir, I have Dahlia with me!"

Great relief washed over me. And then my body tensed right up again. One crucial step down, an even bigger one to come.

"I will be heading to Jordan tomorrow afternoon and I will

call you when I will be close to the border. Her name is Dahlia K. Fareed Mansour. Passport No. . . .”

I texted her back: “I will let you know shortly what to do.”

An hour later I sent her another: “Sorry for the delay, still waiting for a reply from Interior Affairs.”

I was a mess at that point. What if the family changes its mind and goes after May? What if the husband flips? What if Dahlia is stranded at the border? There were a dozen things that could go wrong. I sat coiled.

May and Dahlia were at a monastery in the capital, under the care of the bishop. But they didn't end up spending even one night there. It turned out there was no time to waste. They had to make for the border immediately. The chance was now.

I called Jimmy in Amman and he messaged Ashraf, who was at the Royal Guard compound at the palace. Ashraf then texted May: “Go to the border now. Go to the borders. Did you get my message?”

May and Dahlia flagged a taxi in Damascus bound for the border. The driver almost didn't take them. He was sure that the Jordanians would turn Dahlia away at the border, as she had no visa.

At my desk I could think of nothing else. In my mind I imagined the entire journey. And now they had reached the Jordanian border. Now was the moment of truth. Had the message come down in time to these border agents, the right ones, the ones who would make this decision on May's and Dahlia's life? Had my pleas gotten through?

I texted May: “Remember to show them your identification and where you work.”

May showed the guards at the border her paperwork and called me as they went over it.

———

"Is this really going to work?" she asked me, her voice shaking. "Please tell me this is possible. What must I do?"

I calmed her down, told her I had taken care of it.

"Who exactly are you?" the guards eventually asked May and Dahlia incredulously. "We've received hundreds of phone calls on your behalf!"

The message from the royal palace had made it.

They gave Dahlia a two week visa, which could be extended for three months. It was a miracle. Their taxi driver, hanging around to see how this oddest of fares would play out, couldn't believe they'd done it, that the Jordanians were letting this Iraqi girl into Jordan without a visa. They must really be something special.

At last, my phone buzzed with the best text message of all: "Sir, Dahlia and I are in Amman. We love you!"

That night she and Dahlia reunited with May's mom in Amman. They cried and embraced and looked forward to their new life together, after all hope had seemed lost. May and Dahlia soon made it to the United States and now live here together happily. We've stayed in touch.

I felt enormous gratitude toward the royal family and Ashraf for their help. With their assistance we pulled off this mission of love, the reuniting of a mother and daughter in a land of strife. Syria and Iraq, and the wider Middle East, continue to burn. I have an idea of the human cost, of the individual lives caught up in that desperate region. I have known them, worked with them, seen them up close. I wish I could do more, but reuniting May and her daughter, helping them escape, remains one of the most rewarding things I've ever done.

———

14

The Feds Close In

In the aftermath of the Bronx plea, I believed that I could move on with my life and get the Bronx ethics charges behind me. But on an early September morning in 2006, just weeks after I pled guilty in the Bronx, my world came crashing down.

Using my Bronx plea to justify their investigation—where I admitted to accepting the renovations—federal prosecutors claimed that I owed taxes on the amount I had received, and that I had attempted to illegally eavesdrop on the husband of Jeanine Pirro, the former Westchester County district attorney, at her request, as she believed her husband was having an affair.

I was devastated. I thought the Bronx plea had taken care of any tax issues, and I was sure I hadn't done anything wrong concerning Jeanine Pirro or her husband. But just hours after the federal investigation was reported in the media, federal prosecutors began subpoenaing my colleagues, employees, accounts, and taxes.

Tacopina and Ken Breen began speaking with prosecutors, who were clearly on a mission, and although they refused to tell

us exactly what they were doing or looking for, the media miraculously appeared to know every move they made. Every time an acquaintance of mine got subpoenaed or the federal agents showed up at someone's house, I heard about it from a reporter before I heard it from the actual people involved.

This went on for close to five months. Then in February federal prosecutors had a meeting with Breen and made him an offer—they wanted me to take a plea to one count of federal tax fraud relating to the apartment renovations in my Bronx plea, and one count of conspiracy to eavesdrop, with the stipulation that I would testify against Jeanine Pirro. In exchange, they would agree to a sentence of one year to eighteen months in federal prison.

I told Breen, "There's no way. I can't. A felony conviction will destroy me."

I didn't think I had committed tax fraud, and I knew I didn't eavesdrop. More so, I was not testifying against Pirro when I didn't think she had done anything wrong.

When I refused their offer, they came with the hammer. They began subpoenaing my vendors, clients, business accounts, credit cards, banking accounts, business emails, and just about anyone I'd spoken with between 1999 and 2006.

Then something extremely odd happened. On March 12, 2007, as part of their investigation of me, they subpoenaed Tacopina's financial records.

I considered Tacopina an extremely close personal friend, like family. He was a stocky guy with classic Italian looks. He was smart, a real charmer. But everything I liked about him turned out to be negative later. Between 2002 and 2006 I had given him a number of birthday and Christmas gifts that could be considered quite expensive. In early 2005, when he was trading in an

older model BMW for a newer one, I even paid the difference between the two as a gift to him, a cost of about twenty-six thousand dollars. Together we'd discussed and been involved in a number of business ventures, and he had represented me pro bono in the Bronx case. I learned that the prosecutors were trying to determine whether I'd paid him anything in cash, payments that might easily go unreported and thus be tax violations. More important, I believe that the prosecutors, knowing that Tacopina was representing me pro bono, just as he had in the Bronx, wanted him off the case so I would have to pay for an attorney. Targeting him, creating a conflict of interest, was one clear way to arrange that.

With this conflict, he could not represent me, so Breen took over and immediately sent the federal prosecutors a letter, notifying them that I intended to preserve the attorney-client work product protections and attorney-client privileges that I'd had with Tacopina. We wanted to make sure that Tacopina maintained my attorney-client privileges with him so that the federal prosecutors could not use him or whatever information he had to help build up a case against me.

For the life of me, I could not understand the zeal with which the government was pursuing its investigation, its attempt to turn me into a villain.

Their methods and distortions shocked me, but what bothered me most about all this was how they were turning me into a monster and criminal in the press. Everything they looked at was being secretly fed to the press in order to convict me in the court of public opinion long before I would get a chance to defend myself in court. By no means am I an angel. There are things in my personal and professional life I could have handled differently—such as being more careful about whom I trust and give my friendship

to, and being more aware of how my decisions can be perceived by the public—but the Feds were taking honest mistakes by me and my accountants and alleging they were crimes.

Their investigation spanned the period from July 2006 to November 2007, a sixteen-month pursuit with a vengeance.

On November 8, 2007, I was charged in a sixteen-count federal indictment that made it seem that I was a member of an enormous criminal enterprise. They charged me with honest services fraud, tax fraud, and false statements relating to my children's nanny, a mortgage application, and the renovations issue that had been resolved in the Bronx case. For those renovations I had already been fined and penalized more than $220,000.

I could not understand how they could prosecute me again for this.

The indictment criminalized minor ethical issues and accounting errors—for example, they charged me in the indictment with one count of tax fraud in 2002 due to my accountant's having missed a twenty-thousand-dollar check or wire transfer and failed to claim it in my tax filings; they charged me in another count with failure to report the use of a car, when they knew that that, too, was another mistake by my accountants. As a member of the advisory board of BMW, I was given the use of one of their luxury vehicles every year, which must be claimed as income. My accountants and I had appropriately claimed this in 2004 and 2006, but had missed it in '05. In the aftermath of withdrawing from the presidential cabinet appointment three years earlier, I had paid the taxes, fines, and penalties on my children's nanny, but the federal prosecutors even charged me with that as well.

As Breen and I read through the indictment on the morning of November 9, he said he had never witnessed this sort of overreach-

ing by U.S. prosecutors. He was furious. There wasn't one thing in the indictment that could not have been handled civilly. Instead, they were going out of their way to make everything criminal. Prosecutors too often overcriminalize, overreach, and overpunish. I do believe that mine was a prime example of an overzealous and selective prosecution, the kind we see increasingly around the country.

Although Breen and I couldn't fully understand why they were pushing so hard, it seemed clear to me that Rudy Giuliani's political aspirations at the time had a lot to do with it. Rudy, my mentor, friend, and longtime boss, had announced that he was considering a run for the White House. The more popular he became, the more the press and media focused on me, motivating the prosecutors, and vice versa. It was an out-of-control locomotive.

. . .

On November 15, I watched that locomotive slam into the scales of justice. I learned exactly to what extent federal prosecutors were going to go to win their case when they revealed that Joe Tacopina, my former lawyer, was on their witness list. I was stunned.

I had just met with Tacopina three days before the indictment came down, and he had told me that the prosecutors were targeting him. He also wanted my help with some investment opportunities involving an Italian football team. Unknown to me, as he was discussing this far-flung business deal with me, he was also meeting with and talking to the prosecutors in my case. He had to have known by that point that I was going to be indicted and that he was going to be a witness on behalf of the government against me. I could not believe it. This man was one of my closest friends. He was my lawyer and confidant!

Within days after we learned Tacopina was on the witness list, prosecutors began targeting my lawyer Ken Breen as well. The prosecutors claimed that while interviewing Tacopina, he had discussed with them my conversations with him during the Bronx investigation, and that Breen may have been a witness to those conversations, too—something prosecutors claimed could have created a conflict, and in addition, could make Breen a witness against me as well.

Breen and I were shocked. We knew they had subpoenaed Tacopina's records, but when did they speak to him in person? Why would he agree to speak to them about anything in my case? Why didn't he tell me or Breen that he was meeting with the Feds? As my former attorney, wasn't he obligated to protect my rights?

For the life of us, we couldn't figure out what was going on, but on the night of January 23, 2008, after we had threatened Tacopina with an ethics complaint, he and his attorney, Michael Ross, met with a team of my lawyers at Breen's direction. By the time that meeting was over, we didn't know much, but we knew enough.

Tacopina had met with federal prosecutors to discuss me and the Bronx case as a "gesture of cooperation," according to Ross. During his meeting with the Feds, Tacopina was given immunity from prosecution, as long as the government believed he was telling the truth. I could only conclude that Tacopina was worried only about protecting his own interests. This subpoenaing by the prosecution of a lawyer for the defense, making that defense lawyer a witness for the prosecution, is extremely rare and, I believe in my case, entirely unethical.

But the prosecution got what they wanted: Denying my counsels' request for discovery, Judge Stephen C. Robinson found that the prosecutors were entitled to interview Tacopina and put him

———

on the stand against me and disqualified Breen as my counsel on the grounds that they might want to put him on the stand as well as a witness to my conversations with Tacopina and Tacopina's conversations with the Bronx DA. The judge denied that my attorney-client privilege was violated by any of this. With Tacopina and Breen now neutralized, the prosecutors knew I would be forced to hire a new legal team, which came at a price tag of $1.5 million. Since Hala and I didn't have the cash on hand, we were forced to mortgage our home for the retainer.

Within twenty-four hours after we filed the mortgage application for the retainer, the prosecutors ran into court and filed a *lis pendens* on our home for $187,000, saying that this was what I owed the government in taxes, fines, and penalties for the Bronx apartment renovations, which they were claiming were worth close to $255,000, nearly double what the Bronx district attorney had alleged. As a result, the mortgage, which had been approved, was now rescinded.

This was nothing more than an underhanded way of preventing me from paying for my defense, the Sixth Amendment constitutional right I thought I was guaranteed. They knew what the mortgage was for, and they knew that I had already spent close to a million dollars in legal fees and was hemorrhaging more money than I was making.

The only thing I had left was a 401(k) retirement fund, which I was forced to cash in to use as a retainer for the new legal team. I hired Barry Berke and Eric Tirschwell, of Kramer Levin Naftalis & Frankel, LLP, a prestigious Manhattan law firm specializing in white-collar crime litigation.

With Tirschwell and Berke at my side, the process began. We attended one pretrial hearing after another, but with each hearing

and passing day I began to believe that we had a much bigger problem than just overreaching federal prosecutors and a distorted indictment.

My judge.

. . .

When you are the target of a criminal investigation, it's a fight for your life. A felony conviction is a life sentence. Perhaps not in the literal sense, but once you're labeled a convicted felon in our country you become something of a pariah until the day you die, regardless of the charge, criminal intent, or your guilt or innocence.

As I sat in the courtroom in White Plains, New York, fighting for my freedom and my life, all I wanted and hoped for was a judge who knew the law, had common sense, and would rein in the prosecutors, who I believed were engaging in misconduct.

Instead, U.S. Federal Judge Stephen C. Robinson stunned me. He used the bench as if it were his own personal comedy club— telling jokes, doing movie commentaries, talking about how much he drank, complaining about his salary, seemingly condoning spousal abuse (he once told my attorneys and the prosecutors, who were arguing, to go home and take it out on their wives; "That's what spouses are for," he said), reciting Shakespeare, and talking about his personal love life and dating failures. At times I thought I was in the Twilight Zone.

Another time Robinson regaled us with a story of his mojito-making skills at a Super Bowl party at his home for his staff and clerks, telling us how much they drank. He bragged how most of his jurors loved him, except the ones he'd dated. I almost spat out the water I was drinking. I could not believe my ears. I also

couldn't believe how the press just sat there listening to his demeaning comments about women without crucifying him.

I tried to appear at ease in the courtroom, but Judge Robinson had me on edge. Worse, I felt that my new lawyers, Berke and Tirschwell, were scared to death of him. One minute Robinson was cracking jokes, and the next he was scowling and threatening. Regardless, I still thought that once we got to trial, we'd be okay. Unfortunately, that day would never come.

Just days before trial, Anthony Modafferi, a friend and attorney from New Jersey, sent an email to the *Washington Times* in which he outlined how he believed New York City investigators had suborned perjury and had pressured and threatened grand jury witnesses in the Bronx case against me, and maintained that the federal prosecutors had suppressed and were continuing to suppress that evidence in my current trial. Modafferi had been looking into my prosecution in the Bronx and was considering filing, on my behalf, a federal civil rights action against the New York City Department of Investigation and the Bronx district attorney.

When the federal prosecutors became aware of the email— the *Washington Times* had called the Bronx DA and DOI wanting to know more about Modafferi's claims; the state prosecutors relayed this to the Feds—they were furious and claimed that sharing my federal trial documents and motions with Modafferi violated a protective order signed by Robinson (such a protective order is standard in cases like mine). They threatened me, Berke and Tirschwell, and even Modafferi with contempt, and claimed my new trial team might now have a conflict in the case as well—the conflict being that they did not notify Modafferi of the protective order and that they did not prevent him from releasing information to the *Washington Times*.

———

As a result, Robinson basically suspended my trial team, saying they had a conflict, and ordered me to obtain *yet another* attorney as an independent counsel—costing me more money, of course.

As ordered, I retained a new attorney recommended by Berke, Michael Bachner, to sit in on the conflict issue. Over the next month, in one hearing after another, the prosecutors attacked me and Modafferi, not only for the email to the newspaper, but also for a series of articles that Modafferi had written in which he called my prosecution selective and political, and questioned why I was being treated far more harshly than Democratic cabinet nominees in President Barack Obama's administration who faced similar, if not worse, allegations.

The prosecutors said that Modafferi's statements and articles were false, defamatory, and inflammatory. But the facts spoke for themselves.

Modafferi had written about U.S. Treasury Secretary Timothy Geithner's failure to pay income tax, and President Barack Obama's chief of staff Rahm Emanuel's free use, for five years, of a Capitol Hill town house owned by a pollster with huge contracts with the Democratic National Committee. He also wrote about Adolfo Carrión, Jr., the former Bronx borough president who had been appointed President Obama's director of urban policy, accepting home renovations—in the Bronx of all places—from a contractor who was one of his campaign contributors; about Nancy Killefer, who withdrew her name from consideration after being nominated for chief performance officer, due to her failure to pay nanny tax; and about former Senate majority leader Tom Daschle's failure to pay more than one hundred thousand dollars in income tax.

In his articles Modafferi asked why I, a Republican who had

worked for Giuliani and had supported President George W. Bush, had been the subject of both state and federal investigations, yet not one of the Democrats mentioned above had been subjected to anything close to the same investigative scrutiny by the Justice Department. I understand that "But everybody's doing it" is rarely a winning argument—even if it is in large part true. It's not a good legal defense. But the fact that prosecutions are so often baldly selective does erode the notion of justice. It does something to weaken the whole process, to make it more personal and vengeful in appearance and nature than productive and moral.

Although Modafferi compared me to Democrats, the reality is that no one is supposed to be selectively targeted because of political views or associations, and the laws should be applied consistently and fairly across the board. But they aren't.

Judge Robinson, a former U.S. prosecutor himself, fumed at Modafferi's criticism and assertions. Claiming that the information in Modafferi's email to the *Washington Times* was an attempt to "influence the jury pool," on the morning of October 20, 2009, Robinson revoked my bail and ordered me to be taken into custody.

Within moments I would be in leg shackles and handcuffs.

I couldn't believe what was happening. I had defended, worked, fought, and nearly died for our country many times in the past thirty years and was now being jailed because Modafferi attempted to expose what he believed was government misconduct in my case.

. . .

Earlier that morning at home, as I was about to leave for Westchester and the courthouse, Hala had come into my office with a bottle

of religious oil, placed the oil on her thumb, and drawn the sign of the cross on my forehead. I called out to Celine and Angelina to say good-bye. They answered from their rooms upstairs as they got ready for school. "I'm going—love you!" I yelled, and walked out the door.

Not giving them a kiss good-bye, I felt I'd broken one of my cardinal rules from the time that my son, Joe, was a little boy. I've never wanted to leave the house or let the kids go to bed thinking that I was upset with them. Similarly, I always try to give them a hug and a kiss and tell them I love them as I leave the house, even if I'm just going down the street to the grocery store.

Throughout my career I've heard stories of cops who were killed in the line of duty and never got to say good-bye to their wives or children, and that would haunt forever the family members left behind.

One of the most heroic cops I've ever known was a New York City detective by the name of Joe Vigiano, who was killed on September 11, 2001. Ironically, I had promoted him not long before his death, and at his promotion ceremony he had spoken specifically about how important it is to make sure those close to you know you love them before you leave home.

This truth was never more vividly illustrated for me than in the aftermath of 9/11, as I attended the funerals of so many who died that day. We had one cop who had left his house that morning to go to police headquarters to submit his retirement papers. Upon his arrival, the building was emptying out, everyone racing to the Towers. He went, too. Earlier that morning he probably thought the dangers of his career were over, but tragically he never made it back alive.

That infamous day was the most powerful reminder I've ever

been given that you should never take life for granted and should treat each day as if it's your last. When I left for the White Plains Courthouse that morning, it would be the last time I would see my two little girls for many weeks. Not seeing them to kiss them good-bye, tell them I love them, disturbed me greatly.

Back in the courtroom, I noticed a U.S. marshal standing behind me. I looked toward Michael Bachner on my left and realized there was another marshal behind him. I also knew the press was watching every move, so I just stood up, and as I did, I felt the marshals close in. Although I knew it was their job, I wanted to turn around and say, "Where the fuck do you think I'm going?" But I stayed calm.

Before putting me in shackles and cuffs, one of the marshals asked me to take off my tie. Since I knew the drill, he didn't have to tell me what came next. Tie, cuff links, my gold necklace with a St. Michael's medal on it. On my right wrist was a special bracelet, a memorial band that I commissioned on the first anniversary of 9/11, made of white gold to last forever. NYPD -23—WTC is inscribed on it, along with the unforgettable date. I had worn it every day since I put it on in 2002 in memory of the twenty-three cops who died under my command that day.

Another marshal leaned in and pointed to the American flag pin in my lapel. "Don't forget that," he said. As I took off the bracelet and the flag pin, my anger rose. I looked up and saw the United States seal and flag in the courtroom and was overwhelmed. This is not justice, I thought. In my anger and shock, everything went blank.

The next thing I remember I was sitting in a dark gray jail cell, staring at the wall.

———

15

Losing Rudy

After Rudy Giuliani had left the mayor's office and I'd stepped down from the police department, we created a security consulting firm called Giuliani Kerik, a subsidiary of Rudy's principal company, Giuliani Partners. We had great success and worked on a number of interesting projects: an assessment of Mexico City's criminal justice agencies; a security evaluation of the Peekskill, New York, nuclear power plant; accountability recommendations for the U.S. Department of Justice Organized Crime Drug Enforcement Task Forces Program.

But with the negative press firestorm surrounding my withdrawn nomination for Homeland Security secretary and the Bronx investigation opening on the heels of that, Rudy was getting killed, pulled down in the press because of his mentorship and promotion of and friendship with me.

So I did what I had to do. I resigned from Giuliani Partners at the beginning of 2005.

At first, Tony Carbonetti, Rudy's former chief of staff, told me

that Rudy didn't want me to leave. But I saw no other way out of the guilty-by-association-to-me dynamic that was taking on a life of its own. I called a press conference and publicly announced my resignation.

But things between Rudy and me continued as they had before in terms of our friendship and connection. I had been an integral part of Rudy's mayoral cabinet that led New York City into a renaissance in the 1990s. We had made city history together, done great things. Everything seemed okay.

Every year Rudy hosted a special dinner on September 11 at a downtown steakhouse and invited all the people who were with him on that fateful day in 2001. On that date in 2006, just after the end of the Bronx case against me, Hala and I attended the dinner. We sat with Rudy and talked. He was happy that my case was over and that I'd resolved it as best I could. He gave me a hug. "Hang in there. Everything's gonna be all right," he told me. He said kind words and we laughed and joked together.

A week or two after that night, news broke that I was under federal investigation. I didn't speak to Rudy about it and we didn't talk in the ensuing weeks. I understood why he might want some distance from me at that point. In a sense, the separation was mutual. He wasn't contacting me and I wasn't contacting him. I understood from a legal perspective that if Rudy and I were talking during that time the Feds might start asking me why I was speaking to him, or asking *him* questions about *me*. But I didn't think that this marked a permanent break in our friendship or professional relationship.

A couple of months passed. Come November, Rudy's presidential ambitions were gathering steam. The press and media were gearing up for the 2008 presidential primary two years away, and

Rudy was being talked about as the possible front-runner for the Republican Party. At the end of November there was a poll that ranked Rudy as the most popular out of twenty potential presidential candidates. Barack Obama came in second.

Given that my daughter Celine was only six years old at the time, she had no idea of the difference between a Democrat and a Republican. All she knew was that people were saying that her godfather was going to be the next president of the United States. She was talking about it twenty-four hours a day, as if that were the only thing going on in her little world. She had no idea of what this really meant, of course, but she was convinced that Rudy was going to be president.

One afternoon she walked into my office and asked when she was going to get to see her godfather.

"He's very busy campaigning, sweetheart," I said. "Maybe we can see him before Christmas."

I called Carbonetti and told him I wanted to bring Celine and Angelina by to see Rudy before the holidays, as we often did. I was going to be leaving for the Middle East, to continue my work on national security and prison projects in Jordan, but would be back by mid-December. We could stop by the office or his apartment then. Tony told me that he put it on his list of things to speak to Rudy about and would get back to me with a time. I told Celine we would see her godfather when we did our annual two-day holiday stay in New York City when I got back from my trip.

She was ecstatic. "I want to get him a Christmas present!" she said. She already had it picked out. "I want to get him the president's jumping horse."

"President's jumping horse?"

She looked at me as if I were stupid, as only a six-year-old can

do, and said, "You know, the jumping horse that's in the president's office. We should get him that horse."

I still had no idea what she was talking about.

"Daddy, the horse you have in the room. It's just like the one in President Bush's office." With that, her little hand grabbed mine and she walked me into the living room. She pointed at the Remington bronze statue in the corner, a man riding a horse rising up on its hind legs. She was right.

Called *The Bronco Buster*, it was originally sculpted by Frederic Remington in 1895. *The Bronco Buster* was the first in a series of twenty-two statues Remington made. I had bought mine years before. When I was nominated for secretary of Homeland Security, I brought the whole family with me to the Oval Office. Celine was only four then, but she had obviously made note of seeing the same statue there that day.

I was pretty impressed with her choice and her memory for details. I pulled her onto my lap in front of the computer and we surfed the net looking for a *Bronco Buster* to buy Rudy for Christmas.

"Every president should have one of these," I said, as we looked through one site after another. Celine was so excited that it was almost comical to watch. I couldn't have been happier.

I ordered the *Bronco Buster* and had it delivered to my house. I told Celine that she and Angelina should make Rudy a nice card and when the statue arrived, we would put the card inside that box and then send Rudy the gift. We got the bronze within a day or two. Celine made a sweet card. The box was three feet high and weighed a lot, so Jimmy Grillo, a retired correction captain who had worked for me at Rikers and was still a member of my staff at The Kerik Group, delivered it himself to Rudy's apartment.

Celine was very excited and couldn't wait to see her godfather. I promised her that she would get to see him when I got back from my upcoming trip.

I didn't hear from Rudy or Tony while I was gone. On December 15, I flew back from London to JFK. I sent Tony an email right away, as I was waiting for my luggage. I was taking the girls and Hala to New York City for the next two days.

I received no reply. I called Tony's cell, and there was no answer. I sent another email, but I was getting the message.

Rudy didn't want to see me, didn't want to talk.

I didn't have the heart to tell Celine. The only thing I could say that she would accept was that he was busy campaigning for president, and that's what he had to do if he was going to win. She didn't like it, but the American Girl doll store, *The Little Mermaid* on Broadway, Rockefeller Center, and the lights of Manhattan clouded the Rudy subject for at least the time being, and for that I was relieved.

Our little excursion to New York City was great, but in every spare moment, I was working—speaking to Kim, Debbie, or Jimmy about our projects in Jordan and Kuwait. Kim was in Kuwait meeting with the National Security Bureau and setting up a meeting for me with their director in January in London.

It was just days before Christmas and Santa wasn't prepared. Although we had made our trip to the city and put the tree up at home, it didn't quite feel like Christmas. Hala had done her shopping, but I hadn't done any. Since that's what really puts me in the spirit, I took off and went shopping, loaded the car with gifts, and came back to the house. I immediately felt better and over the next few days Hala and I would wrap some gifts every time the girls were upstairs and out of the way. My thoughts occasionally returned to Rudy and the gift we'd sent him.

———

Throughout the holiday, we had a number of packages delivered to the house. Unless you had to sign for them, they would just drop them outside the front door.

One afternoon, Jimmy came into the house through the garage, as he usually did, and walked upstairs into the kitchen. He told me there was a delivery on the front porch, so I asked him if he could bring it in. I continued to do what I was doing in the kitchen. About ten minutes passed and I wondered what was taking him so long. The door was ajar and I called out to Jimmy. No response.

I walked down the stairs, opened the door, and saw Jimmy just standing on the porch looking at the box.

"What are you doing?" I asked him.

He looked upset but didn't say anything.

"What is it? Did you open it?" I asked.

"I don't have to. I recognize the box."

I was now staring at the box, too, and just then it hit me. It was the same box with the Christmas gift we'd given to Rudy. It wasn't a mistake or a failed delivery. Jimmy himself had hand delivered this to Rudy's Manhattan apartment. Someone had sent it back.

I told Jimmy to open it. I wanted to see what was inside. The beautiful bronze with its packing was there, but Celine and Angelina's handmade Christmas card to their godfather was gone. I had Jimmy pull the whole box apart thinking that there might be a note explaining why the gift was returned to us.

Nothing.

I was embarrassed that Jimmy had seen this, and I was scared to have Celine or Hala see it, so I had Jimmy put it out of sight in the garage.

I was stunned. Could it have been Rudy, or maybe his wife,

Judith? Did they do this because of the federal investigation? I wasn't working with Rudy at the time. He wasn't in government, even though he was preparing a run for the presidency. And what's more, he was my daughters' godfather and had exchanged gifts with them every year before this. I just didn't understand it. What bothered me more than anything was that whoever sent it back took the girls' card and didn't have the courtesy to send a note back with the box.

When I walked back into the house, Hala took a look at me and knew something was wrong. She thought that Joe Tacopina had called with bad news about the investigation, but I told her that I just had a headache and wasn't feeling well.

In the days that followed, I made several calls to Rudy's office, trying to figure out who sent the box back—to no avail. I thought it was possible that one of Rudy's assistants, thinking he was doing the right thing, had sent the package back without Rudy's knowing. Possible, but not likely. If Rudy himself had sent it back, or made the decision to do so, I just wanted to know why.

Over the next few weeks, I received other signs that the bronze hadn't been sent back to us in error. Up until that Christmas, Rudy had never missed Celine's or Angelina's birthday or Christmas. He always sent them cards. That year there was no card for either of them, and unfortunately there hasn't been one since.

Later, Tacopina told me that someone in Rudy's camp had mentioned to him that our gift had been sent back because Rudy was in the process of filing his Federal Election Commission financial disclosures for his presidential campaign and didn't want to list it as a gift. If that's true, it's a sad but real demonstration of the impact of politics on relationships—but I still didn't understand why he had abandoned the girls.

———

It has been sad and disappointing to me, the way he cut off our relationship, because that doesn't seem like the man I knew, professionally or personally. He was like family to me, someone I could never have abandoned. At my NYPD retirement dinner in 2001, in front of nearly two thousand people, Rudy said that I was like the brother he never had.

But you live and learn.

Of course, my reputation and standing were being slaughtered by scandals—and by that point, 2006, this had been going on for about two years—that as correction commissioner I had used COs on overtime to work my wedding; the *Times* calling the lucrative selling of my TASER stock questionable; or worst of all, in many people's eyes, that I'd used an apartment near Ground Zero for my own selfish purposes when it was meant for first responders to the attacks.

The reality was, the COs who were on duty at my wedding were members of my security detail. Whether I was getting married or working in my office on Rikers or sunning myself on Jones Beach, they would have been with me, on duty regardless. The stock transaction that the *Times* called questionable wasn't questionable at all. I sold the stock knowing I was being considered for the Homeland Security position and wanting to put money into our home, to lessen our mortgage. If I hadn't, I wouldn't have been able to take the job. I was on the board of TASER at the time, so the rest of the board was aware of the transaction, as was the SEC. It was all done by the book, but if you read those articles, you would have thought for sure that I had done something illegal or unethical in the transaction. As for the apartment in Battery Park, that apartment had never been set aside for first responders working at Ground Zero, as the press had reported. The truth is I had

been living in my office for the first two or three weeks after the attacks and my chief of staff had contacted the building's management firm. Three vacant apartments were set aside: one for me; one for my staff; and one for the chief of department. There was no apartment in the building set aside for first responders either before or after I was there, but once the first story was written claiming this, almost every other news organization reasserted the falsehood, and they have continued to do so for the past nine years.

It killed me to see Rudy being made to answer for my actions—the press asking him how he felt about me and my scandals, discussing how his support for and association with me reflected on his judgment and character. But I never thought it would end our friendship.

We are two different people, and I wouldn't have handled the situation the way he did. But that's me. I know he's different. He's also a politician. Maybe it was his political instincts taking over, and he saw his relationship with me as just too detrimental to him at that point and had to make a cold cost-benefit calculation. Once a political asset to him, I was now radioactive.

Although I don't like it or agree with his decision, I understand it.

People often ask me if the press attacks on me, the criminal cases, were an attempt to damage Rudy politically. It's a valid question, and yes, much of the negative press was generated by local and national politicians to damage Rudy. However, I also think my profile was substantially enhanced as a result of my relationship with Rudy, making me a choice target for state and federal prosecutors, and providing tons of exposure for them in the bargain. To those commentators who have suggested that I ruined Rudy's chance at the presidency, I say, No way.

———

On a national scale, no one cared that much about my downfall; in fact, most never knew exactly what was going on. At the local level, in the heat of New York, you'd have to be completely blind not to see the political dimension to it.

As I look back and reflect on those years, there's one thing that still bothers me: During my time in Cumberland, Rudy never once called Hala to speak with the girls. He never tried calling any mutual friend of ours to check up on them, ask how they were doing. There were no Christmas or birthday cards. My safe guess is that as a former U.S. attorney Rudy had a sense of what the separation of incarceration does to families—yet not once did he call to help in any way.

On one visit to me in Cumberland in 2012, a now-twelve-year-old Celine asked me, "Daddy, are we ever going to get to see our godfather again?"

"I'm not sure, Celine. I think he's upset with me."

She looked at me, flustered. "That's a stupid answer. *We* haven't done anything to him. Why isn't he talking to me and Angelina?"

I really didn't have an answer for that. Over time they just stopped asking.

Had the tables been turned, I would have looked out for his family. He wouldn't even have had to ask. I know he knows that.

Today, we have not one but *two* Remington bronzes in our home—the original one that now sits in my office, and the one that was meant for Rudy upstairs in a sitting room.

It's been eight years since it was returned to us. When Celine asked me where the second one came from, I just told her it was a gift, from a very dear friend.

———

16

Kerik Needs Help

With my bail revoked, I was on my way to prison, convinced that I was facing a biased judge in a lopsided trial.

The ride was about twenty minutes to the Westchester County Jail in Valhalla. They knew we were coming. The marshals took me into the receiving area and the jail staff came out to remove the handcuffs and shackles. I stepped into the doorway and a sergeant saluted me and shook my hand. "Stay strong, Commish," he said.

A correction officer who worked in the booking area walked close to the sergeant and told him he didn't feel comfortable processing me. The sergeant said all right, so I went over to another correction officer, who shook my hand and said that he would take care of me.

Having run jails, I knew what had to be done. I went along with the program. I told the processing officer that I didn't want any special treatment or to be placed in protective custody, because that would mean segregation from everything and anything. Nobody wants to be in solitary. I knew how mind-numbing it could

be and I didn't know how long I was going to be there. He said that he had just the place for me, but right after he spoke, the phone in the room rang, there were a bunch of "Yes, sirs," and he hung up.

"Well, so much for that. They want you in strict protective custody."

"What's that mean here?" I asked.

"Locked down twenty-three hours a day, and you can only be removed from your cell under the supervision of a sergeant or above and two correction officers after the entire facility is locked down."

That's exactly what I don't want, I thought. This kind of treatment in jail or prison is usually punitive, and I hadn't done anything to deserve it yet.

When they were ready to take me to my cell, a voice came over the loudspeaker: "All movement in the jail must stop at this time—there is no movement in the jail."

One of the sergeants looked over at me and told me that in addition to the escorts, no inmates could be out of their cells anywhere near me, which meant every time I wanted to make a phone call, take a shower, or watch television during my one hour out of my cell during the day, they'd have to have every inmate in the facility put away and I would have to have that three-person escort. I knew this was going to suck for me and for them.

They took me to a cell at the end of a hallway in the mental observation ward so that I would be out of the way and have no contact with other inmates. The last time I was in a jail cell must have been in Jordan, or during a walk-through on Rikers Island about ten years before.

"They call this the James Brown Suite," the sergeant said.

It was an expanded cell with two bunks, one sink, a toilet, and

two lights, one on each wall. At one time it had been two separate cells, but back in 1989, when the singer James Brown was held in the facility, they took out the middle wall and made it a little bigger for the Godfather of Soul.

That first night was difficult, but I think the reality of being imprisoned by the judge hadn't truly hit me yet, and wouldn't until the next morning. The more I thought about it, the more I believed that the prosecutors were getting more desperate by the day and this was a sure sign. Any good investigator or prosecutor will tell you that you have about a ten times greater chance for a resolution in a case if your target is in jail. They now had me at a distinct disadvantage.

At 11:00 p.m. the lights in the jail started going out and like in the Michael Jackson "Thriller" video, the fucking goblins were looking for the moon. The inmates on the other side of the ward started screaming like maniacs, kicking their cell doors. This went on for nearly two hours.

Holy shit, they need to increase their fucking medication, I thought. Or give it to them earlier so it kicks in by midnight.

On the third morning in the cell, I woke to visitors: a deputy commissioner, the warden, and some other senior staff. One of them said, "Commissioner, we're going to have you go down to the clinic to see Dr. Schramm, the director of the Forensic Unit. He'd like to speak to you, and we think there's a place for you there."

About an hour later, I met with Dr. Schramm, who explained that for their convenience (keeping an eye on me) and my own safety, they thought it best that I be housed in the Forensic Unit, but I would have to volunteer to be admitted. It was a larger room, much brighter than my current cell. It seemed peaceful and quiet, and that's what I wanted. "Where do I sign," I said.

Schramm and another doctor offered me something to help me sleep and I declined. I told them that if the media found out I was in there and taking medication, they would report that I was a drug addict. A doctor and a nurse assured me that everything in that unit was confidential, bound by HIPAA's medical privacy laws, but I just laughed—and boy, I was not far off.

At a pretrial hearing a few days later, Judge Robinson publicly disclosed in open court that I was being held in the Forensic Unit of the Westchester County Jail, implying that I was there for psychiatric reasons. The truth was that I had been voluntarily placed there for strict protective custody, as I was a former cop and a public figure; it had nothing to do with my mental state.

Robinson's comments were misleading and outraged the medical staff at the Westchester County Jail. Dr. Schramm, who also taught psychiatric law, told me that he was upset, because it was the first time in his thirty-two years on the job that a judge had ever done that.

I believed Robinson knew exactly what he was doing.

The headlines the next day read "KERIK NEEDS A SHRINK." National news.

Angry, I ordered my attorneys to prepare a motion to recuse Robinson from the case. He had revoked my bail and put me in jail claiming I was attempting to influence a jury pool by way of an email that was not made public. Yet he managed to create horrible and damaging headlines for me by jailing me and then implying I was nuts.

The feeding frenzy of the press was so bad that Robinson pushed the trial date back.

Then things got even more bizarre. At a hearing, Robinson tried to talk me into retaining as my independent counsel an at-

torney by the name of Vincent Briccetti. He called Briccetti his mentor and said he considered him one of the best attorneys in the country.

I was confused. On the record and in open court, the judge was trying to get me to speak to his buddy and mentor, even as Mike Bachner, my counsel, sat right next to me. I thought this was straight-up unethical. I was convinced that we had to get a new judge.

On October 30, my attorneys told Robinson that we intended to file a motion to recuse him from the case. They did so privately at a sidebar, as a courtesy. Robinson stared at Barry Berke with a half-smirk on his face, but his jowls tightened. I could see he was upset, but I didn't care. I wanted to get to trial, and I wanted a judge who was fair and impartial. No way did he fit that bill, I thought.

My attorneys returned to the defense table, leaned over, and said, "He's pissed." Before I could respond, Robinson began talking. I can't tell you exactly what he said, but by the time he finished, I felt as if I'd been shot in the chest. All I remember was him saying that at our next hearing he was inclined to disqualify my legal team.

I could hardly breathe. Not again, I thought. I didn't have any more money for lawyers. The government was going to have me sit in jail for twelve to eighteen months while a new legal team got up to speed, knowing I didn't have the money for another million-dollar retainer. I left the courtroom in a daze.

The U.S. marshals put me in a room to speak to my attorneys. Bachner, Tirschwell, and Berke walked in looking as if they'd seen a ghost. I asked them if there was any chance that Robinson would not disqualify them. They just stood there staring at me.

Tirschwell broke the silence. "Every time he's said he's inclined to do something, he has. I think he's gonna do it."

Before he got the last words out of his mouth, I broke down. Two years of preparing for trial—which was now just days away— close to two million in legal fees, all for nothing. My savings were gone, my retirement gone, my house had a lien on it by the lawyers. I could not believe how this nightmare kept getting worse.

I told them to go see the prosecutors and tell them I quit, that I couldn't go on. "See what kind of deal they'll give me." Berke looked devastated. They all did. Berke asked me if I was sure. "I don't have a choice," I told him.

It was obvious that Robinson disliked me. I was sure that the prosecutors could see it and feel it and were going to do everything in their power to use it to their advantage. Going to trial with him as my judge made it likely that there would be no fairness or impartiality, but I'd still been willing to try. Now, however, if he disqualified my legal team again, I could wait in jail for more than a year before getting to trial. With no more money, I would have to go to trial with a public defender representing me, in front of Robinson, no less. There was no way, I thought. I didn't have a choice.

I quit.

This is not just about me.

As Andrew Kreig, a legal reform advocate and lawyer who runs the Justice Integrity Project, stated in an article on Harvard's Nieman Watchdog website, we need "to reexamine how federal authorities can railroad someone like Kerik into a guilty plea this way." Kreig noted the "unusually aggressive prosecution tactics, such as depriving the defendant of lawyers"; "crippling the defense by imprisoning Kerik pending trial and berating him in public court as exemplifying 'arrogance,' and worse."

Kreig is one of many observers who have taken a look at our system and seen that these tactics are employed far too often in federal investigations.

Back to court.

My attorneys went upstairs and met with the prosecutors. They returned within forty minutes. It was done: twenty-seven to thirty three months in prison.

"What do I have to plead guilty to?" I asked.

"They'll bring you in over the next few days and figure it out," Berke answered. At that point I was removed by the marshals and taken to a holding cell to await the trip back to Westchester.

Nothing in my life had ever shaken me so badly. I couldn't get my head around the politics of it all, the actions of the prosecutors and judge. I've gone after some of the most dangerous men in the world, but I had never, nor would I, stoop to the levels that these men did against me.

I know there is the stereotype of police behaving in a similarly coercive manner, using unfair tactics to get what they want. Some may think that as a cop I must be familiar with such strong-arm tactics. But I can tell you that, in my experience, this use of power is much more common in the prosecutorial world than in policing—mainly because of prosecutorial immunity. Cops can't get away with that stuff. When a U.S. attorney gets caught in misconduct, the overwhelming majority of the time nothing happens. Multiple studies over the past decades have shown that prosecutors are rarely punished for misconduct—that happens in less than 2 percent of cases.

I sat alone on the metal bench in my cell, thinking about how I was going to tell Hala and my family. I had pled guilty in the Bronx case to something I didn't agree with, and now I was doing it all

over again. Just then the cell door opened and a U.S. marshal told me my attorneys were back. When I walked into the room, they were standing there pale-faced.

"We think we know the answer to this, but we're obligated to ask anyway," Tirschwell began. "The prosecutors want to know if there's anything you would like to talk to them about, that could help you at sentencing."

At first I had no idea what they were talking about, but then it hit me. One of my former employees at Giuliani Partners had told me that the prosecutors had badgered him about Rudy Giuliani, his associations in the White House, his campaign schedule, and who paid for his campaign travel and meals.

Was that it? Were they trying to get to Giuliani through me? I looked at the three of them and said, "You guys knew my answer already." I had nothing to say. And with that, I returned to my cell.

Over the next three days, I was taken to the U.S. Attorney's Office, where Berke, Tirschwell, and associates from their office negotiated with the prosecutors on what they wanted me to plead guilty to. It made me sick that the prosecutors and Robinson had spent more than a month asserting that Berke and Tirschwell had such a conflict that it should preclude them from representing me in any way (the prosecutors had put together a nineteen-page letter outlining this), but once I agreed to plead guilty, they had no problem negotiating my plea agreement with those very same lawyers.

. . .

The next morning, November 5, I stood before Robinson to plead guilty to the counts and the language that the prosecutors insisted on. I felt as if I were in a playhouse drama, with a cast of characters

who were all well rehearsed. Everyone had a script, including me, and no one was supposed to deviate from it. Mine was prepared by Berke and Tirschwell and the U.S. Attorney's Office, and it read almost word for word the same as my plea agreement. At this point, a defendant is supposed to tell the judge in his own words what he did wrong. The judge can get an idea of whether the defendant is contrite and sincere. But too often in federal cases, the defendant, in taking the plea, is forced to read in court straight from the prosecution's own language, to read a plea allocution written and structured by the prosecution—meaning they essentially have full control over the process. In my case, the prosecutors threatened to pull the plea if I spoke out against, criticized, or deviated from it in my comments in court in any way.

My eventual cube mate in Cumberland, sixty-six-year-old federal prisoner Rodrigo Gomez, was a prime example of just how horrific this practice can be. A tiny Puerto Rican guy from the Bronx, Gomez had stood up in court and pled guilty to conspiring to possess and distribute five kilos of cocaine and one kilo of heroin. When I personally reviewed his case file when we were in Cumberland together, I realized that his entire plea allocution in court was essentially a lie—every word of it. Gomez knew he was admitting to something he hadn't done, and I have to believe his attorney knew it, the prosecutors knew it, and the judge knew it, too.

Federal prosecutors had told him they would seek twenty-five years to life if he went to trial, or he could plead guilty to ten years. "Nothing I could do," he told me. Deathly afraid, he took the plea deal, but in doing so, he had to say that he conspired with others to possess and distribute five kilos of cocaine and one kilo of heroin.

———

The tragic reality is that Rodrigo Gomez answered his cell phone one day and a guy on the other end asked if he knew anyone who had a half kilo of heroin. Rodrigo explained he wasn't into heroin, but if he heard of anything, he'd let the guy know. The government tied him to a conspiracy, and at six o'clock on a summer morning they took him from his sleep and arrested him. In his possession was one gram of cocaine, the weight of a dollar bill. So Rodrigo Gomez went to federal prison with a ten-year sentence for answering his phone and possessing one gram of cocaine.

As I read through my plea before Bachner and I went into the courtroom, I remember thinking, This isn't justice. This was a victory for the prosecutors. Convictions are supposed to be based on evidence and guilt, not trickery or depriving someone of the Sixth Amendment right to counsel, suppressing evidence, and suborning perjury.

The proceeding began by guaranteeing that I could never appeal or attack my guilty plea in a habeas petition or any future motions.

"Do you understand that you would be able to make a motion if you or your attorney believed that the jury pool has in any way been improperly influenced? Do you understand that you could make a motion to recuse the court if you chose? Do you understand that by pleading guilty today you are waiving those rights, that you are waiving the right to complain on appeal that you could not receive a fair trial, do you understand that?"

"Yes, your Honor."

I also had to waive my right to appeal or attack the plea on the grounds that the government had failed to produce any discovery, Brady, or Giglio material—exculpatory evidence uncovered by

the prosecution that by law must be presented to the defense—even though federal and state prosecutors had worked to deny me access to the evidence in the Caruso federal civil suit. In that suit Caruso claimed that he had been ordered to testify falsely against me in the state case, a claim that the federal prosecutors admitted in a motion would have been harmful to their case against me.

I stood in a powerless fog. With Bachner sitting at my side, and Berke, Tirschwell, and the Kramer Levin legal team sitting in the audience, Robinson once again urged me to retain or speak to Vincent Briccetti, his friend and mentor.

"I think the last time we were together I specifically mentioned an attorney that I knew and had great faith in, Mr. Vincent Briccetti, and offered to appoint him to represent you in this matter in any way you wanted him to, do you understand that?

"I'd be willing to do that free of charge to you. . . . Did I make it clear to you the high regard that I held the attorney that I recommended to you in? I told you that I think I've known him for over twenty years. . . . I told you that he's actually one of the people who trained me. . . . I have the highest confidence in this lawyer, both in terms of his legal acumen and in terms of his ethical understanding and responsibilities. . . . I wanted to offer that to you so there could be no question going forward so that you would have any reason to say going forward that you didn't have the fullest and the brightest counsel that at least this court was aware of. . . . And you understand again that you wouldn't have to pay for Mr. Briccetti, you understand that?"

I was dumbfounded. His pitch for Briccetti was persistent and aggressive.

Bachner was shocked, and all I kept thinking about was Hala

telling me that I should have taken Robinson up on this offer the last time, in order to placate him and at least give myself a semblance of a fair shake from him.

There had to be a motive, I thought, behind this push for me to retain or speak to his friend and mentor. Why weren't the prosecutors objecting? How could they not? I thought. He had disqualified Breen and threatened to disqualify Berke and Tirschwell for alleged conflicts, yet he was trying to replace them with his own recommendation. Was that not a far more substantial conflict?

"Do you understand that you have an absolute right to have conflict-free counsel in this case?" Robinson asked me. What idiot would believe that Briccetti would've been "conflict free" after Robinson had tried to push him on me three different times?

On this, the third occasion, he urged me for nearly fifteen minutes to speak to or retain Briccetti. He then advised me that by moving forward with Bachner as my counsel, I would waive any conflicts of interest that were potentially there—the implication being that because Bachner had been involved in joint cases with Kramer Levin, where Berke and Tirschwell worked, there could have been a conflict. I've since had many people, including attorneys, former U.S. attorneys, and judges, tell me that they've never seen anything quite like this, the government repeatedly going after defense counsel in this manner.

My mind was racing. Was this a trap? As soon as I declined to speak to Briccetti and told Robinson that I intended to move forward with Bachner as my counsel, he dropped another bomb.

He informed me that Bachner, who was sitting right next to me, had not had a full opportunity to review all the Rule 16 discovery, or exculpatory material, in this case, to the extent it existed, and that he had not had the full opportunity to review all

the witness statements and notes and reports in the case, and that there might be other materials in the case that he had not had an opportunity to fully review before that morning.

Then what the fuck are we doing here? I thought to myself, scrambling for answers.

Bachner had come on board only when Robinson ordered me to obtain an independent counsel, and I'm sure there was evidence that he had not seen, that he wasn't aware of. But again, the judge was driving home the heavy price of my accepting the plea arrangement. I would be unable to challenge the government's investigative and prosecutorial methods that led to my plea.

By this point, I was mentally shot, realizing that I was standing before a judge who I am convinced knew exactly what led to my plea agreement, who had urged me to retain his friend and mentor, who had advised me that the attorney who was now representing me knew little to nothing about my case, and who was still content to have me waive every constitutional right that I had.

For the next twenty to thirty minutes, the prosecutors regaled Robinson with their rendition of my misdeeds. Then he ordered me to tell him in my own words what I was pleading guilty to, which I obediently did, reading from the document that the prosecutors and my attorneys had prepared for me.

To this day, the last thing I clearly remember is my refusing to speak to Briccetti and Robinson's then telling me that my counsel had not reviewed all the evidence in my case. From that point on I was completely knocked off balance.

· · ·

In the days after the plea hearing, Bachner and I spoke over the phone. He told me that he was optimistic about my sentencing. He

said it was clear from Robinson's comments at the end of the hearing that he intended to take into consideration my life of public, meritorious service in determining my sentence, and that could only lead to a downward departure from the sentencing guidelines of twenty-seven to thirty-three months.

I had no recollection of what Robinson actually said in that moment, so I reviewed the transcript of the plea hearing, and unlike Bachner, who felt good about the judge's comments, I immediately felt sick to my stomach.

"I never make up my mind about a sentence before reading every bit of information that counsel submits and until I actually hear what counsel say at sentencing . . . under Title 18 Section 3553 (a), I am instructed, and I take these instructions very seriously, that I'm not only to look at the crimes that a defendant has pled guilty to or been convicted of at trial, but I'm instructed specifically to take into account the nature and history of the offense and the characteristics of the defendant, and the defendant's history . . . I think that there is a lot about your life and history that will become important to this court in imposing sentence . . . I think that you've had a full life. And I should be able to take into account that full life and all of the things that you had done, not just the charges here. Because there is much good in that full life, I believe. And I want to take that into account when I consider what is an appropriate sentence."

Based on the words themselves, I could understand Bachner's optimism. However, it had been nearly two years to the day that I had been appearing before Robinson in this matter, and I'd come to know him well, I thought. As I read the transcript of the plea hearing, I was struck by his deliberate appearance of fairness, justice, and logic. I immediately called Bachner back.

———

"That was nothing more than a

"That's not the man I've gotten to kn

and I promise you, the worst is yet to

Five days after my plea, my attor

the real Robinson reappeared. Here

know: pompous, arrogant, threateni

On that day, Hala was in court fo

seen or heard Robinson in action, a

meanor. After admitting that I was no

my bail, from $500,000 to $1.5 mi

strict home confinement. He bragge

fendant for stepping out his front d

suggesting that he'd do the same to

Bachner sat there confused. "Wl

consider all the good in your life?"

some common criminal." Reversing

ditions, he ordered that I not be allo

year-old daughters to and from scl

from my home. He was now punisl

Robinson's behavior at that h

disdain for me. Even the reporter:

pleased with my downfall, questic

bail conditions, which were tran

sary (reporters called my attorne

they'd seen in court).

After three weeks in jail, I wa

my desk at home, I felt I was on b

that night. "Are you sure you've

his family?" he asked me.

I dreaded what was to come.

17

Ties That Bind

In early 2010, my brother started sending me books on the federal prison system, the transition from society to incarceration. I felt that there was nothing in them that I didn't already know. I hadn't been to prison before, but I'd been connected to the prison system, one way or another, for thirty years—walking the tiers in New Jersey; nighttime inspections at Rikers; working on the supermax in Jordan. I found some of the details in these books interesting: the cost of a phone call, how much money you can have with you. But none of this made me feel any better about going inside.

Over the next several days and weeks, friends and family began to show up at my home, many of them upset that I had thrown in the towel rather than go to trial. Instead of spending a bunch of time trying to explain my decision, I just reached over to my inbox on my desk, retrieved the stack of papers clipped together, and handed it to them. "You want to handle this for me?" I asked. It was my attorney's bill for one month, October 2009: $476,708.21. No matter whom I handed it to, it shut them right up.

For close to two years, I had been billed $100,000 to $150,000, and sometimes up to $200,000, per month in legal fees. October's took the cake. It was money we didn't have but were willing to risk, believing that the charges against me were civil and ethical violations, not criminal felonies.

I wanted to go to trial to defend myself, and the United States Constitution is supposed to guarantee me that right, but it just doesn't work like that. I have learned that you have constitutional rights only as long as you have the money to pay for them. The sad thing is that if I can't survive a fight for justice, how can someone less privileged get *any* sort of justice? How do you expect a guy who has no money and no support and who's up against institutional bias to be able to fight for fairness and impartiality? That's 80, 90 percent of defendants. I met many guys in prison who pled guilty to stuff they never should have pled guilty to.

The government prosecutors know that and they use it to their advantage. They can distort and exaggerate their justifications to lock up your property, bank accounts, and other assets. They can drain you and your family of everything you've ever worked for; rip you in the court of public opinion; destroy your family's financial future; and do everything in their power to prevent you from being able to pay for your defense. We need to have robust prosecution—that's necessary for law and order, there can be no doubt about that—but it must be fair. We must have prosecutors who won't break the law to enforce it, or try to win at all costs regardless of fairness or justice.

On February 18, 2010, I walked into the White Plains Federal Courthouse for sentencing, anticipating two things: one, that Robinson would sentence me to the maximum of the agreed-

upon sentencing guidelines (thirty-three months); and two, that he would remand me immediately.

After Robinson explained what the hearing would consist of, Bachner began to lay out my career and all the positive things I'd done in my life. Robinson had said that he was mindful of taking this into consideration. But just as Bachner was getting started, Robinson jumped in. "Let me cut it," he said. He didn't want to hear what Bachner had to say. He wasn't going to allow him to talk about my thirty-year career, my meritorious public service, or the letters of support I'd received.

Then he sentenced me to forty-eight months in federal prison, fifteen months over and above the sentencing guidelines that had been agreed upon by the U.S. attorneys, my lawyers, and the U.S. Department of Probation.

The dozens of cops and federal agents in court to support me were stunned. My friend Geraldo Rivera and his wife Erica were sitting next to Hala. Geraldo cried. Hala felt as if someone had knocked the wind out of her, she told me. As for me, I wasn't surprised. I wasn't devastated. By that point, the case had already beaten me down, taken my business, shamed me in the court of public opinion, and embarrassed my family. What else are you going to do to me? I thought. He did what I expected, what I'd predicted.

Then the prosecutor stood up and demanded that I be jailed immediately. He said I was a flight risk, citing that Hala was a naturalized citizen born in Syria and she still had property and family there. I was furious at his statement for two reasons. First, he knew Hala no longer had property there and just a few distant relatives, but he said that anyway in an attempt to have me remanded. Second, his implication that I would escape to Syria if allowed to

remain out on bail was completely ludicrous. I had worked for the United States in Iraq and had publicly called for sanctions and regime change in Syria. How could he stand in that courtroom and attempt to use such a ridiculous argument? Who did he think would give me an entrance visa to Syria, their intelligence service?

I saw this as yet another example of the distortions these prosecutors presented throughout their investigation and prosecution of my case. They exaggerated and suppressed certain facts to paint the picture they wanted the judge, the press, and the public to see. To them, it didn't seem to be about justice. It was about winning at any cost. Their job is to enforce the law, prosecute people for violations of the law, but they cannot break the law in an attempt to enforce it. As Alex Kozinski, chief judge of the United States Court of Appeals for the Ninth Circuit, recently wrote, as quoted in an editorial in the *New York Times*, "There is an epidemic of Brady violations abroad in the land."

Although Robinson had previously concluded more than once that I was not a flight risk, he still admitted that he intended to remand me when he came to court that day. But I think the prosecutor's claims were so preposterous that Robinson figured he would have looked like an idiot if he agreed. So instead he ordered me to self-surrender to federal prison on May 17.

As Hala and I walked out of the courthouse to waiting reporters, she looked at me and squeezed my hand. "That fifteen extra months was for not hiring his pal Briccetti. I hope you're happy," she told me.

We returned home that afternoon to tell my daughters. I spent the next three months preparing them mentally for my departure. That time between sentencing and surrendering to federal prison was one of the worst periods of my life on a number of different

fronts. By this time, many of my so-called friends had either distanced themselves or completely disappeared. Some I could care less about, but some really bothered me by their absence. As disappointed as I was by those friends who vanished, I was equally surprised by the support I received from others who courageously dug in their heels and stood in support of a friend in the midst of a bad scandal. Not everybody does that.

With each day that brought me closer to prison, I could feel the tension and anxiety levels rise at home. I felt it mostly with Hala and my brother, Don, and then Celine and Angelina, who for the most part didn't think about Daddy's imprisonment unless it came up in conversation.

I wasn't worried about my son, Joe. I assumed he was handling it better than the others, but three weeks before surrendering to prison I learned I was wrong.

Joe was two months from his twenty-fifth birthday and had been a cop for five years already, the last two of which were with the Newark Police Department in New Jersey. In that two-year period, he had made detective and earned an assignment in their elite SWAT team. This is in Newark, which over the past forty years has earned the notoriety of having one of the highest violent crime rates in the country. Three years ago, when Cory Booker was elected mayor of Newark, there was an assumption that he would be the man to turn the city around. But he left for the U.S. Senate without having achieved any significant reduction in crime.

One Friday afternoon, Joe's SWAT team finished up a two-day training session and came to my house afterward for a barbecue. It was nothing special, just hamburgers, hot dogs, beer, and soda. His team leaders knew that I enjoyed Spanish sangria, so they brought some—about ten gallons of it!

Guys who work hard, play hard, and men and women in the military and law enforcement, who depend on each other for their own survival, grow special bonds. I understand this well, so I was happy to see Joe and his team enjoying themselves, talking about their training, telling war stories, busting one another's chops, and laughing until they were blue in the face.

In addition to Joe's team, we'd invited some others to the barbecue, friends from the FBI, DEA, and a number of local police departments. As a good host, I was making my rounds when someone came to me and said that I needed to see Joe right away. I walked over to the table where he was sitting with about fifteen guys. I could see that he was crying. Apparently, guys on his team had just been talking about me and the trial and Joe had broken down and burst into tears. I went over and held him. It didn't make any difference that he was a grown man or that there were all these battle-tested cops sitting there looking at us. I felt as much pain for his suffering as I did for the much younger Celine's or Angelina's. In some ways it was worse.

Although Joe's mother and I separated when he was a year old, I did everything in my power to show him all the love I could as he grew up. Although some of my friends and family said I could have been less of a disciplinarian, there was never a doubt in his mind that I loved him more than life itself. He had now grown into a man who went to work every day risking his life to protect others, which took enormous courage and bravery, yet he was emotionally devastated by what was happening to me. Watching him and feeling his pain tore at my insides and just reinforced in me the truth that there is no pain worse than seeing your own child suffer.

What saved me from breaking down that afternoon were the warriors in Joe's unit, as one by one they came forward offering

him their support, promising me that they would be there for him during my absence. The commander of the Newark SWAT team, Sergeant Frank Rossi, pulled me aside and said, "Boss, don't worry about him while you're gone. I'll look after him personally." Rossi and his team were known for saving lives, but on that day, he and the men in that unit rescued our hearts and emotions. As the evening ended, I felt enormous gratitude.

In my last two weeks home, I tried to spend as much time with Celine and Angelina as possible, and although it was Hala who saw to their every need, I was there when they left for school in the morning, when they came back home, and then when it was time for them to go to bed. As I held them while putting them to sleep, I was afraid for them. It was tearing me up inside, but I had to try to make this, my going away to prison for years, as painless as possible.

About a week before I was supposed to surrender, Celine reminded me that the next day was Mother's Day. She wanted to know what I was doing for Mommy. I felt horrible because I hadn't thought of it, and now there wasn't much I could do anyway, given that I was under house arrest as ordered by Judge Robinson.

A few minutes after Celine brought it up, Joe arrived at the house with lunch and a bouquet of flowers and some balloons for Hala. It was very sweet and I was as happy as I was proud of the man he'd become. He first met Hala when he was ten years old and she was the manager of our dentist's office. In the fourteen years he had known her, he'd come to love her like his own family and they'd become very close. I couldn't have been more pleased.

As I watched him greet Hala in the kitchen, I thought of what a fabulous mother she was to our two little girls. I thought of how lucky they were and how lucky I was that she was there for them. I could not ask for more. At one of the lowest and worst times of

my life, I realized how blessed I was that Hala was there for them and for me.

This was all so different from what I knew as a child growing up. My own mother had abandoned me when I was about three years old. Eventually my father, who lived in New Jersey at the time, found me in Columbus, Ohio, and rescued me from what could have been a disastrous life. My dad later remarried and I grew to love his wife and my stepmother as my own, but the early years before that were rough.

Celine and Angelina had never experienced anything close to that, and we showered them with as much love as we could. As rough and harsh as some people think I am, my heart is soft when it comes to them, at the first sign of a tear in their eyes or a frown on their face. Luckily Hala is there for that, too.

She would constantly keep me in check by telling me what a sap I was and how easily the girls could get over on me, but I didn't care. My love for them was almost painful, and the only thing more painful was knowing that I wouldn't be around them for the next three years.

. . .

On Monday, May 17, 2010, I walked into the reception area of the U.S. Federal Prison in Cumberland, Maryland. I was stripped of my clothes and my personal belongings and issued an identification card by the U.S. Federal Bureau of Prisons. Registration Number 84888-054. I must have twenty different government ID cards from over the years—correction officer, detective, cop, deputy commissioner, commissioner, all these badges, all these markers of who I was, how I served, but now this new one, this red X, trumped all those others.

Inmate.

In that first month and a half or so, I didn't think anything could make me feel any worse about my life or my circumstances, until John Picciano, my former chief of staff, came to Cumberland to visit in early July.

He sat down across from me and looked as if he had just come from a wake. "I've got something to tell you," he said. "If you wrote this into a novel, no one would believe it." While overseeing my trial in 2008 and 2009, John informed me, Judge Robinson sat on the board of the Markle Foundation, a liberal think tank managed by Zoe Baird, President Bill Clinton's nominee for U.S. attorney general. Baird had also been the subject of a nanny scandal like mine and had been pressured by Republicans to withdraw her nomination.

Markle, according to their website, serves as a health-care and national security think tank for the public and private sectors.

In 2009, Markle gave a $249,000 grant to the Huffington Post Investigative Fund, while the Post and its founder, Arianna Huffington, were continually bashing Giuliani and me in the press.

Here are some other notable names of people who either sat on Markle's board or sat on committees in connection with the board, at the time of my pretrial hearings: Senator Tom Daschle, whom Modafferi had written about; Elizabeth Edwards, John Edwards's wife; Van Jones, the former Black Panther and one of President Obama's czars; and Henry Louis Gates, Jr., the Harvard professor and President Obama's friend whom I had criticized publicly in articles in regard to his arrest during an incident at his home in Boston.

John asked me if I knew that Senator Chuck Schumer of New York had nominated Robinson for his judgeship and for his earlier

position as U.S. attorney in Connecticut. Schumer had also nominated his former chief of staff, Preet Bharara, for U.S. attorney for the Southern District of New York. In that position, Bharara oversaw the prosecution of my case.

I told John I knew some of this, yes. "Well, check this out," he said.

On June 24, 2010, right after I arrived at Cumberland, Judge Robinson stepped down from his lifetime appointment as a federal judge to accept a million-dollar partnership at Skadden, Arps, Slate, Meagher & Flom, a prestigious Manhattan law firm with close Democratic Party ties. Less than twenty-four hours later, Senator Schumer nominated someone for a federal judgeship at the White Plains Courthouse, from where Robinson had just resigned.

At this point John just sat there staring at me with a silly look on his face.

"What is it?" I pressed him.

"Guess who Schumer nominated for the judgeship in White Plains?"

He let his question hang in the air before answering it. "Vincent Briccetti."

The name ricocheted around my head. This was the attorney whom Robinson had wanted me to hire as my independent counsel. Was it general political ill will, or were these men boosting their careers on my conviction? I don't know. But I was shocked. Robinson almost had to have been job hunting during my trial, but even worse, he must have known that Briccetti was looking for that judgeship as well, while he was publicly promoting him as one of the best attorneys in the country and urging me to hire him as my independent counsel.

Knowing what I know today, no one will ever convince me that Robinson's conduct leading to my plea and conviction was not premeditated judicial activism. For me the court transcripts speak for themselves. They captured his bias, arrogance, and questionable behavior, including his outrageous public relations campaign for Vincent Briccetti, who is today a U.S. federal judge in the Southern District of New York.

I have nothing against Briccetti. In fact, one of my attorneys told me that Briccetti was as confused as we were by all of this, which raises even more questions about Robinson's motives. In hindsight, looking back at the whole investigation, it stinks. It was a textbook example of prosecutors' caring more about their careers and a conviction than they did about the truth, the evidence, or criminal intent. Everything I was charged with—tax fraud; false statements— could have been handled ethically or civilly, without criminal charges. But that would not have helped their cause.

It's been more than four years since I walked out of that courtroom, and yet what my prosecution and conviction showed me pales in comparison to what I have learned since then about our criminal justice and prison systems.

Some might think, Yeah, but as a cop Kerik caught and fed defendants to prosecutors. He was part of this prison pipeline. Or that Giuliani himself, my mentor, was a prosecutor. Why didn't Kerik care about these issues back in the day? Was he concerned with prosecutorial overreach, fair trials, and overincarceration when he was a cop, or correction and police commissioner?

The truth is that before my trial and incarceration I didn't think these problems were common. I didn't think they were the norm. As a cop I tried to follow the letter of the law. As a drug agent and later a law enforcement executive, I was constantly told by

the prosecutors I worked with that you have to do things in good faith, that you can't violate the rules of ethics, that you've got to be aboveboard, even when it's detrimental to your case.

Times have changed. What I've come to learn is that these failings and misuses of the system are quickly becoming the norm; they're far too common. I'm embarrassed by what I've learned, and more embarrassed by what I never knew.

For starters, no one should ever be wrongfully deprived of the rights to liberty and freedom without just cause, yet in the past twenty-five years alone thousands of people have been wrongfully convicted and sentenced to tens of thousands of years in prison, or, in hundreds of cases, even death. The University of Michigan Law School and the Center on Wrongful Convictions at the Northwestern School of Law have created a unique national registry, a database, of exonerations, giving us a glimpse of how many wrongful convictions have occurred (their registry lists more than two thousand). Many more are still unaccounted for. How is this possible in the United States of America, shining democracy, land of the free?

We hold congressional hearings on athletes' using performance-enhancing drugs, on government agencies' spending too much money on conventions, and on U.S. Secret Service agents' partying in foreign countries, but where is the outrage, the congressional hearings, on a criminal justice system that is increasingly incarcerating citizens, condemning them to prison and stigmatization, and breaking our laws in the name of enforcing them? Where are the hearings to examine and investigate a prison system fraught with fraud, waste, abuse, and corruption, a system that demeans, demoralizes, and degrades those incarcerated?

For nearly two decades, constitutional scholars, judges, and

criminal defense bars have expressed their concerns about the flaws and failures in our criminal justice system. They've found that sentences are too long, punishments too severe, and the sentencing guidelines and mandatory minimums unjust and unwise.

Of course, I myself have put people in prison for ten, twenty, or thirty years or more. These were bad people, who did bad things. These were people from whom I seized tons of cocaine and millions in drug proceeds. These were people who tried to kill me and my partner, and I believed then as I do now that they deserved the sentences they received. However, I have met people in federal prison who are serving the same sentences, if not worse, for nonviolent drug offenses and white-collar crimes, many of them first-time offenders.

There are tens of thousands of nonviolent, first-time, white-collar offenders and drug offenders in prison today serving draconian sentences, individuals who could have been punished with alternatives to incarceration, such as fines and restitution, home confinement or house arrest, and community service. That would allow them to work, pay taxes, and take care of their families. Why aren't they made to give back to their communities? In Cumberland I was housed with doctors, lawyers, accountants, dentists, and politicians. A brilliant neurosurgeon from Baltimore convicted in a tax case, sentenced to ten months. A cardiologist from Washington, D.C., sentenced to eighteen months for Medicaid fraud. Why aren't they put to use, made to serve punishments that include community service, or teaching in our community colleges where students have greater needs?

There are innocent men and women rotting away in prison because they didn't have the money to pay for their defense or don't have the money to pay for an appeal. American citizens should

not lose their constitutional rights because they lack the money to pay for the services needed to exercise them. Most conservative Republicans consider themselves staunch constitutionalists, which I admire and respect. However, if my party, the Republican Party, is what it says it is, then it's time for its members to step up to the plate and seriously address criminal justice and prison reform in this country, to join with the Democrats across the aisle, as we have seen in the Senate Judiciary Committee's support for the Smarter Sentencing Act and the Justice Safety Valve Act—bipartisan support for doing the right thing.

Don't promote yourself as a country of constitutionality and compassion if you honestly believe that putting people in prison and treating them like animals is justified. Stop all the hype that we live in a free and democratic society. I used to ramble on about the same stuff. But now—are we really a country that believes in fairness and compassion? Are we really a country that treats people fairly?

I've met good men—yes, good men—in prison who made mistakes out of stupidity or ignorance, greed, or just bad judgment, but they did not need to be sent to prison to be punished: eighteen months for catching too many fish; two years for inflating income on a mortgage application; three months for selling a whale's tooth on eBay; fifteen years for a first-time nonviolent drug conspiracy in which no drugs were found or seized. There are thousands of people like these in our prisons today, costing American taxpayers billions of dollars when these individuals could be punished in smarter, alternative ways.

Our courts are overpunishing decent people who make mistakes, and our prisons have no rewards or incentives for good behavior. In this alone our criminal justice and prison systems contradict their own mission statements.

For thirty years, I believed the system was honest and fair, and in some ways I still do. But after experiencing firsthand, from the other side, its flaws, failures, and injustices, I tell you that it's not only wrong but dangerous for every American and the future of this country.

There is no greater threat to a free and democratic nation than a government that fails to protect its citizens' freedom and liberty as aggressively as it pursues justice.

I've seen and worked with some of the greatest people in the American criminal justice system, and unfortunately I've seen some of the worst. I also know that when the American people put their minds to doing something, nothing can stop them. It's that strength and determination that we need today to address a problem that over time could destroy our country.

PART III

Reform

18

From the Inside

If you think that a federal prison camp is some kind of resort, think again. There will be no need to bring your golf clubs or swim trunks, just plenty of hand sanitizer and a big wad of cash if you want to avoid catching a flesh-eating MRS disease and you want to remain in contact with the outside world via telephone or email. The place will invariably be a disgusting shithole.

I guess, for some, a cement-block cube with up to five other men, a space originally designed for two, would be considered a luxury accommodation. Maybe your idea of going on vacation is living out of a high school gym locker, being crammed into a space where only one man at a time can stand to get dressed, and eating meals out of a plastic bowl with plastic utensils. For myself and the men I met in Cumberland, the notion of "Club Fed" is a myth.

A phrase that was often repeated by the men was that "the punishment is being *sent* to prison." Meaning that every day of a sentence you're already being soundly punished, *just by being there*, being captive, which is the truth for any person who has experi-

enced incarceration. Do your time and go home? That would be one thing—but the reality is that every day and every night, inmates are subjected to many different forms of additional, gratuitous punishment.

Maybe an explanation is necessary to fill in the uninformed on the nature of the FPC, or federal prison camp. These places were designed as "honor" camps, meant to house first-time offenders, low-level, nonviolent men who broke the law and were sent away. Adult men. Men who presumably could obey the rules while they served their sentences and were not subject to many of the restrictions used in harsher penal settings. The FPCs were never designed to be penitentiaries. They were not meant to be the gulags they have become.

While inmates in these camps aren't chained to the wall and beaten, the noise, the filth, and the lack of basic amenities are collateral forms of punishment designed to break a man's spirit and institutionalize him. Being herded like cattle into the mess hall three times a day and then rushed through substandard meals. Having your cubicle torn apart by officers and all your worldly possessions, as meager as they may be, ripped out of your locker and strewn about the area. Washing with cold water because the water heater broke and wasn't replaced for months. Unnecessary additional punishments and degradation imposed on the inmate. For what purpose? Revenge?

There is a culture among certain correction staffs—imagine this across the country—where it is acceptable to inflict as much punishment on the inmates as the staff can get away with. Not physical punishment, but psychological. I witnessed a constant, ever-present reliance on a systematic form of psychological punishment. Day in and day out, men in prison are treated

like children and then expected to act like men. Humiliation and degradation are all too common. Inmates are verbally abused, harassed, and belittled by staff. They didn't really do it to me, but I watched them do it to others—our unit manager standing there telling an inmate he's "scum," holding his thumb and index finger an inch apart, saying to the inmate, "You're this big. This is all you are to me." This is the unit manager who sets an example for the other staff members.

COs who aren't confident in their jobs, who are often insecure, usually act this way, trying to assert that they're better than the inmates. In a prison or a jail like Rikers, for example, you couldn't embarrass and humiliate the prisoners as they did in Cumberland. Something bad would happen. When I was commissioner, I wouldn't allow it. No reasonable, thinking person involved in corrections would either.

But it's prison, right, and no one is supposed to like it. It's not supposed to be nice. I get it. I understand this thinking, which has informed the paradigm we've created systemwide, for the most part.

And, yes, the inmates have basketball and softball. But they are also subjected to humiliating strip searches, poor sanitary conditions, an unhealthy diet, and arbitrary and capricious administering of antiquated and draconian rules. There are people out there who say that inmates shouldn't have televisions, sports activities, or any other amenity. They have no idea how moronic that is. If you take away these small, basic things so that there is absolutely nothing for inmates to do, you just expedite the institutionalization of these men and women, diminish their social values even more, and really turn them into monsters before they return to society.

Any man who fits the criteria established by the Bureau of

Prisons for eligibility to serve his time in a prison camp should be at home instead, where his punishment for his crime does not have to preclude him from working, paying taxes, or taking care of his family—rather than being put in prison as a thirty-thousand-dollar-a-year drain on the American taxpayer. Men are frequently imprisoned in the federal system hundreds, if not thousands, of miles from their wives and children, often making visitation financially impossible. The bureau's mission statement stresses support from family as a goal for every inmate, and then the same bureau makes it difficult, if not impossible, for family to visit or even call or communicate on a regular basis due to distance and costs. The system is replete with this kind of hypocrisy and Americans are waking up to it. Time for action and reform. The "Land of the Free" incarcerates more of its citizens than any other civilized country in history. To what end?

According to published reports, the federal prison population has grown from 25,000 in 1980 to 216,016 as of March 20, 2014. This is an increase of more than 800 percent over the past thirty-four years. Considering that the U.S. Department of Justice and other federal law enforcement agencies have not come close to an 800 percent increase in enforcement and arrest activity, one has to ask, "What has caused the explosive growth?" I believe the primary answer stems from the elimination of the former federal parole system and the creation of the federal sentencing guidelines and mandatory minimums.

These guidelines and mandatory minimums are extremely detailed, complex, and difficult to understand. They have provided prosecutors unprecedented power over the last twenty years to influence sentencing outcomes and to enhance or prolong a defendant's sentence. The guidelines allow little to no room for non-

incarceration sanctions by the court and do nothing to encourage the use of alternative penalties.

In a speech before the American Bar Association (ABA) in 2003, Supreme Court Justice Anthony M. Kennedy expressed his concerns about the inadequacies and injustices of our correction systems. He called for (1) the federal sentencing guidelines to be revised downward, and (2) a repeal of the mandatory minimums, most of which he felt were "unwise and unjust." He stressed that punishments were too severe and sentences too long. Justice Kennedy has been joined by a growing chorus from all sides of the political and ideological spectrum. U.S. Attorney General Eric Holder, as well as former attorneys general Edwin Meese III, who served under President Ronald Reagan, and Richard Thornburgh, a Republican who served under two presidents, have expressed similar concerns, particularly with regard to sentencing guidelines and mandatory minimums. Many other voices have sounded their support.

Inaction is no longer an option.

My fear is that the lack of attention to the national crisis in our criminal justice system will continue, powered by that old adage "out of sight, out of mind." Our legislators and the American public won't care about a problem if they don't know or believe that it exists. Unless they see it for themselves—either personally or through eye-opening testimony by those who have—they will not act. Based on what I have seen and learned in the federal prison system and on the other side of the bars, inaction is no longer an option.

The U.S. Federal Bureau of Prisons currently has 216,016 prisoners in custody, and according to public records, this is about 35 percent over the rated capacity, meaning that the BOP is housing 35 percent more inmates than there is room for. They manage to do this by double- and triple-bunking inmates in high-, medium-,

and low-security facilities. Overcrowding in any jail or prison environment creates frustration, friction, and confrontation. The possibility of violence against inmates and/or staff increases greatly. To reduce this possibility, prisoners must have access to programs that will keep them occupied and help in reducing recidivism, and "good time" incentives that will encourage them to comply with institutional rules. In addition, prison administrations must do what they can to reduce the overcrowding, as we saw California and Texas do recently.

Currently, there are about twenty-three thousand men being housed in federal minimum-security camps, the lowest classification of housing within the BOP. In Cumberland, there were approximately three hundred inmates who had been convicted of nonviolent drug or white-collar offenses. They posed no threat to society or the community, and they were not escape risks, obviously, or they wouldn't have been there. The housing in a camp consists of dormitory-style units similar to what you'd find on a military base or college campus. There's minimal staffing. There are no fences around most camps, no locks on the doors, and in many ways, I was more restricted during the six months I spent on home confinement before surrendering at Cumberland than I was in the camp. About 85 percent of the prisoners at Cumberland while I was there had been convicted of nonviolent drug offenses. About 20 percent of these were first-time offenders. About 15 percent of the camp's population was white-collar—most of them first-time offenders as well.

When I first got to Cumberland, I encountered a forty-four-year-old black man who suffered from mental illness, was partially blind, and had about a third-grade reading level. He had absolutely no business being there. He belonged in a hospital or treatment center, not a prison. He'd been found mentally incompetent to

———

stand trial by state authorities two or three times, so they turned him over to federal prosecutors who ignored the state's findings and charged him with possession with the intent to distribute crack cocaine. His attorney urged him to accept a plea agreement of 128 months in prison. He signed a plea that he could not read or understand to serve ten years and eight months in federal prison.

After nine years in prison, he was on the verge of being released. During his final month, I watched him pace and wander aimlessly around the compound like an animal in a cage. When I approached and asked him what the matter was, instead of expressing any excitement about leaving prison after nine years, he said he was afraid of getting lost outside. He had to take two buses and this was troubling him.

There was also a twenty-four-year-old gay white inmate at Cumberland who, in 2005, pled guilty in federal court to manufacturing methamphetamine. He was sentenced to forty months, given four years' probation, and ordered to attend a residential drug treatment program. After attending the program and serving twenty-four months, he was released. He found a job, was successfully employed, and was attending evening college classes, he told me. Two years later, he relapsed, began using cocaine, and checked himself into a treatment center to get help. When his probation officer learned of his whereabouts, the young man was sent back to federal prison for thirty-six more months because he'd failed a urine test, a violation of his probation.

He needed treatment—not three more years in prison.

For close to sixteen months, until the day he left Cumberland, I watched this young man sit on his bed, stare into space, and slowly deteriorate. He received none of the therapeutic help he needed. He was dying with his eyes open.

———

My reactions to what I experienced within the federal system were certainly influenced by the fact that I'd worked so hard on Rikers Island to institute and enforce the laws and standards that we were required to. So I was doubly stunned to see at Cumberland how the most basic principles and standards were ignored. There was little to no supervision and no one really cared about the inmates under their control.

In municipal, county, and state correctional systems around the country, the staff is supposed to focus on care, custody, and control. The three Cs. In the federal system, from my "bird's-eye" view, it was custody, some control, and absolutely no care at all.

As for the law-and-order and tough-on-crime advocates who are skeptical of reform, I suggest that they are probably under the same assumption I was until I experienced prison from the inside: that the system makes every effort to rehabilitate the incarcerated. But it does not. For decades now we have been spending billions to simply warehouse inmates. The effort at rehabilitation is nugatory at best.

Many tough-on-crime holdouts are still clinging to worse assumptions than that—including the insidious old notion that "nothing works," which has helped fuel the retributive character of our penal system over the past forty years. Nothing works, so why should we try? Most of these criminals are beyond help, immune to redemption or rehabilitation, this philosophy contends. And still worse is the thinking that criminals don't deserve any help or goodness to begin with, so let them rot and give them nothing. It's the same mentality I encountered when I took over Rikers Island.

The decency, even humanity, of the men and women who go to prison is too often dismissed or overlooked by prosecutors, legislators, and the public.

I think of Blackjack, a muscular black man with gold teeth. I saw him first through the clear window of an office in our wing at Cumberland as he spoke to Courtney, our counselor. I could see that he was pointing at me. Suddenly this tank comes barreling through the door right toward me.

"Yo, Commish, you my man! That's my man!" he shouted.

He had just told Courtney that I looked a lot like the New York City police commissioner, and once Courtney confirmed it was me, Blackjack flew out the door, strode up, and shook my hand.

"We may be on opposite sides of the fence but I've got mad respect for you," he told me. "The way you took care of the city at nine-eleven. My brother worked for you. My sister worked for you."

"How did they work for me?" I asked him.

"They cops. Both of 'em. You took care of the city. You da man!"

"What are you in for, drugs?" I asked him.

"Yo, I ain't no fucking drug dealer." He was insulted. "I'm a credit card man."

If you saw Blackjack you might think, There's a stone-cold thug. And he had the look. When I was a cop, if I had seen him on the street, he'd definitely have been on my radar. He was in Cumberland for about nine months before he got transferred. In that time he had at least three fights, I think. Blackjack didn't give a fuck. He said what he thought, and he'd curse even the COs to their faces if they disrespected him.

But he obviously liked me, always telling whoever was around us when I saw him on the compound, "Yo, don't fuck with the commish! That's my man!"

Blackjack's thanks and loyalty were real, to the point that I was convinced that if anybody *did* say anything negative about me, or

mess with me, he would've punched their fucking lights out. There was a respectful side to him even. I could see it through these interactions. If there were things inside the system that could home in on those qualities and potentialities, the good traits, they could bring them out in men like Blackjack. Now consider the younger men who come into the system and are left there for years. Blackjack becomes their mentor. That's who "rehabilitates" them. Is that what we want as a society, a community? I think not.

I'm not saying that Blackjack himself could have been rehabilitated for sure. But there are tens of thousands of guys like him in prison whom you might reach with the right approach. It is the system's mission and purpose to at least try.

· · ·

To give you a better understanding of my firsthand observations, consider this: Over the past few decades, the system has been overloaded with nonviolent drug offenders serving more than ten years in medium- and low-security facilities. Roughly half of the current 216,016 prisoners in the federal system are in for drug offenses. These offenders eventually drop below their "out" dates and get moved to a minimum-security camp like Cumberland.

The only way to describe the daily environment in these camps is that it compares to a junior high school, but without classes and girls. Grown men sit around like teenage boys talking about old times, drugs, guns, cars, jewelry, women, and sports. Because they have limited contact with the outside world, the prison becomes their home, and the other prisoners their family.

Then you have young, nonviolent, low-level drug offenders who are sentenced to five to ten years and wind up here in the same camp with the older prisoners who are serving out the final years of their

sentences. This is a terrible circumstance for these younger men. Some of them have graduated from high school, a few attended college, but many are uneducated, some completely illiterate (once a guy sitting behind me in the computer room in our wing, trying to bang out an email, asked me how to spell *hurt* and *support*).

However, once they arrive here and mix into their new surroundings and the fear of prison dissipates, they begin their "new education" with the older, institutionalized inmates as their teachers. They learn how to lie, cheat, steal, con, manipulate, and gamble. Their vocabulary diminishes. They swagger more. Many of them seem to have no respect for the privacy of others. A normal conversation consists of yelling and hollering, and minor disagreements often result in threats of violence. Here they learn more about the drug trade than they did on the outside, and they make all the contacts they need to further themselves in criminal activity once back on the street.

Over time, their surroundings begin to demoralize and demean them, and they lose respect, discipline, and responsibility.

At Cumberland, George Butler, known as "Dosey," held court daily, joking and bullshitting the days away as if he were straight out of an Eddie Murphy movie, or sitting around a barbershop (in fact, Dosey was one of Cumberland's barbers) exchanging stories about old times, girls, drugs, violence, and neighborhood news out of D.C. and Baltimore, where many of the inmates at Cumberland were from. Newcomers would bring the latest gossip from the hood: who'd been arrested, how much time they got, where they were sent, who'd been shot, who didn't survive the streets. Dosey seemed like a caricature of himself and he cracked me up. But it's sad to think that no one seems to care about the violence and devastation in their communities.

———

Given the line of work I've been in my whole life, I've never been one to defend drug dealers or criminals of any caliber. But after witnessing the reality of federal prison, I'm concerned about the future of our country, particularly in the minority communities, which are only growing larger.

As difficult as it is for me to say these words, I have to admit that the U.S. criminal justice system will be substantially responsible for the destruction of inner-city kids, black males primarily, if things don't change.

There are a number of factors that bring me to this conclusion—parenting and parental guidance, education and our schools, role models and music, and when all these fail to produce a good child and that kid winds up in trouble with the law, it diminishes his chances by 50 percent. If the kid is caught up in the federal system, I'd say the chances of rehabilitation are closer to zero. The sentencing guidelines in the federal system are so outrageous and ridiculous that no one is benefiting from the amounts of time given to federal criminals, unless they're violent and the purpose of the long sentence is to keep them off the street.

To take a twenty-year-old kid out of D.C. and sentence him to ten years for possessing, distributing, or conspiracy involving drugs is pretty much a death sentence for that kid. With each year he spends inside he deteriorates, and after ten years there is most likely no return. If a young man comes into the system uneducated and does more than five years, he'll leave worse than when he came in. Ten years: far worse and nearly institutionalized. Fifteen and above: Unless there is some miracle reason he should be released, the justice system might as well keep him in for life, because he'll have no real job prospects when he gets out, poor communication skills, and the stigma of being branded "a convicted felon." And

when he fails on the street and gets arrested again, they're going to throw away the key anyway.

One young man who worked in Cumberland's kitchen with me asked me one day, "Hey, why do you call everybody 'sir'?"

"Why not?"

"I'm younger than you," he replied, "and this isn't the army."

I explained to him that it was respect and courtesy and I pretty much call everyone "sir" if I don't know his name.

"Fuck that" was his response.

So much for that, I thought.

Keep in mind that I'm talking mostly about nonviolent drug offenders, many of whose families and communities have already failed them. Many of them are first-time offenders who, with the right guidance, education, and programs, or a mandated military-style boot camp, could leave prison better than when they arrived.

When I was New York City correction commissioner, I ran such a military-style boot camp, or "shock program," on Rikers Island for nonviolent drug offenders who were sentenced to up to one year in jail on state charges. The inmates had to volunteer for the program. Completion of it resulted in a six-month reduction off their one-year sentence. For them, that was the incentive. The tough part was the discipline and determination needed to actually complete the program, which was run by New York City correction officers who were former military boot camp and basic training instructors.

These boot camp inmates were under strict supervision from sunup to sundown. They were taught military drills, respect, honor, patriotism, discipline, parenting skills, and social survival skills, and were given drug-abuse counseling. It was mentally chal-

lenging and physically grueling, but they were highly motivated to get into the program and to complete it so they could get out of jail sooner. The recidivism rates for the boot camp graduates were the lowest in the system. Many men in the federal system today would participate in this type of program or equivalent educational or vocational programs, if they were available and there were incentives to do so. There is neither.

The younger the inmates are and the longer they're imprisoned, the less chance they will have for any type of successful integration back into society.

Unlike their families and community, our criminal justice system must not provide them an option of failure. If we do not shorten their sentences, make their stay more valuable, and get them out of the system faster, smarter, and with a goal to improve themselves, we may as well sentence them to life in prison or death, because that is ultimately what we are doing.

For the nondrug, white-collar offender, the system demeans and demoralizes them as well, but the financial cost to society is greater. Most of these white-collar inmates have led productive and successful lives and have never been in trouble with the law until their cases and convictions. They do not need to be sentenced to years in prison to be punished. Don't misunderstand me: Offenders and lawbreakers do need to be punished, but the punishment should fit the crime, and the punishment should have thought to it.

Many of the men with me in Cumberland struck me as decent people who made a mistake. They did not rob, rape, murder, or commit a violent crime, yet they are also demeaned and demoralized, and financially badly damaged. This often leads to depression, serious health issues, enormous cynicism, and for some, permanent psychological damage. The collateral fallout for their families

is far-reaching. For almost every man in prison, the impact on the next generation is grave.

It's heartbreaking to confront this truth: A father's chances of helping, teaching, guiding, and mentoring his children while incarcerated are close to none. For every day they are separated, the bond between father and child diminishes, and they grow further apart. The system encourages men to communicate with their children and families, but then prevents them from doing so in a number of ways. Phone calls and emails are limited and are far more costly than on the outside. An inmate makes less than twenty cents per hour working within the prison system, but is charged twenty-three cents a minute for phone calls and five cents per minute for emails. Oftentimes, distance and the cost of travel make visits infrequent or preclude them altogether.

No matter where you came from, or what you've been incarcerated for, or how long your sentence, the separation between a parent and his or her kids creates pain and anxiety for both. You cannot teach and mentor a child in absentia. Attempts to discipline your child during a visit or from long distance—by phone or email—can easily create extra friction, added anxiety, and anger. They say that justice is blind. No one comes to understand that better than the children of the incarcerated. If they are too young to realize it today, I promise that over time it is something they will learn and never forget.

Think of it this way: A young man, thirty-one years old, arrested for a first-time, nonviolent drug offense, is sentenced to nine years in federal prison. He has an eleven-year-old son whose *collateral sentence* is that by the time that boy turns twenty, he will have spent nearly half of his lifetime without his father. At perhaps the most critical time in that child's life, when he will need his

father most, he will be without him. If there were alternatives to incarceration, if there were alternative penalties, if there were boot camps, or something other than our reliance on mandated incarceration and draconian sentences, perhaps both father and son could be saved. Instead, with the mandatory minimums and sentencing guidelines, the odds are extremely high that the son will one day replace the father in the living hell of prison.

For mothers or fathers who love, adore, and cherish their children, a day in prison is like a week, a week like a month, a month like a year. Time virtually stands still, while the lives of their children pass them by. For the most part, inmates can only hope and pray that their families have the mental, emotional, physical, and financial wherewithal to make up for their absence. I thank God every day for my wife, Hala, and the love and care she gave our daughters while I was in prison for more than three years.

But what happens to the children who aren't that lucky? This is some of the worst punishment doled out far too easily by a system that in the main is devoid of compassion. And this punishment is ultimately inflicted upon society.

Again, don't misunderstand: I am not saying that lawbreakers should not be punished or go to prison. Some should, but not, in many cases, for the length of time that they are. Their sentences contradict our Founding Fathers' real goals of justice. If there were alternatives, children and families would not have to pay such a high price.

During all the years I spent in the correctional field, I never focused on the collateral damage to the offenders, their families, and, more so, to our society and country. My lack of awareness and recognition was not unique. No, unfortunately, what is clear to me now is that my ignorance was in fact *representative* of the lack

———

of awareness, care, or insight in many of those still active in positions of power and authority in our criminal justice system.

My principal focus was the care, custody, and control of the inmate population, and ensuring that the prisoners received the programs and services they were supposed to receive according to state and federal minimum standards. When I thought of incarceration costs, my only concern was the incarceration cost to house a prisoner within our system. What I never thought about until I lived in prison as an inmate was the collateral economic cost of incarceration to the American taxpayer and to our economy as a whole. The more I've studied this, the more I've been shocked by the reality.

According to recent figures from the government, the average cost to incarcerate a federal prisoner is $28,284.00 annually. A person would naturally assume that an offender sentenced to three years in federal prison would cost the government and the American taxpayers $84,852.00. Wrong! That cost is only to *incarcerate* the prisoner. The collateral economic costs of his three-year incarceration far outweigh the government's out-of-pocket expense, and here's why: If that prisoner earned $100,000 a year before his arrest and incarceration, the government loses the tax income on that, and the economy loses his cost-of-living spending

That is a loss of $300,000 to the economy—$100,000 over three years—plus the nearly $85,000 for his incarceration. Then add in the cost of the investigation that led to his conviction, and the total is now close to half a million. As a result of their imprisonment, many of these men have to file for bankruptcy. Their families are forced to depend on welfare or public assistance. Those are additional, huge losses to the American taxpayer and our economy.

Criminal defendants are often ordered to pay restitution upon their release from prison, but it will be extremely difficult for them to do so. Most of them are left destitute as a result of the prosecution against them and their imprisonment, and their earning capabilities once released will be reduced significantly. Ordering restitution in most cases amounts to nothing more than added symbolic punishment, because once a defendant has been so severely socially and financially incapacitated, where is the restitution money going to come from? This is another enormous financial loss for our economy, not to mention for crime victims who will never recoup their losses.

One of the white-collar prisoners I served time with was a guy who had a very small company that employed five people, including himself. The basic loss to the American taxpayer and our economy for his three-year imprisonment will run in excess of $2 million in direct and indirect costs, not including unemployment benefits for those who lost their jobs when his company closed. So, instead of this man's incarceration costing the economy and American taxpayers an estimated $28,000 per year, it will ultimately cost us about $660,000. Had he been placed on probation and fined and penalized substantially, he would have been punished, justice would have been served, and there would be no loss to the government.

This is only one man. There are thousands within the system with similar crimes and circumstances.

If you say, *Well, guys like that, these white-collar criminals, are scammers and cheats*, then all the more reason for society to get something back from them. Instead, we are paying for their incarceration and losing their contribution to the economy.

They should be given a choice, as with a traffic summons: Pay

up, or go to prison. With drug offenders, especially nonviolent first-timers: Go into a program, learn, work, or else prison.

We're dumbing down society, breaking our own bank, and destroying families and future generations unnecessarily, especially in the federal system. And as long as the federal government keeps paying for it, with taxpayer money, the Justice Department and Bureau of Prisons will continue to warehouse human beings unnecessarily.

19

Return

I couldn't sleep at all my first couple of nights at home. I'd get up and go into my daughters' rooms. Watching them sleeping, thinking about the time I'd lost with them, I'd break down.

I went downstairs one of those first nights to get coffee and I didn't know where the coffee was. I couldn't operate the coffee machine. You come back to your house but your house isn't the same. Your children aren't quite the same either. Your wife is a very different woman, more independent, distant. She's learned to live without you. It diminishes the bonds you may have once had. Nothing is like it was before you left.

These are things you have to deal with psychologically and emotionally when you come home from prison. There's no way around it. And that's if you're a lucky one.

In my office at home I used to always have the TV turned on to the news. But for the first six months I was home I couldn't watch it. The news drove me nuts. It infuriated me. When I tried to watch it, I'd feel the sting of bitterness about what happened

to me. Where is the people's benefit? How has society gained as a result of my incarceration? People may attack me on this and say Kerik's just complaining, but I do believe that a fair, objective look reveals my case and prosecution to have been selective and political.

I don't feel that it was justice. This is just my story. But my story is similar to a million others every year. Guys coming home from prison with a chip on their shoulder. Think about that. Think about all the convicts returning to society like me, feeling this way, with a bitterness burning inside. And the vast majority are not returning to society as I did, to an intact family and a nice house to live in, these privileges that I don't take for granted.

Prison didn't change my patriotism. I love this country. I love the flag.

The first time my son, Joe, ever introduced me at a public event—a dinner for my legal defense fund—he said, "I don't know anybody who's more of a patriot than my dad."

This surprised me. It was one of those things you don't think your kid has really tuned in to or noticed much. I didn't know Joe saw me like that.

But when I see that Budweiser commercial of men and women coming home from Iraq and walking into an airport, and people start clapping for these troops, I see that and it moves me. Patriotic things are extremely emotional for me. Of course 9/11 was a turning point in my life in this regard.

My patriotism is separate from my critique of the system and push for reform. I still believe we have the best country and constitution in the world. But a lot of guys coming back from prison are not like me; they don't think this way. In fact, they hate the government. They're far worse than when they went in. They're

bitter, dismissive of any establishment or authority. Every year there are tens of thousands of individuals added to this group in our society.

. . .

It's been difficult writing this book, having to go back through the experience and relive it. It brings up pain and anger. But this book also drives me. My determination to bring about positive changes in the criminal justice system drives me. What helps me move forward is the thought that this isn't about me anymore, about me and my case. What's done is done. I can't do it over. I can't fight that battle again. I don't look back anymore on my prison time as wasted years. I can't. Instead I think about the reality of a system that has gotten completely lost. My friend Sylvester Stallone wrote me a letter before I surrendered at Cumberland, at the end of which he wrote, "What you did is so minor compared to the sentence . . . and the fury that must be boiling inside of you would be hard to imagine, but don't let it scorch your soul. Instead, use it for fuel to arrive at your next destination."

And I get more fuel from my kids. They are so much of the energy behind me. I have to provide for them. I want to take care of them as much as possible before I leave this earth. I want to set an example for them that you can never quit, never give up. I've had many personal, professional, and political critics. I've been beaten down, but I'm not done. I'm not dead.

It's been amazing to me watching Celine and Angelina, now fourteen and twelve, sit through all the political BS about me. Your kids know who you are and what you are. They can see what's being said about you in the news and read it online, but they know who you really are better than anyone.

Celine and Angelina understand my experience to an extent, but really it's too depressing and complicated to explain fully to a child. And I don't want them to think I'm simply bashing the government. They've been with me at many of the interviews I've done since my release. They understand what I'm talking about when I highlight the collateral damage overincarceration inflicts on kids and families. They felt it.

I recently did a thirty-minute interview with Marvin Scott for WPIX, a local New York City TV station. Angelina sat in the control room and, according to one of Marvin's assistants, she was glued to the monitor the entire time. When it was over, Angelina came over and gave me a high-five and a hug.

"Dad, that was one of the best interviews you've done. You covered everything." She heard me touch on many of the most pressing matters: overincarceration; a loosening of the mandatory minimum sentences and the federal sentencing guidelines; alternatives to incarceration; rehabilitative efforts in prison.

At twelve years old, she gets it. Why don't our legislators and those responsible for changing the system?

· · ·

One of the highlights in my push for reform since I've been back was the panel presentation on criminal justice that I participated in—along with Texas governor Rick Perry and Grover Norquist—at CPAC, the annual Conservative Political Action Conference, in March 2014. This talk was one of the most important events I've done, because of the wide coverage it attracts; our collective conservative message of reform and alternative thinking in criminal justice; and the bipartisan movement we are seeing on the issue where in the past there was partisan division. (Another reason I can't

watch much news these days: political polarization. It's really killing us. It's the Republicans. It's the Democrats. Hillary Clinton recently did well to call out this issue in no uncertain terms, saying that our partisanship is killing the political arena and hurting society.)

Governor Perry has made some real positive criminal justice and penal changes in Texas—ironically enough, the law-and-order capital of the United States. He has proven you can, one step at a time, create sentencing alternatives and close prisons. You can implement reforms, even in places you might think would be unmovable on the issue. If Texas can do this . . .

I found Perry cordial and personable. After our panel discussion, I sat next to him at a table where he was chatting with an elderly black woman from Cleveland. He knew her or her family from somewhere. He seemed charming with her. I thought of how Perry often takes a clubbing in the press. I thought of how the media rarely portrayed me as having a sense of humor, let alone a heart. (And now, in a widely criticized case, Perry finds himself the target of one of the most blatantly selective and politicized indictments I've ever seen.)

But we got our message out.

Even Charles Pierce at *Esquire*, in a piece subtly titled "The Crooks at CPAC," wrote, "To be completely fair, it was the most interesting panel of the weekend so far. . . ." And "[Kerik], at least, is somebody who has learned something from his own past."

Another excellent opportunity to share my insights and recommendations on criminal justice was my presentation to the Government Accountability Office in Washington, D.C., in early 2014. They seemed dumbfounded by my description of our simple yet highly effective TEAMS meetings that helped spur the historic turnaround in New York City's jails.

And still, as I regain my footing and keep after my goal, I feel people's judgments, because I'm an ex-convict now, and much of society still believes that anyone convicted of a crime deserves the maximum punishment, and that the punishment is somehow never enough, that you still haven't paid.

Many people look at you differently, with doubt in their eyes. My fall was very public. I go to restaurants and see people pointing, whispering. Former business associates of mine, who used to constantly hound me for recommendations and meetings, will not even return my phone calls now.

The old saying goes, A conservative is a liberal who's been mugged, and a liberal is a conservative who's been indicted. There's truth in this. But the best insight comes from being able to see things from both perspectives. Fortunately and unfortunately, no one else in our country's history has both had the experience and success in criminal justice and jail and prison management and also spent years in federal prison, as I have. I aim to use my insight to spur reform.

20

A New Direction

Throughout my career I've been gathering, learning, and applying new knowledge. As a correction officer before becoming warden of the Passaic County Jail, I learned the dangers of jails and prisons, both for the staff and the inmates. I'd been a cop before that, but it still opened my eyes. We had every classification of inmate, so I got to see some of the worst. I saw how dangerous it could be for the COs, who secure our country's jails and prisons, and who have earned my respect and admiration.

When I reflect back on my time as a narcotics detective and in the DEA, what comes to mind is violence. In the cases I oversaw there was an enormous amount of violence—homicides, torture. I wrote about this in *The Lost Son*. Bodies were turning up; people were being executed. The brutality was overwhelming. Those years gave me insight into addiction and the damage it does to individuals and their families.

Before dealing with big-time players like the Cali cartel, I did undercover buys in Harlem and Washington Heights. The guys

who sold to me were often really messed up. You'd see it in their faces, plain as day. Some were stone junkies. Now I ask myself, "Was prison good for them?" These low-level dealers selling nickel and dime bags didn't need prison. They needed treatment. They needed to go somewhere for their addiction.

So I'm a proponent of drug courts and diversion programs that offer drug offenders alternatives to incarceration and a felony conviction, such as we've seen a number of states adopt.

But I don't support drug decriminalization. I can't support an action that could increase the possibility that someone becomes addicted to a drug. Maybe some of this comes from my own personal experience, dealing with alcoholism in my family, seeing how it affected the lives of my biological mother, my father, one of my sisters, and the rest of us collaterally. I know firsthand what addiction can do to individuals, families, and society as a whole, when you're incapable of working, incapable of taking care of your children. We should not do anything that creates a greater chance for Americans to be more addicted, and decriminalization, in my mind, heads in that direction.

Running Rikers, I learned the value of accountability, mutual respect among authorities and inmates, and not allowing criminality a place in prison. Then my own trial and conviction gave me an intimate look at disproportionate prosecutorial power, the injustice of the plea bargain system, and the politicization and selectivity of federal cases.

It has been a long road for this country, and for me, in terms of our evolution on matters of criminal justice. But there are positive signs that we may be at a moment in time when we learn from our rough past and create a smarter, more humane, more progressive, more fiscally sound criminal justice system.

It's no secret that I'm not a supporter of President Obama, but I'll be the first one to give him and Attorney General Eric Holder credit for having the courage to take on criminal justice reform, when so many before them didn't have the balls.

In 2013, as part of his "Smart on Crime" initiative, Holder publicly urged Congress to reduce mandatory minimum sentences. (Two years before this, about a year into my sentence, I wrote a white paper, titled "U.S. Criminal Justice System in Dire Need of Repair," which went to members of Congress, the U.S. Sentencing Commission, and Attorney General Holder.)

The reaction to this positive step was telling, though. In response to Holder's initiative, the National Association of Assistant United States Attorneys—federal prosecutors—sent the attorney general a letter. In it they wrote, "[W]e do not join with those who regard our federal system of justice as 'broken' or in need of major reconstruction." An incredible statement in itself.

They went on to tell Holder that they consider the current federal mandatory-minimum-sentencing framework to be "well-constructed and well worth preserving." They protested that mandatory minimums are used only for the most serious crimes. If this were true, I'd have no disagreement with their stance. But federal prosecutors have been too fond of hitting nonviolent, low-level drug offenders with conspiracy counts carrying substantial mandatory sentences.

I lived with these men in Cumberland. Sentencing people to life in prison for nonviolent offenses based on the current draconian guidelines? These practices should be illegal.

What might have stood out most to me in this letter by U.S. assistant attorneys was their assertion that mandatory minimums "are a critical tool in persuading defendants to cooperate," in particular for dismantling gangs and drug operations.

———

If the minimums and the sentencing guidelines were used in just this way, I again would have no objection. But far too often the minimums are used to coerce low-level offenders into accepting plea deals that screw them. Threatening a first-time drug offender with twenty-five years to life so that you can get him to accept the negotiated plea of ten to fifteen years is wrong.

Very often our judicial process comes down to the power of the United States attorney. In their letter to Holder they wrote, "We are exceedingly mindful of the force of that authority and the ethical imperative to steer clear of its abuse in the performance of our official responsibilities." This sounds right in theory, but the practice is something else.

Criminal justice experts from the American Bar Association, the Cato Institute, the National Association of Criminal Defense Lawyers, the ACLU, the Federalist Society, and the Heritage Foundation, among others, have raised serious concerns about overcriminalization by federal prosecutors who are increasingly investigating and criminally prosecuting people for what was once civil, administrative, or regulatory conduct. Have you ever thought that inflating your income on a credit card application or a loan application for a home, car, or college tuition is bank fraud and could land you in federal prison? What about a government employee who falsifies his time sheets or attendance records or uses government property, such as a cell phone or computer, for personal use: Does he deserve prison? Or a banker or corporate executive who buys a client or vendor a generous birthday or Christmas gift? A few years ago, the Justice Department proposed that putting a false name, date of birth, or photo on Facebook could become a felony and conceivably land you in prison.

The reality is that the U.S. attorneys' practice does not match

———

their expressed mindfulness. We continue to see far too many instances of prosecutorial misconduct and Brady violations around the country. And, as I said previously, as long as U.S. prosecutors are not held accountable, as long as they are immune from punishment or rarely if ever punished for misconduct (the notorious Michael Morton case in Texas is a rare example), as long as their performance evaluations are tied to their conviction rates, we cannot leave the system up to their discretion and allow the checks and balances to be weighted in their favor.

In terms of loosening the federal sentencing guidelines, I not only believe that this must be done, but believe that it should be made retroactive. Those inmates sentenced under former mandatory minimums could have their sentences reduced. This would in turn reduce our prison population, thus reducing the money we spend on it. Such retroactive reform was part of both the Fair Sentencing Act and the Smarter Sentencing Act, which have been significant steps in the growing bipartisan movement for progress and change that we've seen over the past few years.

Many states have moved in this direction. According to a Vera Institute of Justice report released in February 2014, twenty-nine states have taken steps to roll back mandatory sentences. States are doing this mostly for economic reasons, and this is important. They do not seem as concerned with the moral reasons, and this must be considered. Why have we evolved into a society that believes the more severe the punishment the better? Why are we willfully turning men and women into monsters and animals by institutionalizing them? People tend not to think of the collateral damage of all this.

Let me say again clearly: Prison serves a purpose, and some people belong in prison, some even for long periods of time—and

even they can still be treated with a measure of humanity while they're in prison. But many of the individuals convicted of breaking the law can be punished with alternatives to incarceration—fines, home detention, probation, community service. People who, for example, catch too many fish, or sell a whale's tooth on eBay, or exaggerate their income on a mortgage application can be punished without prison.

People who need treatment for drug or mental health problems do not belong in prison. They belong in treatment centers. First-time nonviolent and low-level drug offenders should not be treated as hardened criminals and given sentences of ten, twenty, or thirty years to life.

We should also consider programs where first-time nonviolent felony drug offenders enter a guilty plea for their crime but receive a deferred sentence if they complete either a long-term residential drug treatment program or a military-style boot camp. Successful completion could result in the dismissal of charges, thus avoiding a felony conviction and a criminal record, thereby giving these offenders a second chance.

We should consider adopting Virginia's risk-assessment program, which offers shorter sentences and diversionary programs to offenders deemed not likely to repeat crimes.

For those who have paid their debt to society, we must return their civil and constitutional rights and remove their conviction from the record. We need to empower ex-convicts again as U.S. citizens and support them in putting their lives back together. Punishment should not last a lifetime, which is exactly what the label "convicted felon" does.

My conversations with the inmates I lived with in Cumberland, many of whom realized they'd made a mistake and would've given

anything to turn their lives around, revealed that they see the label of *convicted felon* as something that will prevent them from attaining any type of success in the future. Based on what they learn from the older prisoners in the system, the younger men see that label as a till-death sentence.

Hopelessness and despair begin on the day of sentencing when you stand before the court and are reminded that you are no longer an empowered citizen of the United States of America. You are told that your conviction will deprive you of valuable civil rights, such as the right to vote, the right to sit on a jury, the right to bear a firearm, and the right to hold public office. Your conviction could prevent you from holding certain licenses, such as law, real estate, and barber.

In a free and democratic society such as ours, justice should not eternally abrogate one's rights to freedom and liberty, except in the most extreme cases. But day in and day out, this is what it does. In the federal criminal justice system, the only way to expunge that criminal conviction and lifetime label of *convicted felon* is by presidential pardon.

Imagine this: A twenty-year-old United States Marine sniper sold a pair of night-vision goggles on eBay to an international exporter who did not have the appropriate U.S. government export permit. The marine was charged and pled guilty to selling the goggles for export—a felony. As a result of his conviction, he lost his job and his home, and his life and new marriage were completely turned upside down. The federal prosecutor insisted on prison time, so the young man was sentenced to thirty-six months. Now on top of that he will carry the stigma and limitations of being a convicted felon until the day he dies.

This young U.S. Marine, who had barely begun his adult life

and whose only real job was fighting for and defending the very freedoms and liberties that he has lost forever, is now destitute. Unless he is pardoned by the president of the United States, his punishment will last forever. Is that what our Founding Fathers had in mind when they wrote the U.S. Constitution and the laws of our land? I don't think so.

．　．　．

Recent news reports have suggested that law graduates are having difficulties finding employment. I know exactly where they could be quite useful if Congress and the American Bar Association would create a legal assistance program for the inmates who need help the most. Today we have thousands of unemployed former military officers and trainers who could be used as instructors for inmates. You could fund these programs with the cost savings attributed to reductions in prison time and through private investments.

To reduce recidivism, you must reduce the length of time these young men and women spend in our prisons as they currently exist, and make sure that while they're incarcerated they get the education and life improvement skills they need to re-enter society. We have to try to reach lawbreakers, to engage them. Today that is not happening.

So in addition to offering more alternatives to prison and reducing sentences, we need to implement more substantial sentence-reduction initiatives for inmates. These incentive opportunities encourage positive inmate behavior and can substantially reduce the number of inmates within the system by getting them back to society faster. There are several congressional bills sitting in the halls of Congress that would accomplish both.

One such bill or amendment calls for a retroactive enhance-

ment of a federal prisoner's "good time" credit, from 54 days per year to 128 days per year. Instituting this change would create substantial incentives for inmates to comply with institutional rules, which would in turn reduce staff confrontations and inmate-on-inmate violence within the system.

The enhancement of federal good-time credit, which would make it comparable to sentence-reduction incentives in many state prison systems, would also reduce the numbers of inmates. At a time when Congress is desperately searching for ways to cut government spending, good-time credit could reduce the BOP's annual budget by close to $1 billion. Portions of those cost savings could be put back into education and vocational training for inmates and basic BOP staff training.

Most of the New York, Baltimore, and D.C. guys with me in Cumberland lacked education. At one point the camp had 265 inmates and only thirty were in the GED program. Three times that many should have been in it. Historically, prison programs were taught by professionals and real educators like those we had at Rikers Island. At Cumberland those permitted to conduct classes were not actual teachers, had no teaching experience, so the inmate students didn't take the classes or the teachers seriously. There should be positive incentives and reinforcement for educational efforts by inmates, just as there are for the drug treatment programs. I could guarantee that if prisoners were given eighteen months off or, say, 30 percent of their sentence, for attending and passing the GED programs, these men would be studying a lot.

Something else that I believe should change: Our prison system should strive to assist inmates in maintaining more of a connection with their children—because the most damaging thing that I saw, that I experienced firsthand, was the devastation to the families,

the distance created between fathers and mothers and their children. When you're on the inside and you sit in that visiting room and see these guys able to visit with their kids for only a few hours until God knows when—it has a lasting impact on you.

We cannot continue to demean, degrade, and demoralize the incarcerated. People come out of the system worse. The right thing to do is to help them be better.

Unfortunately, there is no survey, inspection, tour, or magic window that would allow judicial leaders and legislators to grasp the raw reality of what it's truly like to live as a prisoner in our country. Without living within the system, one cannot fully see its flaws, failures, and injustice, or have any personal understanding of what it's like to be cast out, stripped of your freedom, then held in nothingness to live by a clock. No matter what your vantage point from the outside—even if you're a prosecutor or a cop or a CO— it is difficult to understand the full effects of incarceration and the damage done to inmates, families, and society as a whole unless you have lived through prison and can see it from the inside out.

I'm not a CO or a cop anymore. I don't arrest people or enforce laws. No longer do I manage jails or build prisons.

But I still believe in this great country of ours, and I am still searching and fighting for justice.

Acknowledgments

I began writing this book the week after I pled guilty in federal court in 2009, and finished it in the last week of October 2014. It encompasses the previous thirteen years of my life, during nine of which I was embroiled in this criminal justice nightmare.

They say you don't know who your friends are until you've been at your worst, and I suppose I had to learn that the hard way, and learn I did. The people I mention below are those who were there for my family and me during one of the most difficult times in my life—old and new friends who went out of their way to help us emotionally, morally, socially, and financially, never asking for anything in return. True friends.

Cindy Adams; Thom Beers; Kenneth Breen; Jeff Smith; Bo Dietl; Dick Grasso; Congressman Peter King; his wife, Rosemarie; and their daughter, Erin Sweeney; Allen and Lenore Kosowsky; Barry and Deborah Morgenstein; Hector Santiago; Mitchell and Robin Modell; Sylvester Stallone; Gary Uher; Raymond Mansolillo; Bill White and Bryan Eure; Athan Tsimpedes and Phillip Segal.

Our neighbors Laura and Arthur Metzler, and our closest friends Nathan and Liza Berman, Simon and Erit Cohen, and Albert and Carolina Manzo have become more like family to us, and

have been there for us in more ways than we can count. Albert became Santa Claus at Christmas and handled the birthdays on my behalf for Hala and the girls.

Geraldo Rivera and his wife, Erica, and Christopher Ruddy constantly checked in on my family.

John Picciano, my former chief of staff, made more than seventy-five trips to FCI Cumberland to visit me during those years, and handled anything and everything my family or I needed.

Dr. Nancy Kymn Rutigliano, a professor at SUNY Empire State whom I have known since 2004, asked me to be a guest lecturer in a master's class in leadership and crisis management that she taught. From prison I answered her students' questions by email for close to two years, allowing me to mentally travel outside Cumberland's walls.

Hala's family and mine could not have done more than they did. But Hala's sisters, Reem and Maysoun, went above and beyond with their help and support. My brother, Don, looked after Hala and the girls like they were his own, and put money in my commissary account every month for three years so Hala wouldn't have to send me any.

For my writing projects I received indispensable help from Francine Cinque, Stacy Harris, and Michelle D. Almodova, who volunteered their time and never asked for anything in return. And I owe a special thanks to Sissaye Gezachew, who lived in the cube next to me at Cumberland for close to two years. He inspired my thoughts, translated my scribble, and edited my horrific spelling and grammar.

My agent, Victoria Sanders, who is more like a friend or family member, always believed in this book and fought to make it

happen. I love her to death. Her assistant, Bernadette Baker-Baughman, was a great help, too.

A special thanks to Mitchell Ivers, vice president and editorial director of Simon & Schuster's Threshold Editions, along with his assistant, Natasha Simons, who guided this project from start to finish. Thanks to the entire Threshold team: Louise Burke (president and publisher), Jennifer Robinson (VP and director of publicity), Lisa Litwack and John Vairo (art directors), Felice Javit and Elisa Rivlin (legal), Susan Rella (managing editor), and Al Madocs (production editor).

A special thanks also to my fellow inmates Gary Antonino, Joseph Burchfield, and Rodrigo Gomez—good men who will be punished for the rest of their lives for the mistakes they made—for helping me maintain my sanity while in prison.

To my collaborator and writing partner on this project, Cullen Thomas, I couldn't have picked anyone better to deal with my insane insomnia and schedule, or a writer who knew and understood the emotional roller coaster that I had been on better than he did.

To Hala, who has given me two of the greatest gifts a man could ever ask for— my daughters Celine, fourteen, and Angelina, twelve. She has lived with and accepted my insanity, schedules, travel to foreign lands, and dangerous assignments and workload and never complained. She has had to endure far more than she could have ever expected when we met. She has been a rock during our most trying times, and a shield of armor that protected my daughters from the cruel world of public life. She has dealt with the investigation, my imprisonment, and its aftermath as well as she can, even as it tore us down and created distance between us. She knows and has felt the collateral consequences of our criminal

justice system better than anyone, and I regret every day that I was the cause of her having to live through it. I am in her debt forever.

To my children: Joseph, who is not only my son but has truly become my best friend. I cannot be prouder of the man he has become—one of honor, strength, and courage. To Lisa and her husband, Josh, for their continued love and support. Last, and most important, to Celine and Angelina, my inspiration for living.

When I left for prison, Celine was a little girl of ten, and a young lady upon my return three years later. Angelina has become my partner in my pushing for criminal justice reform. She will be the first to tell you that she and Celine were punished worse than I was. That's how the system works, but that is not what it was created for.

Joe, Lisa, Angelina, and Celine are my greatest source of strength and motivation. Their love and support inspired me to endure as well as to hold on to hope.

Index